AF326624

How to Talk to Women 5-in-1

The Complete Guide to Feel Confident, Start Smooth Conversations, Never Run Out of Things to Say, Flirt Naturally, and Keep Her Interested

© Copyright 2026 - All rights reserved.

The content contained within this book may not be reproduced, duplicated, or transmitted without direct written permission from the author or the publisher.

Under no circumstances will any blame or legal responsibility be held against the publisher, or author, for any damages, reparation, or monetary loss due to the information contained within this book, either directly or indirectly.

Legal Notice:

This book is copyright protected. It is only for personal use. You cannot amend, distribute, sell, use, quote, or paraphrase any part, or the content within this book, without the consent of the author or publisher.

Disclaimer Notice:

Please note the information contained within this document is for educational and entertainment purposes only. All effort has been executed to present accurate, up-to-date, reliable, and complete information. No warranties of any kind are declared or implied. Readers acknowledge that the author is not engaging in the rendering of legal, financial, medical, or professional advice. The content within this book has been derived from various sources. Please consult a licensed professional before attempting any techniques outlined in this book.

By reading this document, the reader agrees that under no circumstances is the author responsible for any losses, direct or indirect, that are incurred as a result of the use of the information contained within this document, including, but not limited to, errors, omissions, or inaccuracies.

TABLE OF CONTENTS

INTRODUCTION
CONNECT WITH INTENTION

Human connection is not a luxury. It is a biological necessity. For thousands of years, our ancestors survived because they could talk, cooperate, and build bonds. If you feel a surge of nerves when you think about talking to a woman you find attractive, you are feeling a literal survival instinct. Your brain treats social rejection with the same intensity as physical pain. This is not just a feeling; it is a measurable physiological event.

Scientific research shows that social exclusion activates the same regions of the brain as physical injury. A study published in the journal *Science* by Naomi Eisenberger found that the anterior cingulate cortex lights up during social "burns." When you hesitate to start a conversation, your body is trying to protect you from that pain. But here is the truth: that same brain is also wired for rewards. When you connect deeply with another person, your brain releases oxytocin and dopamine. These chemicals lower stress and improve your health.

This book is about moving past the fear and toward the reward. We are going to look at how to talk to women through the lens of science, psychology, and honest human intent. We will not use tricks or scripts that feel fake. Instead, we will focus on how you can show up as a high-value man who communicates with clarity and purpose.

The Biological Mandate for Socializing

Why do we talk at all? Evolutionary psychologists, such as Robin Dunbar, argue that language evolved as a form of social grooming. In smaller primate groups, monkeys pick bugs off each other to build trust. Humans developed language to do the same thing on a much larger scale. This is known as the "Social Brain Hypothesis."

Dunbar's research suggests that our brain size is directly linked to the size of our social circles. We are built to handle about 150 meaningful relationships. Conversation is the tool we use to manage those spots. When you talk to a woman, you are essentially auditioning for a spot in her social world, and she is doing the same for yours.

Many men fail in these interactions because they forget this biological root. They treat conversation like a performance or a test. They think they need to win or convince her of something. This creates pressure. True connection happens when you move from a mindset of "What can I get?" to a mindset of "What can we share?"

The Nervous System and Social Engagement

To understand connection, we must look at the "Polyvagal Theory" proposed by Dr. Stephen Porges. This theory explains how our autonomic nervous system regulates our social behavior. When you feel safe, your "social engagement system" is active. Your heart rate slows, your voice takes on a melodic tone, and you can pick up on subtle facial expressions.

However, when you feel threatened—even by a simple social interaction—your body shifts into "fight or flight" mode. Your voice becomes flat, your face loses its expressiveness, and you stop being able to process the nuances of what a woman is saying. You aren't being "weird" on purpose; your nervous system has simply shut down your social tools.

How do we fix this? We do it by training the body to remain calm under social pressure. By understanding that your racing heart is just a biological signal, you can learn to stay in the "social engagement zone." This book will show you how to maintain that calm so your true personality can shine through.

The Problem with the Modern World

We live in a strange time for human interaction. We are more "connected" than ever through screens, yet more isolated in person. A 2018 study by Cigna found that loneliness has reached epidemic levels, with nearly half of adults reporting they sometimes or always feel alone.

This isolation has made us rusty. We spend hours looking at curated images on social media, which skews our perception of reality. We see "perfect" people and think we are not enough. This creates a barrier before we even open our mouths.

When you decide to "Connect with Intention," you are breaking this cycle. You are choosing to be present in a world that is increasingly distracted. That presence is rare, and because it is rare, it is highly attractive. Women notice when a man is actually looking at them and listening, rather than just waiting for his turn to speak or checking his phone.

The Impact of Digital Fatigue

Constant screen time has changed how we process eye contact and body language. A study from the University of California, Los Angeles (UCLA) showed that even five days without screens improved the ability of preteens to read human emotions. As adults, we face a similar decline. We have lost the "feel" for the natural rhythm of a conversation.

Because people are starved for real attention, your ability to provide it becomes a competitive advantage. When you can hold eye contact without looking away in discomfort, you signal high status and high emotional intelligence. You are telling her that you are comfortable in your own skin. This is more powerful than any pick-up line ever written.

To connect with intention, you must focus on three core areas: **Confidence, Competence, and Character.**

1. Confidence: The Internal Foundation

Confidence is not about thinking you are better than everyone else. It is about "Self-Efficacy," a term coined by psychologist Albert Bandura. It is the belief in your ability to handle a situation. In social terms, it means knowing that no matter how a conversation goes, you will be okay.

We will look at how to build this through "Power Posing" (as studied by Amy Cuddy) and cognitive reframing. We will move away from seeking external validation and toward building internal certainty.

2. Competence: The Skill Set

Competence is the "how-to." It involves knowing how to start a conversation, how to read body language, and how to keep a flow going. Think of this like a muscle. You wouldn't expect to bench press 300 pounds on your first day at the gym. Conversation requires the same steady practice.

Many men feel stuck because they think social skills are "innate." Science tells us otherwise. Neuroplasticity—the brain's ability to form new connections—means you can learn these skills at any age. We will provide the drills and mental models to make this possible.

3. Character: The "Why"

Character is your intent. Why are you talking to her? If your intent is just to get a number to prove your worth, she will feel that pressure. If your intent is to see if she is someone you actually like, the interaction changes. It becomes a shared discovery.

Character also involves integrity. Are you saying things you actually mean? Women have a highly developed "congruence detector." If your words don't match your true intent, it creates a "gut feeling" of unease in them. We will teach you how to be congruent.

The Science of First Impressions

You have likely heard that first impressions happen fast. Science says they happen even faster than you think. Researchers from Princeton University found that it takes only a tenth of a second for a person to form an impression of a stranger's face. Attributes like trustworthiness and competence are judged almost instantly.

This does not mean you need to be a male model. It means that your intent is often visible before you say a word. Your posture, your eye contact, and the way you take up space tell a story.

> "The human face is the most significant social stimulus in our environment." — Dr. Alexander Todorov, Princeton University.

If you walk up to a woman with rounded shoulders and your eyes on the floor, your body is telling her you are a threat or a burden. If you stand tall and offer a genuine smile, you are telling her you are a source of value.

The Role of Mirror Neurons

Why does your mood affect her so much? The answer lies in "Mirror Neurons." These are specialized brain cells discovered by Italian researchers in the 1990s. They fire both when you perform an action and when you observe someone else performing that same action.

If you approach a woman while feeling anxious and tense, her mirror neurons will pick up on that tension. She will start to feel anxious too, often without knowing why. Conversely, if you approach with warmth and relaxation, she is more likely to feel relaxed in your presence. This is why "working on yourself" is the most effective way to improve your interactions with others.

Moving Beyond Surface-Level Talk

A common complaint from women is that conversations with men often feel surface-level. They feel like they are being interviewed.

- "Where are you from?"
- "What do you do for work?"
- "Do you like it here?"

While these questions are fine for the first thirty seconds, they do not build connection. To "Connect with Intention," you must move toward "High-Value Disclosure." This involves sharing small pieces of your own perspective and asking questions that allow her to do the same.

The 36 Questions Study

A famous study by psychologist Arthur Aron explored whether intimacy could be accelerated by asking specific questions. He used a list of 36 questions designed to lead to "sustained, escalating, reciprocal, personalistic self-disclosure." He found that pairs who asked these deeper questions felt significantly more connected than those who stuck to small talk.

We are not going to ask you to carry a list of 36 questions on a date. However, we will use the principles behind them. We will learn how to ask "The Why" instead of "The What." Instead of asking "What do you do?", we might ask "What led you to choose that career?" This invites a story rather than a data point.

Why Intention Matters More Than "Lines"

If you search for advice on talking to women, you will find thousands of pick-up lines. Most of them are terrible. They are designed to be "clever," but they usually come across as performative. They create a "frame" where you are trying to impress her.

When you have a clear intention—such as "I want to see if this person is as interesting as she looks"—you don't need a script. Your brain is a highly advanced social computer. When you give it a clear goal, it finds the words for you.

The goal of this 5-in-1 guide is to give you a framework, not a script. We want you to be the architect of your social life. By the time you finish these five books, you will understand the mechanics of attraction, the flow of dialogue, and the psychology of long-term interest.

The "Spotlight Effect" and Social Anxiety

One of the biggest hurdles to talking to women is the "Spotlight Effect." This is a psychological phenomenon where people tend to believe they are being noticed more than they actually are. A study by Thomas Gilovich at Cornell University proved that we overestimate how much others pay attention to our flaws or social blunders.

In reality, most people are too worried about their own "spotlight" to notice yours. When you realize that the woman you are talking to might be just as nervous as you are, the pressure drops. You can stop focusing on your own performance and start focusing on making her feel comfortable.

What to Expect in the Following Books

This collection is structured to take you from the "inside out."

- **Book 1: Build the Mindset to Feel Confident.** We start with your internal state. You cannot build a skyscraper on a swamp. We will fix the foundations of your self-esteem and body language. We will look at "Cognitive Behavioral" techniques to stop negative thoughts before they stop you.

- **Book 2: Start Smooth Conversations.** We look at the logistics of the approach. How do you walk up? What is the first thing you say? We will use situational awareness to make every opening feel natural.

- **Book 3: Never Run Out of Things to Say.** We solve the awkward silence problem. You will learn techniques like "The Echo Effect" and "Free Association" to keep the energy high. We will discuss the "Flow State" in conversation.

- **Book 4: Flirt Naturally.** This is where we move from "friendly" to "romantic." You will learn the subtle art of banter, teasing, and reading green lights. We will examine the psychology of "Play" and why it is essential for attraction.

- **Book 5: Keep Her Interested.** Finally, we look at the long game. How do you maintain a connection? How do you lead with purpose and build a relationship that actually lasts? We will discuss "Attachment Theory" and how it influences long-term success.

The Importance of the Growth Mindset

Psychologist Carol Dweck coined the term "Growth Mindset." People with a fixed mindset believe they are just not good with women. People with a growth mindset believe that social skills are a set of behaviors that can be learned and improved.

Every interaction you have is a data point. If a conversation goes poorly, it is not a reflection of your worth as a man. It is simply a lesson in what to adjust next time. Even the most "naturals" you see in public had to learn these lessons. They just started earlier or failed more often until they got it right.

As you read this book, I want you to commit to being a social scientist. Observe the world. Test these techniques. See what works for you.

Overcoming the "Nice Guy" Paradox

Many men struggle with the "Nice Guy" syndrome, a concept popularized by Dr. Robert Glover. These men are often kind, but they hide their true intentions because they fear conflict or rejection. This lack of honesty actually makes women feel less safe.

Being "intentional" means being honest about your attraction. It means being a "Good Man" rather than a "Nice Guy." A Good Man has boundaries, has a backbone, and is clear about what he wants. We will show you how to be assertive without being aggressive.

Setting Your Personal Goals

Before we move into Book 1, take a moment to define what success looks like for you. Success is not just getting a date. Success is:

- Being able to walk into a room and not feel invisible.
- Expressing your true personality without a filter.
- Handling a "No" with a smile and moving on with your day.
- Finding a partner who actually fits your life and values.

Connection is a two-way street. You are not just trying to be "chosen" by a woman; you are choosing her too. This shift in perspective—from "supplicant" to "selector"—is the heart of being a confident man.

A Note on Ethics and Respect

Everything in this book is built on the foundation of mutual respect. We do not support manipulation. The goal is to become the best version of yourself so that you can attract the best partners. Authentic attraction is about highlighting your true strengths, not hiding your flaws behind a mask.

When you connect with intention, you respect her time, her boundaries, and her personhood. This respect is not "weakness." It is the highest form of social intelligence.

Summary of Core Concepts

Concept	Definition	Scientific Basis
Social Grooming	Conversation as a tool for trust building.	Dunbar's Social Brain Hypothesis
Polyvagal Theory	How the nervous system affects socializing.	Dr. Stephen Porges
Reciprocal Disclosure	Sharing personal info to build intimacy.	Arthur Aron's 36 Questions
First Impressions	Rapid judgment of character and intent.	Princeton First Impression Study
Growth Mindset	The belief that social skills are improvable.	Dweck's Mindset Theory
The Spotlight Effect	Overestimating how much others notice us.	Gilovich's Cornell Study
Mirror Neurons	Brain cells that sync emotions between people.	Rizzolatti's Research

The Path Forward

You are about to start a process of change. It will require you to be honest with yourself. It will require you to take small risks. But the result—a life filled with meaningful, exciting, and deep connections with women—is worth every bit of effort.

The modern dating world is full of noise. This book is the signal. We will cut through the confusion and give you a clear, science-backed path to becoming the man you want to be.

Stop waiting for the right moment. The right moment is the one you create. Let's start by building the mindset that makes everything else possible.

BOOK ONE
BUILD THE MINDSET TO FEEL CONFIDENT

INTRODUCTION
FIND YOUR INNER STRENGTH

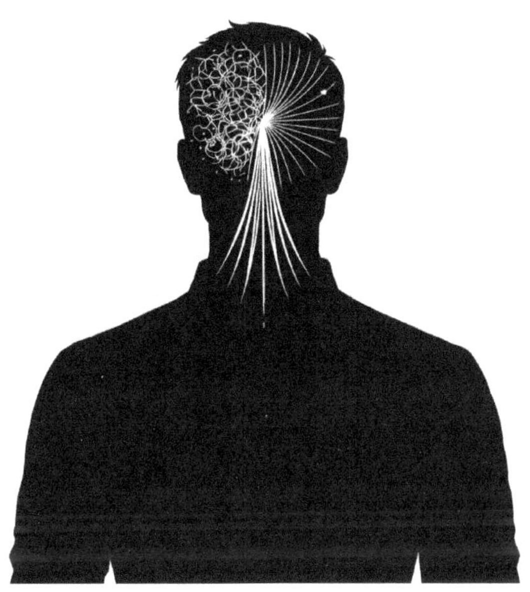

Confidence is often treated like a mystery. People talk about it as if it is a gift you are born with or a prize you win. You see a man walk into a room, stand tall, and talk to a woman with ease. You might think he has something you do not. You might think he was just lucky to be born that way. Science tells a different story. Confidence is a result of specific mental habits and physical actions. It is a skill you build through practice and clear logic.

To feel confident, you must first change how you see your own mind. Many men believe their personality is fixed. They think they are "just shy" or "not good with people." This is a mistake. Your brain is plastic. This means it can change at any age. Neuroscientists call this "neuroplasticity." When you repeat a thought or an action, you create physical paths in your brain.

If you spend years telling yourself you are socialy awkward, you build a path for that belief. But you can also build a new path. You can train your brain to feel steady and capable. This book starts here. We will not look at how to fake a smile. We will look at how to rebuild your internal foundation. When your foundation is strong, the words you say will have weight. You will not need to look for approval because you will already have it from yourself.

The Biology of Confidence and Fear

Your body is a chemical factory. The way you feel at any moment is the result of hormones and neurotransmitters. When you feel "unconfident" or nervous, your body is likely producing high levels of cortisol. This is the stress hormone. It is built to keep you safe from predators. In the past, if a lion was chasing you, cortisol helped you run faster. Today, your brain sees a social risk as a lion. It sends cortisol through your veins, which makes your heart race and your palms sweat.

To counter this, you need to trigger different chemicals. Testosterone and serotonin are the markers of a confident state. Research from Harvard University shows that even simple shifts in posture can change these levels. When you take up space and stand with your chest open, your testosterone rises and your cortisol drops. This is not just "body language." It is a biological hack. You are telling your brain that you are safe and in control.

Social confidence is also tied to the "Amydgala." This is the part of the brain that handles fear. When you are about to talk to a woman, your amygdala might fire a warning. It is trying to protect you from the "pain" of rejection. But rejection is not physical. It is a social signal. By understanding that your fear is just an old biological reflex, you can learn to ignore it. You can acknowledge the feeling and then act anyway. This is the definition of courage.

The Myth of the "Natural"

We often look at men who are successful with women and call them "naturals." This term is misleading. Most of these men learned their skills through trial and error. They simply failed enough times to figure out what works. In psychology, this is related to "Self-Efficacy." This concept was developed by Albert Bandura. It is the belief that you can produce a specific result.

A "natural" is just someone with high self-efficacy in social situations. He believes he can handle the talk, so he is not afraid to start it. He does not see a failed conversation as a disaster. He sees it as a lesson. He has a "Growth Mindset," a term from Dr. Carol Dweck. He knows his social skills are like a muscle. He goes to the "social gym" every day.

You can do the same. If you feel behind, it is only because you haven't put in the reps yet. This book is your training plan. We are going to break down the mental blocks that keep you from acting. We will replace your old, negative stories with new, fact-based ones.

The Three Layers of Social Worth

To build the mindset to feel confident, you must understand where your value comes from. Most men look for value in the wrong places. They look at their bank account, their car, or how women react to them. This is "External Validation." It is dangerous because it can be taken away. If a woman is mean to you, your confidence crashes. If you lose your job, your self-worth vanishes.

True confidence comes from "Internal Validation." This is built on three layers:

1. **Competence:** Doing things well. This doesn't have to be social. If you are a good cook, a skilled coder, or a strong athlete, you have competence. This builds a baseline of "I am a person who can do things."

2. **Integrity:** Doing what you say you will do. When you break promises to yourself, you lose self-respect. If you say you will go to the gym and then you don't, your brain records that you are not a man of your word. When you keep your promises, your internal confidence grows.

3. **Self-Acceptance:** Knowing your flaws and being okay with them. You do not need to be perfect to be confident. You just need to be honest. A man who knows he is not the tallest or the richest but doesn't hide it is very attractive. He is "Congruent." His inside matches his outside.

Many men approach women like they are asking for a job. They are "supplicants." They want the woman to give them something—attention, a phone number, or a date. This puts all the power in her hands. It makes the man feel small.

Intentional connection is different. You are not asking for a job. You are the "CEO" of your own life, and you are looking for a "partner." When you have this mindset, you don't worry about if she likes you. You worry about if you like her. You ask yourself: "Is she interesting? Is she kind? Does she have a good vibe?"

This shift changes your body language. You stop leaning in too much. You stop laughing at jokes that aren't funny. You become a "High-Value Man." High value is not about money. It is about how much you value your own time and attention. When you value yourself, others follow suit.

The Science of "Social Status" and Perception

Humans are social animals. We are hardwired to track our place in the hierarchy. This is why "status anxiety" is so common. We worry about what others think because, in the past, being kicked out of the tribe meant death. But the rules have changed. The "tribe" is now millions of people. One bad interaction does not mean you will die.

A study from the University of New South Wales found that people who are more "self-compassionate" have more social success. They don't beat themselves up over small mistakes. Because they are kind to themselves, they are more relaxed. This relaxation is contagious.

When you walk into a room, people are not looking for your mistakes. They are looking for a "vibe" to follow. If you are comfortable, they will be comfortable. If you are anxious, they will feel tense. This is the "Mirror Neuron" system at work. Your internal state becomes the "emotional thermostat" for the room. By fixing your mindset, you fix the environment around you.

Cognitive Reframing: Changing the Script

Your brain runs on scripts. These are the automatic thoughts that pop up when you face a challenge.

- **Old Script:** "She's too pretty. She probably has a boyfriend. She won't want to talk to me."
- **New Script:** "She looks like someone who enjoys a good conversation. I'll go say hello and see what her energy is like."

Cognitive Behavioral Therapy (CBT) uses a method called "Reframing." You take a negative thought and check it against the facts.

- **Fact:** You don't know if she has a boyfriend.
- **Fact:** You have had good conversations before.
- **Fact:** The "risk" is just a few seconds of talking.

When you break down your fears with logic, they lose their power. You move from the emotional brain (the limbic system) to the logical brain (the prefrontal cortex). This gives you the "Presence" needed to connect.

Understanding the Internal Critic

Everyone has an internal critic. It is that voice that tells you that you aren't good enough. In psychology, this is often linked to the "Super-ego" or early childhood experiences. While we don't need to spend years in therapy to talk to women, we do need to handle this critic.

Think of your internal critic like a "security guard" who is too excited. He thinks everything is a threat. When you see an attractive woman, he yells "STOP! DANGER!"

To feel confident, you don't try to kill the critic. You just stop letting him drive the car. You thank the guard for trying to keep you safe, and then you step out of the car and approach anyway. Over time, the guard gets quieter. He realizes that talking to women doesn't result in death. This is called "Habituation." Your brain gets used to the stress and stops reacting so strongly.

The Role of Body Language in Mindset

We will cover body language in detail in Chapter 2, but it is important to understand its role in your mindset now. The relationship between your mind and body is a two-way street.

If you feel confident, you stand tall. But if you stand tall, you also start to feel confident. This is the "Feedback Loop" of the nervous system. When you pull your shoulders back and widen your stance, you send a signal to your brain: "I am the alpha in this space." Your brain responds by releasing the chemicals that match that role.

Try this right now:

1. Slump your shoulders and look at the floor. Try to say "I am a powerful man." It feels fake.

2. Now, stand up. Put your feet shoulder-width apart. Lift your chin. Look straight ahead. Say it again. It feels much more real.

Your body is a tool for changing your mind. Use it.

Summary of Mindset Shift

Old Mindset	New Mindset
Seeking Approval	Giving Approval
Avoiding Rejection	Seeking Connection
Fixed Personality	Growing Skillset
Supplicant Role	Selector Role
External Validation	Internal Worth

Practical Exercises for This Week

To start building this mindset, you need small wins. You don't need to ask for a date yet. You just need to prove to your brain that you are a social person.

- **Exercise 1: The 3-Second Rule.** When you see someone you want to talk to, go within three seconds. Do not let your brain start "overthinking." The longer you wait, the more "danger" signals your brain will create.

- **Exercise 2: Eye Contact Drills.** As you walk down the street, make eye contact with five people. Give a small nod and a smile. If they look away, that's fine. If they smile back, that's a win.

- **Exercise 3: The Morning Mirror.** Look at yourself in the mirror every morning. Acknowledge one thing you did well the day before. This builds your "Internal Validation" muscle.

The Path to Your Best Self

Building a confident mindset is not a "quick fix." It is a shift in how you live your life. It is about becoming a man who is grounded in his own value. When you feel confident, you don't need "lines" because you are the message. Your presence speaks for you.

In the next chapters, we will build on this foundation. We will look at exactly how to use your body, how to stop the negative thoughts, and how to face your fears. But it all starts with your decision today. Decide that you are a man who can learn, grow, and connect.

CHAPTER 1

REWIRE YOUR BRAIN FOR SOCIAL SUCCESS

The belief that you are "stuck" with a certain personality is one of the most destructive lies a man can believe. You might think that your silence in social settings or your heart-pounding anxiety is a permanent part of your DNA. It is not. The human brain is not a finished product; it is a work in progress. Every time you think a thought or perform an action, you are physically changing the structure of your mind.

To feel confident when talking to women, you do not need a personality transplant. You need to understand how to guide this physical change to work for you rather than against you.

The Forest of the Mind

Neuroplasticity is the scientific term for the brain's ability to reorganize itself by forming new neural connections throughout life. For decades, the medical community believed the brain stopped developing after

20

childhood. We now know this is false. Research by neuroscientists like Dr. Michael Merzenich has shown that the brain remains plastic well into old age.

This means the "socially awkward" version of you is simply a set of well-worn neural pathways. If you want to become the version of you that speaks with ease, you must stop walking down those old paths and start carving new ones. This process is not magic. It is biological construction.

Think of your brain like a forest. If you walk the same trail every day, that trail becomes wide, clear, and easy to follow. If you try to walk through the thick brush where there is no trail, it is difficult and slow. Most men have spent years walking the "trail of hesitation." When they see a woman they like, their brain automatically takes the easiest path: the path of fear and withdrawal. Rewiring your brain means intentionally hacking through the brush of your discomfort until a new, confident trail becomes the easiest path to take.

Ultimately, your goal is to move these social skills from the **Prefrontal Cortex** (where you have to think about them manually) to the **Basal Ganglia**, which is the seat of automatic habits. When a skill reaches the Basal Ganglia, you stop "trying" to be confident and simply *are* confident.

The Anatomy of the Social Brain

To change the brain, you must understand the hardware you are working with. Social interaction is handled by a complex network of regions often called the "Social Brain." The key players in this network are the prefrontal cortex, the amygdala, and the mirror neuron system.

The prefrontal cortex is the "CEO" of your brain. It is located right behind your forehead and handles logic, planning, and personality expression. This is the part of you that knows you should go say hello. The amygdala, however, is the "alarm system." It is a small, almond-shaped cluster deep in the brain that processes emotions, especially fear. When the amygdala detects a "threat"—like the potential for social rejection—it can shut down the prefrontal cortex. This is known as an "Amygdala Hijack."

When you experience an Amygdala Hijack, your logical brain goes offline. This is why you might "freeze" or "blank out" when you try to talk to an attractive woman. You aren't stupid; your CEO has simply been locked out of the building by the security guard.

Beyond Extinction: The Inhibitory Learning Model

For years, we thought that "facing your fears" simply erased the fear memory. Recent research from Dr. Michelle Craske at UCLA shows that the original fear stays etched in your brain forever. To rewire yourself, you aren't deleting the old path; you are building a more powerful **"Safety Memory"** that eventually suppresses the original fear response.

This requires a shift in how you practice. To build a robust safety memory, you must remain in the presence of the social stimulus until your **ventromedial prefrontal cortex (vmPFC)** successfully transmits an inhibitory signal to the amygdala. If you approach a woman but then quickly "flee" before your heart rate drops, you actually reinforce the fear. You must stay long enough for your brain to receive the data that "I am still alive, and this is safe."

The Danger of "Safety Behaviors"

Many men use what psychologists call **"Safety Behaviors"** to cope with social anxiety during a date or approach. These include:

- Checking your phone constantly.
- Avoiding eye contact.
- Relying on a memorized script.
- Staying quiet to avoid negative judgment.

While these feel like they protect you, they actually prevent rewiring. Your brain thinks the reason you survived the interaction was the "safety behavior," not the fact that the situation was safe. To truly rewire your brain, you must intentionally drop these behaviors and allow yourself to be fully "exposed" to the social moment.

The Social Mirror Neuron Pathway

In the 1990s, we discovered mirror neurons—cells that fire both when you act and when you watch someone else act. However, 2024 fMRI research has distinguished between two different pathways: a **non-**

social pathway (focused on hand movements) and a **social pathway** (focused on faces and emotions).

The social pathway is heavily linked to the **limbic system** (the emotional center) and the **insula**. This means that a woman's brain isn't just "mirroring" your gestures; it is mirroring your internal state. If you are masking deep anxiety with a "cool" line, her insula will detect the incongruence, creating a "gut feeling" of unease. This is why working on your internal wiring is the most important "tactic" you will ever learn.

Overcoming the Negativity Bias

The human brain has a built-in "negativity bias." From an evolutionary perspective, it was more important to remember where the lion lived than where the delicious berries grew. Survival depended on focusing on what could go wrong. In the modern world, this bias makes you hyper-aware of every "bad" social interaction while you quickly forget the "good" ones.

If you talk to ten women and nine of them are friendly but one is rude, your brain will fixate on the one who was rude. You might even use it as "proof" that you shouldn't try again. This bias creates a skewed reality. To rewire your brain, you must train yourself to notice and weigh positive social data more heavily.

One way to do this is through "Positive Scanning." This is a technique where you intentionally look for three small social wins every day. A win could be a smile from a cashier, a brief laugh with a coworker, or a woman holding eye contact for a second longer than usual. By focusing on these wins, you are forcing your brain to build neural pathways for "social success." Over time, your brain will start to look for these opportunities automatically.

The Role of Myelin in Social Skill

When we talk about "muscle memory" in sports, we are actually talking about "myelin." Myelin is a fatty substance that wraps around the axons of your neurons. It acts like insulation on a wire. The more you repeat a specific action, the thicker the myelin sheath becomes on that neural circuit. Thicker myelin means the signal travels faster and with less "leakage."

This is why social skills feel clunky at first. If you haven't practiced starting conversations, your neural circuits for "opening" are like thin, uninsulated wires. The signal is slow and weak. But as you repeat the action, you "myelinate" that circuit. This is why "naturals" seem so smooth. They aren't thinking about what to do; their signals are traveling at high speeds through heavily insulated pathways.

You cannot think your way to thick myelin. You have to act. Every time you push through the "awkward" phase of a conversation, you are laying down another layer of insulation.

Cognitive Reframing: Turning Anxiety into Excitement

Physiologically, anxiety and excitement are almost identical. In both states, your heart rate increases, your breathing quickens, and you feel a "buzz" of energy. The difference is the "label" your brain puts on those sensations.

If you label the buzz as "anxiety," your brain prepares for a disaster. If you label it as "excitement," your brain prepares for a challenge. A study by Alison Wood Brooks at Harvard Business School found that people who said "I am excited" before a stressful task performed better than those who said "I am calm."

Instead of trying to suppress the nerves you feel when approaching a woman, reframe them. Tell yourself, "My body is gearing up for a high-stakes social interaction. This is energy I can use." This simple shift in labeling prevents the amygdala from taking over. It keeps the prefrontal cortex engaged. You aren't "scared"; you are "primed."

The Power of Visualization and Mental Rehearsal

Your brain has a hard time distinguishing between a vivid imagination and a real event. We can use this to our advantage through "Mental Rehearsal." Elite athletes and surgeons use visualization to improve their performance. By imagining a successful outcome in detail, they are actually firing the same neural circuits they would use in the real world.

Research in the journal *Neuropsychologia* showed that mental practice can lead to physical brain changes similar to actual practice. To rewire your brain for social success, spend five minutes a day visualizing a smooth interaction. Don't just imagine "winning." Imagine the details:

the sound of the room, the feeling of your feet on the floor, the tone of your voice, and the woman's positive reaction. Most importantly, visualize yourself handling a "hiccup" or a brief silence with total calm.

Breaking the Loop of Rumination

Rumination is the act of obsessively thinking about past failures or future fears. It is a "closed-loop" system that reinforces negative neural pathways. If you spend an hour thinking about a time you felt embarrassed, you are effectively "practicing" being embarrassed. You are myelinating the "failure" circuit.

To stop rumination, you must use "Pattern Interrupts." This is a technique from Cognitive Behavioral Therapy (CBT). When you catch yourself in a negative thought loop, you must physically and mentally break the pattern. This could be as simple as standing up and stretching, or counting backward from 100 by sevens. The goal is to force the brain to switch from the emotional centers to the logical centers.

Once you have broken the loop, replace the thought with a "proactive" one. Instead of "Why did I say that stupid thing?", ask yourself "What is one thing I will do differently next time?" This moves the brain from a state of "defense" to a state of "problem-solving."

The 1% Rule of Social Exposure

You do not rewire your brain by doing something massive once. You do it by doing something small consistently. In the world of habit formation, this is often called the "1% Rule." If you try to jump into the most high-pressure social situation immediately, your amygdala will likely scream and retreat, reinforcing your fear.

Instead, look for "Micro-Challenges." These are actions that are slightly outside your comfort zone but not terrifying.

- **Day 1-3:** Make eye contact and smile at three strangers per day.
- **Day 4-7:** Ask a stranger for the time or directions, even if you don't need them.
- **Day 8-10:** Give a brief, genuine compliment to a service worker ("I like your energy" or "That's a great watch").

Each of these small acts is a "vote" for your new identity. Each one sends a signal to your brain that social interaction is safe. As these small acts become "easy," your comfort zone expands. This is "Systematic Desensitization." You are slowly turning down the volume of your fear response until it is no longer a barrier.

Summary of Rewiring Techniques

Technique	Goal	Scientific Basis
Positive Scanning	Overcome Negativity Bias	Neuroplasticity / Dopamine
Inhibitory Learning	Build dominant safety memories	Dr. Michelle Craske
Drop Safety Behaviors	Prevent stealth avoidance	CBT for SAD
Cognitive Reframing	Turn Anxiety into Excitement	Physiological Arousal Labeling
Mental Rehearsal	Pre-wire success pathways	Hebbian Theory
Pattern Interrupts	Stop Rumination	PFC Engagement
Micro-Challenges	Expand Comfort Zone	Systematic Desensitization

Your Brain is the Tool, You are the Architect

Rewiring your brain is the most important work you will do. Everything else—the body language, the conversation starters, the flirting—depends on this foundation. If your brain is wired to see women as "judges" or "threats," no amount of "lines" will help you. But when you wire your brain to see them as "potential connections" and yourself as a "capable communicator," everything becomes easier.

Remember that discomfort is not a sign that something is wrong. Discomfort is the feeling of a new neural pathway being formed. It is the sound of the "CEO" taking back the building. Embrace the clunkiness of the learning process. You are building a high-performance social machine, one thought and one interaction at a time.

CHAPTER 2

ADOPT STRONG BODY LANGUAGE AND PRESENCE

Your body speaks before you do. Long before you utter a single word to a woman, your physical presence has already broadcasted a wealth of information about your status, your emotional state, and your intentions. This is not a matter of opinion; it is a hardwired biological reality. In the animal kingdom, and among humans, non-verbal signals are the primary way we determine who is a leader, who is a threat, and who is a potential partner. If your mindset is the software of confidence, your body language is the hardware that runs it. To talk to women with genuine impact, you must align your physical carriage with your internal goals.

Anthropologists and sociologists, such as Dr. David Givens, have noted that human attraction is a "non-verbal negotiation." Most of the "choosing" happens in the first few seconds of an encounter based on silent cues. When you walk into a bar, a coffee shop, or a bookstore, women are subconsciously scanning for signals of health, protection, and social ease. If your body language screams "I am trying to hide," no amount of clever conversation will bridge that gap. However, when you adopt a presence that says "I am comfortable in this space," you invite interest rather than suspicion.

We are going to move beyond simple advice like "stand up straight." We will look at the biomechanics of presence, the hormonal impact of posture, and the specific "tells" that signal high value. By the end of this chapter, you will understand how to occupy space with purpose and how to use your physical self to anchor your confidence.

The Hormonal Feedback Loop of Posture

One of the most significant breakthroughs in understanding body language came from the study of "Power Posing." While some specific claims in early studies were debated, the core principle remains solid: our physical posture influences our internal chemistry. A famous study by researchers at Harvard and Columbia Universities looked at how "high-power" vs. "low-power" poses affected hormones.

High-power poses—postures that are open and expansive—were associated with an increase in testosterone and a decrease in cortisol. Testosterone is the hormone of dominance and focus. Cortisol is the hormone of stress and inhibition. When you stand in a way that opens your torso and takes up space, you are literally telling your brain to be more assertive and less afraid. Conversely, low-power poses—folding your arms, hunching your shoulders, or touching your neck—increase cortisol and lower testosterone.

This creates a loop. If you feel nervous, you shrink your body. Shrinking your body increases stress hormones, which makes you feel more nervous. You can break this loop by "faking" the physical state of confidence. By holding a powerful posture for even two minutes, you can shift your chemical baseline. This makes it easier to approach a woman because you aren't just "acting" confident; you are biologically more confident.

The Geometry of Attraction: Open vs. Closed

In social psychology, the most important distinction in body language is "Open" vs. "Closed." This is rooted in our survival instincts. Our most vulnerable areas—the throat, the solar plexus, and the groin—are located on the front of our bodies. When we feel threatened, we instinctively protect these areas. We cross our arms over our chest. We turn our bodies away. We look at the ground.

When you approach a woman with closed body language, you are signaling that you are either afraid of her or that you have something to hide. Neither is attractive. To project presence, you must maintain an "Open Front."

- **Shoulders:** Keep them back and down, not hunched toward your ears.
- **Chest:** Keep it pointed toward the person you are engaging with.
- **Hands:** Keep them visible. Putting your hands in your pockets or behind your back is a "low-trust" signal.

Research into "Honest Signals" by MIT Professor Alex Pentland shows that people are more likely to trust and be attracted to those who show high levels of "fluidity" and openness. If your movements are jerky or stiff, it signals high cortisol. If your movements are smooth and your posture is open, it signals that you are the master of your environment.

Occupying Space: The Mark of High Status

In any social group, high-status individuals take up more space. They sit with their legs comfortably apart. They drape an arm over the back of a chair. They walk with a wide, grounded stride. This is not about being "macho"; it is about demonstrating that you do not feel the need to "minimize" yourself for others.

Many men, especially those who are tall or large, try to make themselves "smaller" to avoid being seen as aggressive. This actually backers. It makes you look uncomfortable and untrustworthy. Presence comes from being "comfortably large."

- **The Grounded Stance:** Stand with your feet at least shoulder-width apart. Distribute your weight evenly. When you "fidget" or shift your weight from foot to foot, you signal "flight" energy. A grounded man stays still.

- **The "V-Shape":** Aim for a posture where your shoulders are the widest point and your waist is narrower. Even if you aren't in perfect athletic shape, standing with your shoulders back creates this visual "power frame."

- **Respecting the "Bubble":** While taking up space is good, you must also respect "Proxemics." This is the study of how humans use space in communication, popularized by Edward T. Hall. Standing too close too fast is aggressive. Standing too far away is fearful. The "sweet spot" is usually about three feet (arm's length) for an initial approach.

The Power of the Gaze: Eye Contact and Dominance

Eye contact is perhaps the most intense form of non-verbal communication. It can trigger the release of phenylethylamine, a chemical associated with attraction and "love at first sight." However, there is a fine line between a "confident gaze" and a "creepy stare."

High-value eye contact is characterized by "Comfortable Intensity."

1. **The 70/30 Rule:** In a conversation, you should maintain eye contact about 70% of the time while listening and about 50% while speaking. This shows you are engaged but not trying to "stare her down."

2. **The "Slow Blink":** Rapid blinking is a sign of high anxiety and "deception" in the brain's processing. Slowing your blink rate signals a calm nervous system.

3. **Breaking Eye Contact:** When you do look away, look to the side, not down. Looking down is a submissive signal. Looking to the side implies you are simply thinking or observing the environment.

A study in the *Journal of Research in Personality* found that pairs who were told to look into each other's eyes for two minutes reported significantly higher feelings of affection than those who looked at each other's hands. When you are talking to a woman, your eyes should tell her that she has your full attention. This "presence" is rare in a world of smartphones and constant distraction.

Micro-Expressions and the "Smize"

While you can control your shoulders and your stance, your face often betrays your true feelings through "micro-expressions." These are involuntary facial expressions that last only a fraction of a second. Dr. Paul Ekman, the world's leading expert on facial expressions, has shown that humans are incredibly good at "sensing" when a smile is fake.

A real smile—known as a "Duchenne Smile"—involves the contraction of the *orbicularis oculi* muscle around the eyes. This creates the "crow's feet" and makes the eyes look "warm." A fake smile only involves the mouth.

To project presence, you don't need to grin like a maniac. In fact, a "static" grin can look needy. Instead, aim for a "slight, knowing smile." This implies that you are having a good time and that you have a secret worth knowing. When you do smile, make sure it reaches your eyes. This signals "Congruence"—that your internal state matches your outward expression.

Hand Gestures and "Palm Displays"

Your hands are tools of persuasion. In evolutionary history, showing your palms was a way to prove you weren't carrying a weapon. Today, palm displays are still a powerful signal of honesty and openness.

- **Use "Illustrators":** These are hand gestures that emphasize what you are saying. Research shows that people who use their hands to describe ideas are viewed as more energetic and intelligent.

- **Avoid "Adapters":** These are "self-touching" behaviors, such as scratching your neck, adjusting your watch, or rubbing your hands together. These are signals that you are trying to "self-soothe" because of high stress.

- **The "Steeple":** Bringing your fingertips together in a steeple shape is a classic signal of confidence and intellectual authority. Use it sparingly to emphasize a point.

When you are approaching a woman, keep your hands out of your pockets. Visible hands reduce the "threat" response in her brain and make you appear more approachable.

Walking with Purpose: The "Alpha" Gait

How you walk into a room sets the stage for every interaction that follows. A "confident gait" is characterized by:

1. **Stride Length:** Longer, purposeful strides rather than short, hurried ones.
2. **Arm Swing:** Allow your arms to swing naturally from the shoulders. Stiff arms look defensive.
3. **Head Position:** Keep your head level. Imagine a string pulling you up from the crown of your head. Do not look at your feet.

A study by researchers at the University of Durham found that people could accurately judge a person's "social dominance" and "adventurousness" just by watching a video of them walking. By slowing down your walk and keeping your head up, you signal that you are not in a rush and that you are "at home" in your surroundings.

Presence as a "Shield"

Presence is not just about what you do; it is about what you *don't* do. A man with strong presence is "unreactive." If a loud noise happens, he doesn't jump. If a woman says something challenging, he doesn't immediately become defensive or start explaining himself. He remains centered.

This "non-reactivity" is a high-status signal. It implies that you are the "rock" in the environment. In the context of talking to women, this means you can handle "tests" or "teasing" with a calm smile. Your body language doesn't change because your internal state is secure.

Summary of Presence Cues

Cue	Confident Action	Low-Value Action
Torso	Open, shoulders back	Closed, arms crossed
Feet	Wide, grounded	Narrow, shifting weight
Hands	Visible, palm displays	In pockets, self-touching

Cue	Confident Action	Low-Value Action
Head	Level, chin slightly up	Looking down at phone / floor
Movements	Slow, deliberate	Fast, jerky, reactive

Practical Exercise: The "Presence Audit"

This week, I want you to conduct a "Presence Audit" on yourself.

1. **The Window Reflection:** As you walk past shop windows, check your posture. Are your shoulders hunched? Is your head down? Fix it immediately.

2. **The "Wait" Drill:** Whenever you are waiting in line, stand in a "Power Pose" (within reason). Feet wide, hands out of pockets, chest open. Observe how people treat you differently compared to when you are "shrinking."

3. **The Eye Contact Challenge:** In your next interaction, try to notice the eye color of the person you are talking to. This forces you to hold eye contact long enough to establish a real connection.

Presence is a physical habit. Like any habit, it feels "fake" at first because it is "new." But as you "myelinate" these pathways, standing tall and looking people in the eye will become your default state. You are no longer "trying" to look confident; you *are* confident because your body is sending that signal to your brain every second of the day.

CHAPTER 3

STOP SELF-SABOTAGE AND NEGATIVE SELF-TALK

You can have the most open body language in the world and a brain rewired for success, but if you have a "traitor" in your own head, you will eventually stumble. This traitor is the voice of self-sabotage—the internal dialogue that whispers "she's too good for you," "you're going to mess this up," or "remember how awkward you were last time?" In psychology, this is known as negative self-talk, and it acts as a biological handbrake on your social potential.

To connect with intention, you must move from being a victim of your thoughts to being the observer and commander of them. This is not about "positive thinking" in a vague, superficial way. It is about

Cognitive Restructuring. It is a systematic process of identifying the logical fallacies your brain uses to keep you "safe" (but lonely) and replacing them with high-accuracy, high-value assessments of reality.

The Neurobiology of the Internal Critic: Why Your Brain Attacks Itself

To dismantle the voice of self-sabotage, we must first understand why it exists from a biological standpoint. Your brain's primary directive is not your happiness or your romantic success; it is your **survival**.

For hundreds of thousands of years, the greatest threat to a human's survival was social exclusion. If you were cast out of the tribe, you died. Therefore, your brain developed a hyper-sensitive "early warning system" designed to prevent you from doing anything that might result in social shame. This system is centered in the **Amygdala** and the **Insular Cortex**.

When you think about approaching a woman, your Insular Cortex—which processes social pain and "gut feelings"—senses a risk of rejection. It interprets this risk as a threat to your life. To stop you from taking that risk, it generates negative thoughts as a deterrent. These thoughts are effectively "mental electric fences" designed to keep you inside your comfort zone. The voice saying "you aren't good enough" is actually a primitive safety mechanism. The problem is that in the modern world, this fence is preventing you from living a full life.

The Default Mode Network (DMN) and Rumination

The physical "home" of your self-talk is the **Default Mode Network**. This is a series of interconnected brain regions that become active when you aren't focused on a specific task. Research by Dr. Judson Brewer at Yale University has shown that in people with high social anxiety, the DMN is hyperactive and highly "self-referential."

Instead of observing the world, the DMN turns the "camera" inward, analyzing every perceived flaw. When you sit at a bar and think, *"Everyone is looking at me and judging my outfit,"* that is your DMN over-processing. By learning to "quiet" the DMN through mindfulness and external focus, you can physically reduce the volume of the internal critic.

The Architecture of the Internal Critic: Psychological Frameworks

Self-sabotage is rarely a random occurrence. It usually follows a structured script. To break the script, we can look at two major psychological frameworks: **Transactional Analysis** and **Schema Theory**.

1. Transactional Analysis (TA)

Developed by Dr. Eric Berne, TA suggests we have three "ego states": The Parent, The Adult, and The Child.

- **The Critical Parent:** This is the voice of self-sabotage. It repeats the criticisms you heard from authority figures, peers, or society. It uses words like "should," "must," and "never."
- **The Adapted Child:** This is the part of you that feels the "sting" of that criticism. It feels small, judged, and rebellious but paralyzed.
- **The Adult:** This is the logical, data-driven part of you.

Self-sabotage happens when the **Critical Parent** dominates the **Child**. To gain confidence, you must strengthen the **Adult**. The Adult doesn't say "I'm a god"; the Adult says "I am a man who is going to walk over and start a conversation. If it goes well, great. If not, I have data for next time."

2. Schema Theory

Dr. Jeffrey Young developed Schema Theory to explain deep-seated patterns we use to interpret the world. Common schemas that lead to social self-sabotage include:

- **Defectiveness/Shame:** The belief that you are internally flawed and that if people get close, they will see it.
- **Social Isolation:** The belief that you are different from others and don't belong.
- **Failure:** The belief that you are fundamentally inadequate in areas of achievement (including social achievement).

When you understand that your negative thoughts are just "schemas" (old mental filters), you can start to distance yourself from them. They aren't the truth; they are just "old software" running on a new computer.

In Chapter 1, we touched on distortions. Here, we dive deeper into how they specifically sabotage your interactions with women.

Emotional Reasoning

This is the fallacy that because you *feel* a certain way, it must be true. *"I feel awkward, therefore I must BE awkward and she must see it."* **The Fix:** Remind yourself that feelings are not facts. You can feel like a nervous wreck while appearing perfectly calm to an outside observer. In fact, studies on the "Illusion of Transparency" show that people consistently overestimate how much their internal state is visible to others.

Personalization

The belief that you are the cause of every external event. If a woman looks at her watch while you are talking, you assume you are boring her.

The Fix: Consider the "Three Alternative Causes" rule. Maybe she has a deadline. Maybe her feet hurt. Maybe she's expecting a call. By widening your perspective, you stop the internal critic from making everything about your "deficiency."

Overgeneralization

Taking one bad experience and turning it into a "universal law." "I tried to talk to a girl at the gym once and she was cold; therefore, all women at the gym hate being talked to."

The Fix: Demand evidence. Is it logically possible for 4 billion women to have the exact same reaction? No. Replace "always" and "never" with "sometimes" and "this time."

The Neuroscience of Shame and the "Freeze" Response

When self-sabotage becomes intense, it often manifests as **Shame**. Shame is different from guilt. Guilt says, "I did something bad." Shame says, "I *am* bad."

Neurobiologically, shame triggers a "dorsal vagal shutdown." This is the extreme end of the Polyvagal Theory discussed in the introduction. When you feel deep shame about your social abilities, your body doesn't just feel anxious; it feels heavy, tired, and defeated. Your eyes drop, your heart rate actually slows in a depressive way, and you lose the ability to speak fluidly.

To combat this, you must recognize shame as a **physiological state**, not a personality trait. When you feel that heavy "I shouldn't be here" sensation, you need to use "Up-regulating" techniques. These include:

- **Physiological Sighs:** Two quick inhales through the nose followed by a long exhale through the mouth. This resets the carbon dioxide balance in your blood and signals the brain to move out of the "freeze" state.

- **Cold Exposure:** Splashing cold water on your face triggers the "mammalian dive reflex," which can break a shame-based thought loop instantly.

The Power of "Selective Attention" and the RAS

Your brain is bombarded with millions of bits of data every second. To keep you from going insane, it uses the **Reticular Activating System (RAS)** to filter what you notice.

If you believe you are "socially invisible," your RAS will filter for evidence that supports that. You will notice the person who bumps into you without apologizing, but you will literally "not see" the woman who made eye contact and smiled.

To stop sabotaging yourself, you must "re-program" your filter. This is called **Selective Attention**. You must give your RAS a new mission: *"Look for signals of interest and friendliness."* When you walk into a room, tell yourself: *"I am looking for people who are open to a conversation."* Suddenly, the "green lights" you were previously blind to will start to pop out. This isn't "magic"; it's basic sensory filtering.

Cognitive Defusion: Becoming the Observer

One of the most powerful tools in modern psychology for stopping self-sabotage is **Cognitive Defusion**, a core component of Acceptance and Commitment Therapy (ACT).

Most men are "fused" with their thoughts. If the thought *"I'm boring"* pops up, they believe they ARE boring. Defusion is the process of creating space between you and the thought.

The Ladder of Defusion:

1. **Level 1 (Fused):** "I am boring." (This feels like an absolute truth).
2. **Level 2:** "I am *having the thought* that I am boring." (This creates a tiny bit of space).
3. **Level 4 (The Label):** "Oh, there's the 'Boring Script' again. Thanks, brain, for trying to protect me."

By labeling the thought as a "script" or "noise," you take away its power. It can still be there, but it no longer dictates your actions. You can walk up to a woman *while* having the thought that you are boring. The thought doesn't have to stop you.

The "Inner Defender" vs. The "Inner Critic"

A groundbreaking technique involves personifying your thoughts. If you have an "Inner Critic" that bullies you, you need to develop an "Inner Defender."

Imagine you are in a courtroom. The Inner Critic is the prosecution, listing all the reasons why you are inadequate. Currently, you have no defense attorney. You are just letting the prosecution win. Your job is to build the "Defense" case.

Example Case:

- **Prosecution (Critic):** "You haven't had a date in six months. You're losing your touch."
- **Defense (Defender):** "Actually, in those six months, we have been focusing on our career and fitness. We have been choosing to stay single to work on ourselves. Furthermore, we talked to three new people this week, showing clear improvement in social courage."

By actively talking back to the critic with **facts**, you lower its credibility. The goal isn't to be "arrogant"; it's to be **fair**.

The Biological Case for Self-Compassion

Many men think self-compassion is "soft" or "weak." They believe that being a "hard taskmaster" to themselves is the only way to improve. Science proves the opposite.

Dr. Kristin Neff's research shows that self-criticism triggers the **Threat Defense System** (Cortisol and Adrenaline). This puts you in "survival mode," where your social skills actually decline. Self-compassion, however, triggers the **Care-Satiation System** (Oxytocin and Endorphins).

When you are compassionate to yourself after a social "failure," you lower your cortisol. This allows you to stay "socially engaged" and try again. A man who beats himself up stays in his room for a week. A man who uses self-compassion stays out and talks to the next person. Which one is "stronger"?

Practical Exercises

To truly stop self-sabotage, you must move from theory to "homework."

1. The "So What?" Descending Arrow

Take your biggest social fear and ask "So what?" until you reach the bottom.

- *Fear:* "I might run out of things to say." -> *So what?*
- *Answer:* "It will be awkward." -> *So what?*
- *Answer:* "She'll think I'm weird." -> *So what?*
- *Answer:* "I'll feel embarrassed." -> *So what?*
- *Conclusion:* "I'll be a bit uncomfortable for 5 minutes, then I'll go home and my life will be exactly the same."

2. The Daily "Social Evidence" Log

Your internal critic is like a bad lawyer. It ignores all the evidence of your success. To counter this, keep a log. Every night, write down three things that went "okay" or "well" socially.

- "A stranger thanked me for holding the door."
- "I made a joke and my coworker laughed."
- "I held eye contact with a woman for two seconds."

3. The Pattern Interrupt

When you catch yourself in a "rumination loop" (replaying a mistake), you must physically break the circuit.

- The 5-4-3-2-1 Technique: Name 5 things you see, 4 you can touch, 3 you hear, 2 you smell, and 1 you can taste.

This forces the brain to move from the Default Mode Network (thinking about the past) to the Task Positive Network (experiencing the present).

Summary of Cognitive Tools

Tool	Purpose	Scientific Basis
Cognitive Restructuring	Challenge irrational thoughts	Beck's CBT
Transactional Analysis	Strengthen the "Adult" ego state	Dr. Eric Berne
Cognitive Defusion	Distance yourself from "noise"	ACT / Mindfulness
Selective Attention	Re-program your social filter	RAS / Neuroscience
Self-Compassion	Reduce cortisol and anxiety	Neff's Care System
Pattern Interrupts	Stop the rumination loop	DMN vs. TPN

Conclusion: You are the Commander of the Ship

Self-sabotage is a habit of the mind, not a character flaw. It is the result of an old biological system trying to protect you in a world that no longer requires that protection. By identifying your distortions, analyzing the cost of your negativity, and practicing the art of defusion, you clear the mental path to connect with intention.

You are the driver of the bus. Your thoughts are just noisy passengers. They can yell, they can complain, and they can tell you to turn around—but they cannot touch the steering wheel. That power belongs to you.

CHAPTER 4

FACE SOCIAL FEARS WITH EXPOSURE EXERCISES

The final wall between you and the ability to connect with intention is not a lack of knowledge, but a lack of **Habituation**. You can understand the biology of the brain, adopt the posture of a king, and silence your inner critic, but if your nervous system still perceives a social approach as a life-threatening event, you will remain paralyzed.

To dismantle this paralysis, we must move from the laboratory of the mind into the field of action. This chapter is about **Systematic Desensitization**—the gold standard of clinical psychology for treating phobias and social anxiety. In the 1950s, psychologist Joseph Wolpe developed the concept of exposure therapy based on a simple biological principle: if you are exposed to a feared stimulus repeatedly in a safe environment without anything bad happening, your brain eventually stops sounding the alarm.

This process is called **Extinction**. For the modern man, this means we must systematically "bore" the amygdala until talking to a beautiful woman feels as mundane as ordering a cup of coffee.

The Science of Inhibitory Learning: Beyond "Getting Used to It"

For years, psychologists believed that exposure therapy "erased" fear. We now know this is incorrect. According to the **Inhibitory Learning Model** developed by Dr. Michelle Craske at UCLA, the original fear memory stays in the brain forever. What we are doing is building a **new**, more powerful "Safety Memory" that inhibits the old "Fear Memory".

When you avoid a social situation, you reinforce the belief that staying home kept you safe. When you face the situation, you create a "Competing Memory"—a record of you talking to a stranger and surviving. The goal of this chapter is to make your Competing Memories so numerous and robust that they become the default response of your nervous system.

Crucially, modern research suggests we should focus on **Anxiety Tolerance** rather than just waiting for the anxiety to go away. The goal isn't necessarily to feel "calm" immediately, but to prove to your brain that feeling anxious is not dangerous. You are training yourself to stay in the pocket while the fire is hot.

The Neurobiology of Extinction and "Staying Power"

When you perform an exposure exercise, your brain undergoes a process called **Long-Term Depression (LTD)** of the synapses in the amygdala. This is a physical reduction in the strength of the neural connections that trigger the fear response. Simultaneously, the **Ventromedial Prefrontal Cortex (vmPFC)**—the part of your brain responsible for emotional regulation—begins to send "inhibitory" signals to the amygdala. It essentially says, "I see the beautiful woman, but the alarm is not necessary."

To strengthen the vmPFC, you must utilize **"Staying Power"**. You must remain in the social situation until your anxiety drops or until you have successfully "violated" your expectation of disaster. If you approach a woman but then flee while your heart is still racing, you accidentally send a signal to your brain that you "escaped" a predator, which actually reinforces the fear. You must stay long enough for the heart rate to drop and the brain to log the data: "I am still alive, and I am safe."

Identifying and Dropping "Safety Behaviors"

A major breakthrough in 2025 research is the identification of **Safety Behaviors**—subtle crutches we use to "survive" a social interaction. These include:

- Checking your phone to look "busy."
- Rehearsing your exact lines in your head over and over.
- Avoiding direct eye contact or looking at your feet.
- Speaking very softly to minimize attention.

While these feel like they protect you, they actually prevent neural rewiring. Your brain thinks the only reason you weren't rejected was because of the phone or the script, not because the situation was safe. To maximize your growth, you must intentionally drop these behaviors and allow yourself to be fully "exposed" to the moment.

The Fear Hierarchy: Your Social Training Log

We do not start by asking for a date with the most attractive woman in the room. If you do that while your anxiety is at a level 10, your brain will likely go into **Sensitization**—a process where the "trauma" of the event actually makes the fear worse. Instead, we use a **Fear Hierarchy** (or an Exposure Ladder). You must rate each task on a scale of 0 to 10 using **SUDs (Subjective Units of Distress)**.

- **0-3:** Mildly uncomfortable but easily manageable.
- **4-7:** Moderate anxiety (sweaty palms, racing heart, but logical thought remains).
- **8-10:** High anxiety/Panic (urge to flee, "blanking" out).

Your goal is to stay in the **4-7 range**. This is your "Growth Zone." In this zone, your brain is releasing a precise cocktail of norepinephrine and dopamine that facilitates the growth of new neural connections.

These exercises are designed to desensitize your **Peripheral Nervous System** to the presence of others and to correct your sense of "Personal Space."

1. The Proximity Endurance Drill

Many socially anxious men have an overactive "Peripersonal Space" boundary. Their brain perceives anyone within a 5-foot radius as a potential threat.

- **The Task:** Go to a high-density area (a mall, airport, or busy street). Your only task is to remain in the "Personal Space" (within 3 to 4 feet) of others without looking at your phone or listening to music. You must be "fully present" in the crowd.

- **The Reps:** Perform this for 20 minutes, 3 times this week. Record your SUDs every 5 minutes. You will notice that by minute 15, your anxiety naturally "plateaus" and then drops. This is the biological process of habituation in action.

2. The "Functional" Inquiry (Social Warm-up)

Athletes warm up their muscles; you must warm up your "social muscles." This exercise removes the "intent" and focuses on the "mechanics."

- **The Task:** Ask five strangers for the time, directions, or a recommendation for a nearby coffee shop.

- **The Focus:** Pay attention to your voice. Is it thin and quiet? Or is it coming from your diaphragm? Aim for a "Level 5" volume—clear enough to be heard over background noise.

- **The Reps:** 5 successful interactions. Note how many people are actually helpful. Your brain needs this data to realize that "strangers" are generally "allies."

Once the presence of others feels neutral, we introduce "Friction"—small moments of social tension designed to prove you are resilient and to dampen the "Shame Response" in your **Insular Cortex**.

3. The Compliment-and-Exit (The "Drive-By")

Giving a compliment is an act of high-value social leadership. It shows you are a man who notices beauty or quality and isn't afraid to acknowledge it.

- **The Task:** Give a genuine, non-sexual compliment to a stranger ("Great shoes," "That's a cool book," "You have great energy") and **keep walking**. Do not wait for a conversation.
- **The Logic:** This practices the **Approach Mechanic** while removing the "What do I say next?" pressure. It proves to your brain that you can "impact" someone's day positively without needing anything in return.
- **The Reps:** 10 compliments.

4. The "Shame Attack" (The Cognitive Reframe)

Developed by Albert Ellis, the founder of REBT, this involves doing something slightly "odd" on purpose to prove that social disapproval is not fatal.

- **The Task:** Ask for a discount at a grocery store where they clearly don't give discounts (e.g., "Can I get 10% off these eggs?"), or ask for a "Whopper" at a Starbucks.
- **The Logic:** When the cashier says "No," your brain will want to feel shame. You must stand there, smile, say "No problem, just thought I'd ask," and finish your transaction calmly. You are "immunizing" yourself against the word "No."

Phase 3: Targeted Exposure and Intentional Connection (SUDs 7-9)

Now we apply the skills to the specific context of intentional connection. We are targeting the **Dopaminergic Reward System**— teaching it that the "risk" of approach is worth the "reward" of connection.

5. The Observational Opener (The "Warm" Approach)

Approaching a woman you find attractive is the ultimate test of your new mindset. We avoid "lines" because lines are a "Safety Behavior"—a crutch used to hide your true self.

- **The Task:** State a genuine observation about the environment or her "vibe." "I couldn't help but notice you look like you're having the most focused conversation in the room," or "I saw you reading that—is it actually as good as everyone says?"

- **The Science:** This moves into **High-Stakes Vulnerability**. You are showing interest, which is the highest risk for the ego. By staying in the conversation for at least 60 seconds, you allow your nervous system to move from "Fight/Flight" back into "Social Engagement."

6. The "Anxiety Admission" (The Vulnerability Stake)

If you feel your heart racing or your voice shaking during an approach, do not hide it.

- **The Task:** Say, "I'll be honest, my heart is racing a bit because I was nervous to come talk to you, but I liked your style too much to pass by."

- **The Logic:** This is based on **Paradoxical Intention**. By naming the fear, you move it from the "unconscious" (where it controls you) to the "conscious" (where you control it). It also triggers the "Pratfall Effect," where people who show small, honest flaws are perceived as more likable and high-status than those who act like "perfect" robots.

Handling Rejection: The "Social Recovery Velocity"

The biggest barrier to exposure is the fear of being told "no." You must reframe rejection as **Neutral Physiological Data**. When a woman says "no," your brain's **Dorsal Anterior Cingulate Cortex (dACC)** fires. This is the same region that processes physical pain.

However, true mental fitness is measured by your **Social Recovery Velocity (RV)**—the speed at which you return to your emotional baseline after a "No".

- **Low RV:** You get rejected and go hide in the bathroom for 20 minutes, replaying the event.

- **High RV:** You acknowledge the "sting," take a deep breath, and within 60 seconds, make a small comment to someone else—the bartender or a guy at the next table.

By re-engaging immediately, you prove to your brain that the "Social World" is still intact. You are becoming **Antifragile**—a system that actually gets stronger from stress and disorder.

Summary of Exposure Exercises

Level	Exercise	Biological Target	Target SUDs
Foundation	Proximity Drill	Peripersonal Space Neurons	2
Bridge	The Time-Check	Basal Ganglia (Habit formation)	3
Friction	Compliment-Exit	Ventral Striatum (Reward)	5
Mastery	The Observational Opener	Prefrontal Cortex (Integration)	7

Conclusion: The New You is on the Other Side of Boredom

Confidence is not a "feeling" you wait for; it is a **physical state** you earn through exposure. By the time you finish these exercises, you will have a library of memories proving that you are safe, capable, and resilient. You will no longer need to "get hyped up" to talk to someone. You will simply do it because the "fence" of your anxiety has been torn down.

CHAPTER 5

PROJECT VALUE THROUGH AUTHENTIC SELF-WORTH

In the architecture of social dynamics, "Value" is the invisible currency that dictates the flow of every interaction. Most men approach the world with a "scarcity" mindset, believing they must perform, entertain, or impress to earn the attention of a high-quality woman. This is the fundamental error of the "supplicant." Authentic self-worth, however, is not a performance; it is a **projection of internal reality**.

When you possess authentic value, you no longer seek to "get" something from an interaction. Instead, you become the source of the interaction's energy. This chapter will dissect the evolutionary, biological, and psychological components of value, providing you with a roadmap to shift from a man who seeks validation to a man who provides it.

1. The Evolutionary Blueprint of Social Value

To understand why certain behaviors are perceived as "high-value," we must look at the environment in which our brains evolved. For 99% of human history, social status was the primary determinant of survival and reproductive success.

Sexual Selection and Honest Signaling

In evolutionary biology, **Zahavi's Handicap Principle** suggests that high-quality individuals often display "handicaps"—behaviors or traits that are "costly" to maintain—to signal their superior fitness. In a social context, a man who is calm, relaxed, and takes his time speaking is signaling that he is not threatened by his environment. He has enough "social surplus" to not be in a hurry.

Conversely, a man who is twitchy, hurried, and constantly checking for approval is signaling that his environment is a threat. He is "low-value" because he lacks the resources (internal or external) to be at ease.

Parental Investment Theory

According to **Parental Investment Theory**, the sex that invests more in offspring (females) is more selective. This means that, biologically, women are hardwired to look for "Value Indicators" that suggest a man has the resources—emotional, social, and physical—to provide stability.

These indicators include:

- **Social Intelligence:** The ability to navigate complex group dynamics.

- **Emotional Resilience:** The ability to remain centered under pressure.

- **Ambition and Drive:** The potential to acquire future resources.

When you project authentic self-worth, you are sub-communicating that you possess these traits. You are signaling that you are a "safe" and "rewarding" investment of her time and energy.

2. The Neurobiology of Status and Confidence

Your sense of self-worth isn't just a "feeling"; it is a chemical state. Two primary hormones and one neurotransmitter dictate how you view yourself and how the world views you: **Testosterone, Cortisol, and Serotonin.**

The Serotonin System: The Calm of the Leader

Serotonin is often called the "status neurotransmitter." Research by Dr. Robert Sapolsky on primate hierarchies found that the highest-ranking males had the highest levels of serotonin. Crucially, this serotonin didn't just make them "happy"; it made them **calmly dominant**.

High serotonin allows you to process social information without an overactive amygdala. It keeps you from overreacting to slights or "tests." When you have high serotonin, you move slower, breathe deeper, and hold eye contact longer. These are the physical "tells" of a high-value man.

The Testosterone-to-Cortisol Ratio

Confidence is physically represented by a high testosterone-to-cortisol ratio.

- **Testosterone** drives the "approach" behavior and reduces fear.
- **Cortisol** drives the "avoidance" behavior and increases anxiety.

A man who projects value has "Low-Stress Dominance." He is assertive (Testosterone) but not frantic (low Cortisol). If you are "High-Testosterone but High-Cortisol," you come across as aggressive, unstable, and insecure. Authentic self-worth is the ability to maintain your drive while keeping your stress system inhibited.

3. The Psychology of the "Selector" vs. the "Supplicant"

Most social advice focuses on "what to say." But the "what" is irrelevant if the "why" is rooted in supplication.

The Supplicant Mindset (Seeking Validation)

The supplicant enters an interaction as a "buyer" who cannot afford the product. He uses "Safety Behaviors" to protect his ego:

- **Self-Deprecation:** Insulting himself before anyone else can.
- **Approval-Seeking Questions:** "Do you like this?" or "Is this okay?"

- **Physical Shrinking:** Making himself smaller to avoid being perceived as a threat.

The Selector Mindset (Providing Value)

The high-value man enters as a "judge" or "selector." His internal dialogue is not *"Does she like me?"* but rather *"Is she the kind of woman I want in my life?"* This shift is rooted in **Self-Determination Theory (SDT)**, which posits that humans have three innate needs: Autonomy, Competence, and Relatedness. A man with high self-worth meets his own needs for autonomy and competence. He doesn't look to a woman to "complete" him or validate his existence. Because he is already "full," he can offer relatedness as a gift.

4. Boundaries: The Guardrails of Self-Worth

You cannot have value without the ability to reject that which does not serve you. In social dynamics, **Boundaries are the ultimate "Honest Signal" of self-worth.**

The "Nice Guy" Trap

Many men suffer from "Nice Guy Syndrome," a term popularized by Dr. Robert Glover. They believe that if they are "nice" (meaning they have no boundaries and always agree), they will be rewarded with sex or love. In reality, this behavior is seen as manipulative and low-value. It signals that the man has no internal compass and is willing to sell his integrity for a moment of approval.

How to Set High-Value Boundaries

Setting a boundary is not about being a jerk; it's about being **Congruent**.

- **Scenario:** A woman is being flaky or disrespectful of your time.

- **Low-Value Response:** "It's okay, I don't mind waiting. When can we meet instead?" (Supplication).

- **High-Value Response:** "I value my time, so I'm going to go ahead with my other plans. Let me know if you want to reschedule when you're less busy." (Boundary).

The high-value response is powerful because it shows that you have a "Life Path" that continues with or without her. This is the definition of **Outcome Independence**.

Outcome Independence is the ability to engage in an interaction without being attached to the result. It is the realization that your value is a "constant," not a "variable" that changes based on a woman's reaction.

The Economics of Attention

In any market, that which is rare is valuable. If your attention is given freely to anyone who smiles at you, it has low market value. If your attention is reserved for those who meet your standards, its value skyrockets.

By practicing Outcome Independence, you are effectively "raising your price." You are signaling that you have an **Abundance Mindset**—the belief that the world is full of opportunities and that no single interaction is "make or break."

The "Takeaway" Technique

When an interaction is going well, a high-value man is the first to end it. He might say, "It was great meeting you, but I have to get back to my friends/work." This "Takeaway" proves that you are not "starved" for her attention. It leaves her wanting more and reinforces your status as a man with a full, interesting life.

6. Sub-Communication: The Language of the Subconscious

Only a small fraction of your "Value" is communicated through words. The rest is sub-communicated through your **Vocal Tonality** and **Micro-Expressions**.

Vocal Tonality: The "Breaking Rapport" vs. "Seeking Rapport"

- **Seeking Rapport:** Ending sentences with a rising pitch (like a question). This signals that you are looking for confirmation.
- **Breaking Rapport:** Ending sentences with a flat or falling pitch. This signals authority and certainty.

High-value men speak with "Breaking Rapport" tonality. They state their truths as facts, not as suggestions for the other person to verify.

The "Pregnant Pause"

Low-value men are terrified of silence. They feel they must fill every gap to keep the woman from getting bored. High-value men **own the silence**. Using a "Pregnant Pause" before answering a question shows that you are thinking, that you are not reactive, and that you are comfortable with the tension of the moment.

7. Social Proof and the Power of Preselection

We are social animals. We look to the "herd" to see who is valuable. This is the concept of **Social Proof**.

The Vetted Man

If other women find you attractive and comfortable, you are "Preselected." This is why a man walking with two female friends is often approached more than a man walking alone. He has been "vetted" by other members of the "tribe."

How to Build Social Proof Solo

You don't need a harem to show social proof. You can build it by being the "Mayor of the Room":

- Greeting the staff by name.
- Introducing people to each other.
- Being a "Social Hub" rather than a "Social Satellite."

By being the person who "adds" value to the environment, you become the person that others want to be near. This is **Radiant Value**.

8. Vulnerability: The Ultimate Power Play

There is a common misconception that high-value means being a "robot" who never shows emotion. In fact, the opposite is true.

The Pratfall Effect

Research into the **Pratfall Effect** shows that highly competent people become *more* attractive when they make a small mistake or admit a flaw. Why? Because it shows they are so secure in their core value that they don't need to hide their humanity.

A man who can laugh at himself, admit he's nervous, or share a "dorky" passion is signaling **Extreme Self-Worth**. He is saying, "I am so high-value that this small flaw doesn't even dent my armor." This is the peak of authentic confidence.

Authentic self-worth is a muscle. It is built through a series of "Internal Wins":

1. **Keep promises to yourself:** If you say you'll go to the gym, go. This builds **Self-Trust**.

2. **Speak your truth:** Stop "filtering" your opinions to please others.

3. **Exercise your "No":** Practice setting small boundaries in your daily life.

4. **Acknowledge your growth:** Look at the progress you've made in Chapters 1-4.

You are no longer the man you were when you started this book. You are a man who understands the biology of his brain, the language of his body, and the worth of his soul. You are ready to stop "trying" to be confident and simply **be** confident.

CONCLUSION

LIVE AS A CONFIDENT MAN

You have reached the end of the first stage of your journey, but in the architecture of personal transformation, this is not a finish line—it is the completion of the foundation. Many men seek the "house" of social success—the relationships, the respect, and the romantic connections—without ever pouring the concrete of the mindset. They try to build on sand, and when the first wave of rejection or social friction hits, the structure collapses.

By completing these first five chapters, you have poured the concrete. You have addressed the **Neural Plasticity** of your brain, the **Biomechanics** of your presence, the **Cognitive Filters** of your mind, the **Habituation** of your nervous system, and the **Internal Valuation** of your soul. Now, we must discuss how to inhabit this structure. To "Live as a Confident Man" is to move from the laboratory of learning into the arena of daily life, where the theory becomes bone-deep reality.

What does it actually mean to "live" this? There is a pervasive cultural myth that a confident man is the loudest person in the room, the one constantly telling jokes or demanding center stage. This is a misunderstanding. Authentic confidence is **Quiet**. It is the absence of the need to prove anything.

The Confident Man is "Grounded." In physics, "grounding" provides a path for excess electrical charge to safely dissipate into the earth. Socially, a grounded man does the same with emotional "charge." If someone insults him, the charge dissipates because he knows his value. If a beautiful woman ignores him, the charge dissipates because his self-worth is not a variable. He is the "Rock" around which the river of social chaos flows.

Pillar I: Integration of the Plastic Mind (The Maintenance of Growth)

We began in Chapter 1 by understanding that your brain is not a static machine. To live as a confident man, you must treat your **Neural Plasticity** as a lifelong hygiene practice. The brain is efficient; it wants to return to the path of least resistance. If you stop challenging your social comfort zone, the "Safety Neurons" will begin to reclaim the territory you've won.

The "Social Gym" Protocol

Living as a confident man requires a "maintenance dose" of social stimulus. Just as an athlete does not "finish" fitness, you do not "finish" confidence.

- **Daily Novelty:** Talk to one person you don't know every single day, regardless of your mood. This keeps the **Prefrontal Cortex** dominant over the **Amygdala**.

- **The "Update" Loop:** Every evening, briefly review your social interactions. Not to criticize, but to "tag" the wins. This reinforces the **Dopaminergic pathways** associated with social success, making the "Confident Identity" your brain's new default mode.

Pillar II: Embodied Leadership (The Physicality of Being)

In Chapter 2, we learned that the body speaks first. To live as a confident man is to adopt an **Open Front** as your permanent default state. This isn't just about how you stand when talking to a woman; it is how you stand when you are alone in your kitchen, how you sit at your desk, and how you walk down a sidewalk when no one is watching.

Proprioceptive Awareness

The Confident Man has high **Proprioception**—he is acutely aware of where his body is in space. He does not "leak" energy through fidgeting, foot-tapping, or nervous glances.

- **The "Scanning" Habit:** Periodically throughout the day, perform a "Body Scan." Are your shoulders creeping toward your ears? Is your jaw clenched? Drop the tension.
- **The "Slow Down" Rule:** Confident men move slower than anxious men. To live this, practice "The 10% Rule": walk 10% slower, speak 10% slower, and wait 10% longer before responding to a question. This signals to your nervous system—and the world—that you are in control of your time.

Pillar III: The Silent Command Center (The End of Self-Sabotage)

Chapter 3 taught you to silence the "Internal Critic." To live as a confident man, you must move from "fighting" your thoughts to "dismissing" them. You become the **Discerning Gatekeeper** of your own mind.

From "Defusion" to "Identity"

Eventually, you will reach a point where the negative self-talk doesn't just "lose its power"—it stops appearing altogether. This happens through the process of **Identity Shift**.

- **The Old Script:** "I'm trying to be confident."
- **The New Script:** "I am a man who connects with others."

When your identity changes, your thoughts align. A confident man doesn't have to "convince" himself he is worthy; he simply operates from that assumption. If a negative thought does appear, he treats it like a "spam email"—he sees it, recognizes its source, and hits "delete" without reading it.

Chapter 4 introduced the "Exposure Ladder." To live as a confident man is to move from **Systematic Desensitization** to **Antifragility**. Nassim Taleb defines "Antifragility" as a system that actually gets *stronger* from stress and disorder.

Seeking the "Social Burn"

An anxious man views social friction as a wound. A confident man views social friction as a "repetition" in the gym.

- **Scenario:** You approach a woman, and she is cold.
- **Anxious Response:** "I failed. I should stop." (Fragile).
- **Confident Response:** "My nervous system just got a high-intensity workout. I am now more resilient than I was five minutes ago." (Antifragile).

To live this, you must intentionally seek out "Social Burn" once a week. Put yourself in a situation where you are the "least important" person in the room, or where you have to speak up in a group. By constantly testing the "edges" of your fear, you ensure that the center of your confidence remains unshakable.

Pillar V: The Radiance of Value

Finally, we come to the lesson of Chapter 5: **Authentic Self-Worth**. Living as a confident man means you are a **Source of Value**, not a consumer of it.

The "Vibe" of Abundance

Most men walk into a social setting looking to "take"—to take a woman's attention, to take a friend's approval, to take the room's energy. The Confident Man walks in to "give."

- He gives **Attention** (through deep listening).
- He gives **Approval** (through genuine compliments).
- He gives **Security** (through his grounded presence).

This is the ultimate secret of attraction: people are drawn to those who make them feel better about themselves. When your self-worth is high, you have an "overflow" of positive regard that you can share with others. This makes you "magnetic" in the most literal sense of the word.

The Confident Man in Relationships

Living this way changes how you interact with women. You move from "The Chase" to "The Connection." Because you don't *need* her validation, you can actually *see* her for who she is. You become a "Detector of Quality" rather than a "Seeker of Sex."

The Power of the "Clean Slate"

A confident man doesn't bring the "ghosts" of past rejections into a new interaction. Every woman he meets gets a "Clean Slate." He assumes she is friendly and interesting until she proves otherwise. This **Positive Assumption** is a self-fulfilling prophecy; because he treats her like a friend, she is much more likely to respond as one.

The Confident Man in the World (The Higher Purpose)

Confidence is not an end in itself; it is a tool. Why did we go through the trouble of rewiring your brain and facing your fears? Not just so you can "get more dates." We did it so you can live a **Big Life**.

Confidence allows you to pursue the career you want, to stand up for the people you love, and to express your unique personality without the "muffling" effect of anxiety. A confident man is a "net positive" for the world. He creates more than he consumes, and he leaves every environment better than he found it.

The "Ripple Effect"

When you stand tall and speak your truth, you give the people around you "permission" to do the same. Your confidence is contagious. By transforming yourself, you subtly transform your entire social ecosystem.

Sustaining the State: The "Confidence Dip"

It is important to be realistic: you will have bad days. There will be days when your sleep is poor, your stress is high, and your "Internal Critic" finds a way back in. This is the **Confidence Dip**.

The "Baseline" Rule

The goal of Book 1 was not to make you "perfect," but to raise your **Baseline**.

- **Before Book 1:** Your "Bad Day" was a 2/10 (Panic/Avoidance) and your "Good Day" was a 5/10.

- **After Book 1:** Your "Bad Day" is a 5/10 (Mildly nervous but functional) and your "Good Day" is a 9/10.

When the dip happens, don't panic. Don't tell yourself "I lost it." Simply return to the basics. Fix your posture. Take a deep breath. Do a low-stakes exposure exercise. Your "hardware" is already built; you just need to clear the temporary "software" glitch.

Moving Toward Connection

You have successfully navigated the "Internal World." You are now a man who is "Ready." But "Ready" is only half the battle. You have the engine, the fuel, and the steering wheel, but you still need to learn the "Map" of the social world.

In **Book 2: Master the Art of Meeting and Connecting**, we will take this powerful, grounded mindset and apply it to the specific mechanics of the human interaction. We will cover:

- How to start a conversation in a way that feels natural and non-threatening.

- How to read "Subtle Interest" signals that most men miss.

- How to move from "Small Talk" to "Deep Connection."

- The ethics and empathy of high-value interaction.

The Final Charge

The world is waiting for you. There are thousands of women who are looking for exactly what you have just become: a man who is comfortable in his own skin, who speaks his truth, and who treats others with genuine value.

The "fear" will never completely vanish—nor should it. Fear is the "energy" of the unknown. To live as a confident man is to see that fear, smile at it, and say: **"Let's see what happens next."**

REFLECTION QUESTIONS
CHECK YOUR PROGRESS

You have traversed the foundational landscape of social confidence. In the previous five chapters, we moved from the microscopic level of synaptic firing to the macroscopic level of social signaling. However, information without **Integration** is merely noise. In the field of educational psychology, the "Testing Effect" suggests that the act of retrieving information from your memory actually strengthens that memory more than simply re-reading it.

This reflection chapter is designed to force that retrieval. It is not merely a "check-box" exercise; it is a **diagnostic tool** for your nervous system. Before you move on to the tactical maneuvers of Book 2— where we discuss the "How" of conversation—you must ensure your "Software" and "Hardware" are fully synced. If you carry a "bug" in your self-worth or a "glitch" in your body language into a social interaction, no amount of clever openers will save you.

Metacognition is "thinking about your own thinking." To live as a confident man, you must become a master of this internal observation. Research from the **Max Planck Institute for Human Cognitive and Brain Sciences** shows that individuals with high metacognitive ability are more resilient to stress and better at navigating complex social hierarchies.

By answering the following assessment sections, you are engaging your **Prefrontal Cortex** to audit your **Limbic System**. You are essentially "debugging" your confidence.

Section I: The Neurobiology of Your New Identity

In Chapter 1, we established that the brain is plastic. You are no longer "a guy who is shy"; you are a man in the process of **Neural Renovation**.

1. The Amygdala Audit:

Think back to a social situation from the last 48 hours where you felt a "ping" of anxiety.

- Did you recognize the physiological shift as a "false alarm" from your amygdala?
- Were you able to "label" the emotion in the moment (e.g., "I am feeling social threat")?
- *Integration Task:* Describe the physical sensation of that anxiety. Was it a tight chest? A dry throat? By precisely identifying the sensation, you reduce its power.

2. The Growth Mindset Calibration:

When you made a social "mistake" recently (e.g., a joke that didn't land), what was your immediate internal response?

- **A:** "I'm bad at this and I'll never learn." (Fixed Mindset)
- **B:** "My brain just received data on what doesn't work. This is a rep in the gym." (Growth Mindset)
- *Integration Task:* If you chose A, write down the "Neural Correction." How would a man with a 10/10 growth mindset describe that same event?

Section II: The Physicality of Presence

In Chapter 2, we discussed the "Broadcast" of your body. Your physiology is the "base station" of your confidence.

3. The Proprioception Check:

As you are reading this right now, where is your tension?

- Scan your jaw, your shoulders, and your breath.
- Are you "taking up space" in your seat, or are you "huddled" over your screen?
- *Integration Task:* Perform the **High-Power Pose** (shoulders back, chest open, chin slightly up) for 60 seconds. Note the shift in your mental clarity. This is your "Baseline State."

4. The Eye Contact Barrier:

During your recent interactions, where did your eyes go when the conversation became slightly tense or personal?

- Did you look down (Submissive)?
- Did you look to the side (Dismissive)?
- Or did you hold the gaze with a "soft" focus (Grounded)?
- *Integration Task:* Practice "The 70/30 Rule" today. Aim to hold eye contact for 70% of the time while listening and 30% while speaking.

Section III: The Cognitive Debugger

Chapter 3 focused on the "Traitor in the Head." We must ensure your internal dialogue has moved from "Prosecutor" to "Defender."

5. Cognitive Distortion Identification:

Review your thoughts from the last week. Can you find an example of:

- **Mind Reading:** "She thinks I'm boring."
- **Catastrophizing:** "If this goes badly, my social life is over."
- **Fortune Telling:** "I know she's going to say no."
- *Integration Task:* Take your most common distortion and write a "Counter-Evidence Statement." For example: "I cannot read her mind. The evidence shows she is still standing here talking to me, which suggests she is interested."

6. Cognitive Defusion Practice:

When a negative thought arises, are you still "fused" with it?

- Do you say "I am a loser"?
- Or do you say "I am noticing a thought that I am a loser"?
- *Integration Task:* Spend five minutes observing your thoughts as if they were clouds passing over a mountain. You are the mountain. The thoughts are just weather.

Section IV: The Action and Habituation Audit

Chapter 4 was the "Social Gym." Knowledge without action is a hallucination of progress.

7. The Fear Hierarchy Review:

Where are you currently on your Exposure Ladder?

- Have you completed the "Low-Stakes" interactions (Time checks, directions)?
- Have you felt the "Boredom of Habituation" yet?
- *Integration Task:* Identify the next "Step" on your ladder. What is the specific action that feels like a 6/10 on the SUDs scale? Commit to doing it within the next 24 hours.

8. Rejection Resilience:

Describe the last time someone was "not interested" or "cold" toward you.

- Did you take it personally (Personalization)?
- Or did you see it as "Incompatible Data"?
- *Integration Task:* Write down three reasons why someone might be "cold" that have absolutely nothing to do with your value (e.g., they just had a bad phone call, they are late for a meeting, they are shy).

Section V: The Projection of Value

Chapter 5 explored the "Currency" of social value. This is the most "subtle" but powerful layer of Book 1.

9. The Supplicant vs. Selector Test:

In your recent conversations with women, who was "auditioning" for whom?

- Were you trying to prove how "cool" or "successful" you are?
- Or were you observing her to see if she met your standards?
- *Integration Task*: Define your "Top 3 Social Standards." What are three traits a woman *must* have for you to be interested in her (e.g., sense of humor, intelligence, kindness)? Having these standards is the foundation of the **Selector Mindset**.

10. Boundary Strength:

When was the last time you disagreed with someone or said "No" to a request that didn't serve you?

- Did you feel a "need" to apologize for your boundary?
- *Integration Task*: Practice "The Unapologetic No" today. If someone asks you for something you don't want to do, say "I can't do that, but thanks for asking." No excuses, no over-explaining. Note the surge in self-respect that follows.

The Integration Field Test: "The 10-Minute Grounding"

To graduate from Book 1, you must perform this final "Mindset Field Test."

The Mission: Go to a public place (a coffee shop, a park, a lounge). Sit or stand there for 10 minutes without a phone, a book, or a friend.

- **The Physical Goal:** Maintain an open, relaxed posture. Do not fidget.
- **The Mental Goal:** Use your "Selective Attention" to look for "Green Lights" (people smiling, interesting details in the architecture, positive energy).
- **The Emotional Goal:** If you feel the urge to "hide" or check your phone, acknowledge the feeling, label it ("There is the safety-seeking urge"), and choose to remain present.

The Pass/Fail Criteria:

- **Pass:** You remained present, grounded, and observant for the full 10 minutes. You felt the anxiety spike and then subside (Habituation).

- **Fail:** You checked your phone, you hunched your shoulders, or you left early because of discomfort. (If you fail, repeat tomorrow).

Summary of Book 1 Progress

Foundation	Status (1-10)	Primary Tool to Use
Neuroplasticity		Labeling the Amygdala
Presence		High-Power Posing
Mindset		Cognitive Reframing
Courage		The Exposure Ladder
Self-Worth		The Selector Mindset

Moving Forward: The Transition to Connection

You have successfully audited your internal world. You are no longer a victim of your biology; you are the architect of it. You have built a "Confidence Baseline" that is significantly higher than when you began Chapter 1.

However, a lighthouse—no matter how strong and grounded—is useless if it doesn't know how to signal the ships. In **Book 2: Master the Art of Meeting and Connecting**, we will take this "Grounded Man" and put him into motion. We will move from **Mindset** to **Mechanics**.

We will discuss:

- How to open a conversation so naturally that she doesn't even realize it's an "approach."

- How to use "Situational Awareness" to never run out of things to say.

- How to read the subtle body language cues that say "Please keep talking to me."

You are ready. The foundation is set. The concrete is dry. It is time to build the structure.

BOOK TWO
START SMOOTH CONVERSATIONS

INTRODUCTION

BREAK THE ICE WITHOUT STRESS

You have spent the duration of Book 1 building an internal fortress. You have rewired your neural pathways, optimized your hormonal profile through posture, silenced the internal critic, and habituated your nervous system to the presence of social pressure. You are now a man of "Grounded Value." However, even the most powerful engine is useless if it cannot engage the gears to move the vehicle. In the world of social dynamics, "engaging the gears" is the act of **The Open**.

Breaking the ice is the single most criticized and over-analyzed aspect of social interaction. For decades, the "pickup" industry focused on complex routines and canned lines, while the "self-help" industry focused on vague platitudes like "just be yourself." Both failed because they ignored the fundamental **Neurobiology of Social Initiation**. Breaking the ice is not about the words you say; it is about the **State** you transmit and the **Safety** you establish in the first three seconds of an encounter.

In this book, we move from the "Internal" to the "External." We will master the mechanics of starting conversations naturally, anywhere, without the crushing weight of stress or the fear of looking like a "creeper." This introduction serves as the strategic framework for your transition from a man who is "Ready" to a man who is "Active."

The Neurobiology of the "Ice": Why Initiation Feels Like a Threat

To "break the ice" is to overcome a massive amount of biological inertia. When you see a woman you want to talk to, your brain initiates a sequence of events known as **Preattentive Processing**. This happens in milliseconds, long before your conscious mind has a chance to form a sentence.

The Thalamic Shortcut

Information from your environment travels to the **Thalamus**, the brain's "relay station." From there, it takes two paths. The "High Road" goes to the Sensory Cortex and the Prefrontal Cortex for logical analysis. The "Low Road" goes directly to the **Amygdala**. If you are socially anxious, the Low Road wins. Your Amygdala flags the social approach as a "High-Risk Conflict," triggering the release of cortisol and adrenaline.

The Role of the Ventrolateral Prefrontal Cortex (VLPFC)

The "Ice" is actually a state of **Social Inhibition** controlled by the VLPFC. This area of the brain acts as a "brake." It is evolutionary designed to keep you from doing something that might get you kicked out of the tribe. In the modern world, this brake is hyper-sensitive. It scans for reasons *not* to act: "She's on her phone," "She looks busy," "People are watching." Breaking the ice is the act of manually overriding this brake using **Top-Down Regulation**.

The Physics of Social Interaction: Potential vs. Kinetic Energy

To understand why breaking the ice is stressful, we can look at the physics of energy. An anxious man sitting in a corner has high **Potential Energy**. He is "wound up," full of stored tension and "what-if" scenarios. The moment he tries to move, that potential energy has to be converted into **Kinetic Energy** all at once. This creates a "jolt" in his system—and that jolt is felt by the person he is approaching as "nervous energy."

The Flywheel Effect

The key to stress-free initiation is **Social Momentum**. Imagine a massive, 10-ton steel flywheel. To get it to turn even one inch requires an immense amount of energy. But once it is spinning, its inertia keeps it moving with very little effort.

If you walk into a social environment and stay silent for an hour, your flywheel is at a dead stop. When you finally decide to approach a woman you find attractive, the energy required is astronomical. Your anxiety will be at its peak because you are trying to jump from "Zero" to "Sixty" in one second.

The Momentum Protocol:

To break the ice without stress, you must be in a state of Social Flux. This means you are talking to everyone from the moment you leave your house.

- **Level 1:** Greet the neighbor or the mail carrier.
- **Level 2:** Make a small observation to the barista or the bouncer.
- **Level 3:** Crack a joke with a group of guys by the bar.

By the time you see the woman you are genuinely interested in, your flywheel is already spinning. The "approach" isn't a massive leap over a canyon; it's just the next logical step in a day already filled with connection.

The "Safety First" Principle: The Female Perspective

To break the ice effectively, you must understand the **Female Neurobiology of Threat Detection**. For a woman, a stranger approaching her is a "High-Variance" event. Her brain's **Insular Cortex**—the area responsible for social intuition and disgust—is hyper-tuned to "Incongruence."

If you approach with "High-Need" energy (supplication) or "Sneaky" energy (trying to hide your intent), her brain registers a "Predatory Signal." This triggers an immediate "shutdown" or "shielding" response. Breaking the ice "without stress" means approaching in a way that provides **Immediate Psychological Safety.**

The Three Pillars of Safety:

1. **Transparency:** Her brain wants to know *why* you are there. "I noticed you" or "I had to come say hi" provides a logical anchor for the interaction.

2. **Open Body Language:** As mastered in Book 1, your front must be open, hands visible, and posture relaxed. This signals that you are not hiding a weapon (ancient brain) or a motive (modern brain).

3. **The "False" Time Constraint:** Giving her a subconscious "out" by signaling that you aren't going to stay forever. Simply angling your body slightly away or mentioning you are "heading back to your friends" lowers her defense.

The Three-Second Rule: Bypassing the Ruminative Loop

In the world of social dynamics, there is a famous concept called the **Three-Second Rule**. It states that you must initiate the approach within three seconds of noticing the person. While it sounds like a "pickup" gimmick, it is actually a profound biological hack.

Avoiding the Default Mode Network (DMN)

When you wait longer than three seconds, your brain's **Default Mode Network** kicks in. This is the part of the brain responsible for "self-referential thought" and "future simulation." In other words: **Overthinking.**

- **At 1 second:** You notice her. You feel a spark of interest (Dopamine).

- **At 4 seconds:** Your DMN starts simulating rejection. "She'll think I'm weird," "Everyone is looking."

- **At 10 seconds:** Your VLPFC "brake" is fully engaged. You are now paralyzed.

By acting within three seconds, you bypass the "Critical Filter." You move before your brain has the chance to tell you why you shouldn't. This creates a state of **Spontaneous Congruence**. Because you didn't have time to rehearse a "line," your voice remains grounded and your "Vibe" remains authentic.

The Philosophy of the "Giver" vs. the "Taker"

The ultimate way to break the ice without stress is to change your **Fundamental Intent**. Most social anxiety stems from the fear of not "getting" what you want.

The Consumer (Taker) Intent:

The Taker approaches because he wants something: a phone number, a date, or validation. This creates "Performance Anxiety." If he doesn't get the number, he has "failed." This desperation is sub-communicated through his micro-expressions and is highly unattractive.

The Provider (Giver) Intent:

The High-Value man approaches with "Provider" intent. He is there to **give** value to the environment.

- He gives a moment of **presence**.
- He gives a **genuine observation**.
- He gives a **spark of energy** to an otherwise mundane day.

When you are the one "Giving" the interaction, you cannot "Fail." Even if she isn't interested, you have still offered value. This shift in intent is the "Cheat Code" to social freedom. You are no longer "breaking the ice" to get inside; you are breaking the ice to bring the warmth.

The Anatomy of a Stress-Free Initiation

Component	The Anxious Approach	The Grounded Approach
Timing	Wait for "The Perfect Moment" (10+ mins)	3-Second Rule
Intent	To "Get" a result	To "Give" a positive interaction
Momentum	Standing start (Zero social reps)	High Momentum (Talked to 5 people already)

Component	The Anxious Approach	The Grounded Approach
Energy	Potential (Pent-up tension)	Kinetic (Flowing and relaxed)
Safety	Ambiguous / Sneaky	Transparent and Open

Transitioning from "Mindset" to "Mechanics"

In Book 1, we focused on the **Being**. In Book 2, we focus on the **Doing**. However, the "Doing" must always be a reflection of the "Being." This book is your **Field Manual**, and it is structured to build your skill set layer by layer:

- **Chapter 1: Read the Room and Timing:** Developing the "Social Radar" to know when a woman is open to being approached and when she is in a "Closed" state.

- **Chapter 2: Use Situational Openers that Work:** Moving away from "lines" and toward "Observations." You will learn to use the environment as your wingman.

- **Chapter 3: Practice Active Listening for Real Connection:** Using the **Mirror Neuron System** to create deep rapport in minutes, not hours.

- **Chapter 4: Handle Rejection with Grace and Logic:** How to handle the word "No" so well that it actually increases your social status.

- **Chapter 5: Move from a Greeting to Real Talk:** How to move from a 30-second "icebreaker" into a real, meaningful conversation.

The "Momentum Mission" (Your First Field Assignment)

To prepare for Chapter 1, you must begin building your Social Momentum. Today, your goal is not to "approach" for a number. Your goal is simply to "Open the Valve" of your social energy.

The Task: Have five "one-sentence" interactions with strangers you are *not* attracted to.

- "That's a great color on you."

- "Do you know if this place has good WiFi?"

- "Man, the line is moving fast today."

The Goal: Notice how the more you talk, the "lighter" your chest feels. You are converting your potential energy into kinetic energy. You are ready to break the ice.

CHAPTER 1

READ THE ROOM AND TIMING

You are now standing on the edge of the social arena. Your mindset is grounded, your posture is open, and your intent is to "give" value. But before you take a single step or utter a single word, you must engage the most critical skill in the social arsenal: **Calibration**.

Imagine a sniper on a rooftop. He does not simply look through the scope and pull the trigger. He measures the wind speed, the distance, the humidity, and the movement of the target. He gathers data. Only when the variables align does he take the shot.

In social dynamics, most men are "spray and pray" machine gunners. They barge into conversations, interrupt deep moments, and ignore the subtle "Stop" signs that women broadcast. They lack **Situational Awareness**. This chapter is about turning you into the sniper. It is about developing a "Social Radar" so sensitive that you can distinguish between a woman who is begging to be distracted and a woman who wants to be left alone, all from across a crowded room.

This is not just about "politeness." It is about **Efficiency** and **Success Rate**. When you learn to read the room, you stop wasting energy on "Red Light" targets (who will reject you) and start focusing on "Green Light" targets (who are waiting for you). You stop fighting the current and start swimming with it.

1. The Neurobiology of Social Perception: Your Brain's Radar System

To understand how to read a room, we must first look at the hardware you are using. Your brain has a specialized network designed specifically for interpreting the intentions of others. This is primarily centered in the **Superior Temporal Sulcus (STS)**.

The STS is the part of the brain responsible for processing "Biological Motion." It tracks where people are looking (gaze direction), how they are moving (posture), and what their hands are doing (intention). When you walk into a venue, your STS is frantically calculating: *Is that person a threat? Is that person a mate? Is that person angry?*

The Fusiform Face Area (FFA)

Working in tandem with the STS is the **Fusiform Face Area (FFA)**. This region processes facial identity and micro-expressions. It can detect a "Duchenne Smile" (a genuine smile that engages the eyes) versus a "Pan Am Smile" (a fake, polite smile) in less than 200 milliseconds.

The problem for most modern men is that their "Radar" is jammed by their own anxiety. When your Amygdala is screaming "Don't get rejected!", it inhibits the STS and FFA. You become "Socially Blind." You stop seeing *her* and only see your own fear.

The first step of reading the room is to **Externalize Your Focus**. You must consciously switch your brain from "Internal Monologue" (What do I say?) to "External Data Collection" (What is she doing?).

2. The Macro-Read: Assessing the "Energy Temperature"

Before you look at a specific woman, you must read the **Context** of the environment. Every venue has an "Energy Temperature," and your approach must match it. If you bring "High Energy" (loud voice, big gestures) into a "Low Energy" environment (a library or quiet coffee shop), you trigger the group's immune system. You become a disturbance.

High-Energy Environments (The "Mating" Grounds)

- **Examples:** Nightclubs, busy bars, festivals, house parties.
- **The Context:** These environments are designed for social friction. The noise level is high, meaning verbal communication is difficult.
- **The Calibration:** You must rely on **Non-Verbal Dominance**. Your movements must be slower than the crowd (to show stability), but your energy must be "up." You cannot be the "quiet guy in the corner" here; you will be invisible. Physical touch and proximity happen much faster here.

Low-Energy Environments (The "Sanctuaries")

- **Examples:** Bookstores, grocery stores, coffee shops, museums.
- **The Context:** People are here for a specific task or for solitude. Their "Social Shields" are up by default.
- **The Calibration:** You must use a **"Gentle Entry."** You cannot barge in. You must respect the "Personal Bubble" (Peripersonal Space) much more strictly. Your voice should be lower, and your opening must acknowledge the potential interruption ("I know you're reading, but...").

Transitional Spaces (The "Flow" Zones)

- **Examples:** Sidewalks, subways, waiting lines.
- **The Context:** People are in motion. They have a destination.
- **The Calibration:** You have a very short window. You must possess **"Stopping Power"**—the ability to safely halt their momentum without startling them. We will discuss the "Merge" technique later in this chapter.

3. The Micro-Read: The Traffic Light System

Once you have calibrated to the room, you scan for individual targets. To simplify the complex data your STS is receiving, we use the **Traffic Light System**. This filters women into three categories based on their **Availability Signals**.

Red Light: The "Hard Stop" (Do Not Approach)

A "Red Light" signal means the woman is actively signaling "Do Not Disturb." While "Pickup Artists" will tell you that you can "crack" any set, the High-Value Man respects boundaries. Approaching a Red Light requires immense skill and often yields low returns.

The Signals:

- **The Audio Block:** Wearing large, noise-canceling headphones. (Earbuds are a "Dark Yellow," but full cans are a Red).

- **The "Scowl" Focus:** She is typing furiously on her laptop with a furrowed brow. This is "High-Cognitive Load." Interrupting her will trigger anger, not attraction.

- **The Closed Circle:** She is in a group of friends who are standing shoulder-to-shoulder in a tight circle (O-Formation), facing inward. Their backs are to the world.

- **The Speed Walk:** She is moving rapidly, eyes fixed on the horizon, likely late or escaping a situation.

The Protocol: Abort. Your time is better spent elsewhere. Respecting a "No" before it is even spoken is a sign of high social intelligence.

Yellow Light: The "Idle" State (Proceed with Caution)

This is the most common state. The woman is neither inviting nor rejecting. She is simply existing. Most men mistake "Yellow" for "Red" because she isn't smiling. Remember: **Neutrality is not Rejection.**

The Signals:

- **The "Fake" Scroll:** She is looking at her phone, but her thumb isn't moving fast. She is looking up every few seconds. She is likely using the phone as a "prop" to avoid looking awkward while alone.

- **The Wandering Gaze:** She is standing alone (or with a friend), but her eyes are scanning the room. She is looking for stimulation.

- **The Open Stance:** She is talking to a friend, but their feet are planted in a "V-Formation" (open to the room) rather than facing each other directly. This is a subconscious invitation for a third person to join.

- **The Earbud Dangle:** She has one earbud in, or she is holding her headphones. She is "accessible."

The Protocol: Approach. The Yellow Light is a "Green Light" waiting for a catalyst. That catalyst is you.

Green Light: The "Invitation" (Go Immediately)

These are signals of active interest or high receptivity. If you see a Green Light and do not act, you are actively rejecting *her*.

The Signals:

- **The Sustained Gaze:** She locks eyes with you for more than one second, or she looks, looks away, and then *looks back* (The Double Take).

- **The Preen:** Upon seeing you, she fixes her hair, adjusts her dress, or checks her reflection. This is a biological "mating display."

- **The Proximity Hover:** She moves from the other side of the room to stand near you (e.g., ordering a drink right next to you at an empty bar).

- **The Duchenne Smile:** She smiles at you with her eyes crinkling at the corners.

The Protocol: You have a 3-second window. Go now.

4. The Science of Gaze Detection: The "Wi-Fi" Connection

Of all the signals, **Eye Contact** is the most powerful. Humans are the only primates with a visible white sclera. Evolutionary biologists believe this evolved specifically to facilitate **Cooperative Eye Hypothesis**—we *want* others to know where we are looking.

Your eyes are your "Social Wi-Fi." When you lock eyes with a woman, you are "pairing" devices.

The "Look-Back" Rule

If you catch a woman looking at you, do not immediately look down. That signals submission (Low Status). Do not stare aggressively (Threat).

- **The High-Value Response:** Hold the gaze for a split second longer than feels comfortable, give a slight, knowing smirk, and then slowly look away *to the side*.

- **The Confirmation:** If she looks down and smiles, she is submissive/interested. If she looks away and keeps a neutral face, she might just be scanning. If she looks back at you within 45 seconds, it is a confirmed Green Light.

Pupil Dilation

If you are close enough to see her pupils, look for dilation. Under the influence of **Dopamine** and **Oxytocin** (attraction chemicals), the pupils expand to let in more light/data. This is an involuntary, honest signal of interest.

5. Reading Group Dynamics: The "V" vs. The "O"

Approaching a woman who is with friends is often easier than approaching her alone, provided you can read the **Group Geometry**.

The "O" Formation (Closed)

If the group is standing in a tight circle, shoulders touching or overlapping, they are in a "Closed System." They are likely discussing something private or are highly bonded. Breaking into an O-Formation is physically difficult and socially aggressive. You have to tap someone on the shoulder, which interrupts the flow.

- **Verdict:** Wait for the formation to shift.

The "U" or "V" Formation (Open)

If the group is standing in a semi-circle or "horseshoe" shape, leaving an open space facing the room, they are in an "Open System." That empty space is a vacuum waiting to be filled.

- **Verdict:** You can step into the empty space and address the group as a whole. "Hey guys, quick question..."

Identifying the "Gatekeeper"

In every group of women, there is usually a "Protector" or "Gatekeeper." This is often the less attractive friend or the "Mother Hen" of the group. If you focus only on the girl you like (The Target) and ignore the Gatekeeper, the Gatekeeper will shut you down ("We need to go to the bathroom").

- **The Strategy:** Win the Gatekeeper first. Direct your opening question and your first 30 seconds of attention to the *group* or the Gatekeeper. Once she approves of you, she will "allow" you to talk to the Target.

You have identified a Yellow or Green Light target. Now, *when* do you speak? Timing is the difference between an "Interruption" and an "Integration."

The "Conversation Lull"

If two people are talking, observe the rhythm of their conversation. Do not speak while they are rapidly exchanging sentences (high engagement). Wait for the **Lull**—that moment of silence where they both look around or sip their drinks.

- **The logic:** In a lull, the group is "starved" for new stimulus. You arriving is a relief, not a bother.

The "Inhalation" Rule

If you must interrupt a solo person or a group, watch their breathing.

- **Never interrupt on the Inhale:** When someone inhales sharply, they are preparing to speak. If you cut them off, you are physically stifling their expression.

- **Interrupt on the Exhale/Pause:** When they have finished a sentence and are breathing out, their "turn" is over. This is the biological "gap" for a new speaker.

The "Merge" (Moving Targets)

Approaching a woman walking down the street is the hardest maneuver. You cannot chase her from behind (Predator behavior). You cannot jump in front of her (Obstacle behavior).

- **The Technique:** You must walk *parallel* to her for a few steps, match her speed, and then initiate the "Head Turn."

- **The Merge:** "Excuse me ..." (spoken over your shoulder). Once she turns and slows down, *then* you stop and turn fully. You must bridge the gap between "Stranger walking" and "Conversation."

7. Environmental Awareness: Using the Room as a Wingman

The final piece of reading the room is using the environment itself to time your approach. This is called **Triangulation**.

Instead of approaching her directly ("Hi, I'm John"), you comment on a third object that you both are experiencing.

- **The Queue:** If the line at the coffee shop is taking forever, that shared frustration is a timing window. "I think we're going to age five years before we get our lattes."
- **The Event:** If a song comes on at the bar that everyone hates (or loves), that is a timing window.
- **The Disruption:** If a glass breaks, a dog barks, or the lights flicker—**Speak Immediately**. The disruption breaks everyone's "autopilot." The person who speaks first after a disruption becomes the temporary "Leader" of the room.

8. Summary: The Calibration Checklist

Before you engage, run this 3-second diagnostic:

1. **Energy Check:** Am I matching the energy of the venue? (High vs. Low)
2. **Traffic Light:** Is she Red, Yellow, or Green?
3. **Group Geometry:** Is it an "O" (Closed) or a "V" (Open)?
4. **Timing:** Is there a lull? Is she breathing out?
5. **Go.**

If the lights are Yellow or Green, you must act. The "Perfect Moment" does not exist. There is only the "Available Moment." The sniper doesn't wait for the wind to stop completely; he adjusts for the wind and takes the shot.

Action Steps: The "Social Radar" Drills

You cannot learn to read a room by reading a book. You must go into the field.

Drill 1: The Traffic Light Audit Go to a busy public place (a mall food court or a park). Sit on a bench. For 10 minutes, do nothing but assign a color (Red, Yellow, Green) to every woman you see.

- *Note:* Look for the "fake scroll." Look for the "V-formation" feet.
- *Goal:* Realize how many "Yellows" there actually are. The world is not as "Red" as your anxiety tells you.

Drill 2: The Eye Contact "Tag" Walk through a shopping district. Make eye contact with five strangers.

- *Task:* Hold the gaze until *they* look away.
- *Observe:* Which way did they look? Down (Submission)? Away (Dismissal)? Did they smile?
- *Goal:* Desensitize yourself to the intensity of the "Gaze."

CHAPTER 2

USE SITUATIONAL OPENERS THAT WORK

You have mastered the art of "Reading the Room." You can identify the high-traffic social zones, you can spot a "Green Light" from thirty feet away, and your internal radar is tuned to the subtle shifts in group geometry. You are standing in the perfect position at the perfect time. Now comes the moment that paralyzes 99% of men: **The Open.**

In the old paradigm of social advice, "The Open" was a performance. You were told to use "canned lines," elaborate stories, or "neg" a woman to get her attention. These methods failed for a simple biological reason: they are **Incongruent**. When you use a line that someone else wrote, your micro-expressions and vocal tonality don't match the words. The woman's brain—specifically her **Superior Temporal Sulcus**—detects this mismatch as a "deceptive signal." She feels a "creep vibe" because what you are saying doesn't match who you are being.

Authentic confidence requires a different approach. We are going to use **Situational Openers**. These are comments, questions, or observations based on the immediate shared reality between you and her. By using the situation, you bypass her "Stranger Danger" filters because you aren't coming at her with a script; you are simply acknowledging the world you are both already in.

1. The Neurobiology of the "Shared Reality"

Why are situational openers so effective? It comes down to the **Common Ground Theory** in linguistics. For a conversation to feel "safe" and "natural," both participants must feel they are occupying the same mental space.

When you use a canned line, you are forcing her to enter *your* world (which is a world of performance). When you use a situational opener, you are inviting her to join you in the *real* world.

The Role of the "Social Bridge"

Your brain's **Mirror Neuron System** is designed to sync with the people around you. When you point out something in the environment—the long line, a weird piece of art, or a great song—you are creating a "Social Bridge." You are essentially saying, "I am experiencing the same reality as you." This immediately lowers the cognitive load for her because she doesn't have to figure out "what you're doing." You're just two people noticing the same thing.

2. The Three Pillars of the Situational Opener

To construct an opener that works, you need to follow three fundamental rules: **Low Stakes, Observation-Based, and Non-Seeker.**

Pillar I: Low Stakes

The opener should be so casual that it doesn't require a "big" response. If you ask a deep, heavy question immediately, you trigger "Social Pressure." A low-stakes opener is something she can answer with three words or even a nod. Ironically, the less "important" your opener feels, the more likely she is to engage with it.

Pillar II: Observation-Based

Don't reach for a topic. Look at what is happening *right now.*

- **The Environment:** The décor, the weather, the crowd.

- **The Activity:** What she is doing (reading, waiting for a drink, looking at a menu).

- **The Shared Experience:** The fact that the music is too loud or the coffee smells incredible.

Pillar III: The "Non-Seeker" Vibe

In Book 1, we discussed being a "Giver" rather than a "Taker." Your opener must reflect this. You aren't asking for her number yet; you are "giving" a momentary observation. You should speak as if you are thinking out loud. This is called **"Throwaway Delivery."**

3. The "Contextual Trio": Three Types of Situational Openers

There are three primary ways to open based on your environment. Mastering these ensures you are never "stuck" for a topic.

A. The Indirect Opinion (The "Soft" Open)

This is the most "socially safe" way to start. You ask for a quick, low-stakes opinion on something in the immediate vicinity.

- **Example (Bar):** "I'm trying to decide if that's the best or worst cocktail on the menu. What's the verdict on yours?"

- **Example (Grocery Store):** "I've been staring at these avocados for five minutes. Do you have a secret for picking the one that isn't a rock?"

- **The Logic:** People love giving their opinions. It places them in a position of "Expertise," which makes them feel good.

B. The Observational Statement (The "Ghost" Open)

This isn't even a question. It's a statement about the environment. You don't even necessarily look at her when you say it; you look at the thing you are talking about.

- **Example (Waiting in line):** "I think we're going to be three years older by the time we get to the front of this line."

- **Example (Art Gallery):** "I can't tell if that's meant to be a sunset or a very angry cat."

- **The Logic:** This is "Low Pressure." If she doesn't respond, you haven't "failed" because you were just commenting to the room. If she laughs or agrees, the door is open.

C. The "Direct-Contextual" Open

This is for when the "Green Lights" are strong. You acknowledge her presence directly but tie it to the context.

- **Example (Gym):** "I see you here every Tuesday and you're always crushing it. I had to come over and ask—what are you training for?"
- **Example (Coffee Shop):** "That book looks intense. On a scale of 1 to 10, how much is it ruining your afternoon?"
- **The Logic:** It shows you are observant and bold, but because it's tied to what she is actually doing, it doesn't feel like a "random" intrusion.

4. The "Time Constraint" Technique

The #1 reason women "shut down" an opener is the fear that they will be trapped in a 20-minute boring conversation. To solve this, you use a **False Time Constraint (FTC).**

Before you even speak, you signal through your body language that you are "on your way" somewhere else. You might be angled slightly away, or you might lead with:

- *"I can only stay for a second, but I had to ask..."*
- *"I'm actually headed to meet my friends, but I noticed..."*

By telling her you are leaving soon, you remove the "Trap." She can relax and enjoy the interaction knowing that you aren't going to cling to her all night. This is the **Paradox of Availability**: The less "available" you seem, the more she wants to keep you there.

5. Vocal Tonality: The "Sub-Communication" of the Open

It's not what you say; it's how it sounds. As we learned in Book 1, your voice is a direct wire to her **Amygdala.**

- **The Mistake: "Seeking Rapport" Pitch.** ending your sentence with a rising pitch, like a question? This sounds like you are asking for permission to speak. It signals low status.

- **The Masterclass: "Breaking Rapport" Pitch.** End your opener with a flat or slightly downward inflection. This signals authority and certainty. You aren't "asking" if your observation is okay; you are stating it as a fact.

The "Volume Match": If the room is quiet, speak softly. If the bar is loud, speak with "Chest Voice." Your volume must be calibrated to the "Energy Temperature" of the room (Chapter 1).

6. The "Bridge to the Hook": What Happens After the Opener?

An opener is just a key. Once the door is open, you need to "Hook" the conversation. A "Hook" is the moment she becomes an active participant.

To move from the opener to the hook, you use **"Free Information."** *
You: "That book looks intense. Scale of 1 to 10?"

- **Her:** "Oh, it's an 11. It's about quantum physics."
- **The Hook:** You don't just say "Cool." You take the "Free Information" (Quantum Physics) and build on it. "Quantum physics? Okay, so you're either a genius or you're trying to build a time machine to escape this coffee shop."

7. Summary: The Situational Opener Checklist

1. **Stop Overthinking:** Use the 3-Second Rule.
2. **Look for the "Third Object":** Don't talk about her; talk about the environment.
3. **Low Stakes:** Make it easy for her to answer.
4. **FTC:** Signal that you aren't staying forever.
5. **Grounded Tone:** Speak with a downward inflection.

Action Steps: The "Commentator" Drill

Today, your mission is not to get numbers. Your mission is to become a "Social Commentator."

The Task: Go to a public place (grocery store, park, mall). Make 10 observational statements to strangers.

- "Man, it's freezing in here."
- "That's the biggest dog I've ever seen."

- "I think we're the only ones not on our phones right now."

The Goal: See how many people smile or agree. You will realize that the "Ice" is much thinner than you thought. Once you can open a stranger about a dog, you can open a beautiful woman about her book.

CHAPTER 3

PRACTICE ACTIVE LISTENING FOR REAL CONNECTION

You have successfully broken the ice. The "Situational Opener" has done its job: it bypassed her stranger-danger filters, established a shared reality, and created a small spark of engagement. But as many men find out the hard way, the "Open" is only the invitation. The "Conversation" is the dance.

Most men fail in the second to fifth minute of an interaction because they treat conversation like an interview or a performance. They are so trapped in their own **Dorsolateral Prefrontal Cortex (dlPFC)**—the part of the brain responsible for planning and logical sequencing—that they stop actually hearing what is being said. They are simply waiting for their turn to speak, frantically rehearsing their next line while the woman provides "Free Information" that they completely ignore.

To move from a greeting to a real connection, you must shift from **Reactive Talking** to **Active Listening**. This is not a passive act of silence. It is an aggressive, high-energy cognitive process where you use your brain to "map" her internal world. When you listen actively, you trigger the **Mirror Neuron System** in both brains, creating a physiological state of "Neural Coupling." This is the scientific definition of "Chemistry."

1. The Neurobiology of the "Click": Neural Coupling

When two people are truly engaged in a conversation, something remarkable happens in their brains. Research using fMRI shows that the brain activity of the listener begins to mirror the brain activity of the speaker with a slight delay. This is known as **Neural Coupling**.

The Role of the Superior Temporal Sulcus (STS) and Parietal Cortex

As she speaks, your STS processes her speech and intentions, while your Parietal Cortex maps her spatial metaphors. If you are listening deeply, your brain actually begins to anticipate what she will say next. This "predictive coding" makes her feel deeply understood on a sub-cortical level. She won't say, "I love how his Parietal Cortex is mapping my metaphors"; she will say, "I feel like we just *clicked*."

The Dopamine Reward of Being Heard

Being listened to triggers the same reward centers in the brain as food or money. When you give a woman your full, undivided attention, you are providing a "Dopaminergic Gift." In a world of digital distractions, a man who can truly listen is a rare, high-value commodity.

2. The Three Levels of Listening

To master this, you must move through three distinct levels of auditory and emotional processing.

Level 1: Internal Listening (The Amateur)

At this level, you are focused on *yourself*. You hear her words, but you are primarily thinking about:

- "What should I say next?"
- "Do I look cool right now?"

- "Is she liking me?" **Result:** The conversation feels staggered and "clunky." You miss the emotional subtext and often interrupt just as she was about to share something vulnerable.

Level 2: Focused Listening (The Professional)

At this level, you are like a laser. You are focused entirely on her. You notice her tone, her pauses, and her choice of words. You aren't thinking about your next line; you are thinking about *her* line. **Result:** You pick up on "Free Information" and can ask relevant follow-up questions. The conversation flows because you are responding to what was actually said.

Level 3: Global Listening (The Master)

At this level, you are listening to everything *around* the words. You notice the shift in her body language, the way her eyes light up when she mentions her dog, and the "energy" of the room. You are listening with your skin as much as your ears. **Result:** You can "label" her emotions and create deep rapport instantly. You pick up on the things she *isn't* saying.

3. The Mechanics of the "Deep Hook"

In Chapter 2, we mentioned the "Hook." Active listening is how you find the **Deep Hook**. Most men only listen for "Nouns" (What she does, where she is from). A confident man listens for **Values and Emotions** (Why she does it, how she feels about it).

The "Free Information" Mine

Every sentence a woman speaks contains 2-3 pieces of "Free Information."

> **Her:** "I just moved here from Chicago for a job in bio-tech, and I'm still trying to find a good pizza place."

- **The Amateur Hook:** "Oh, bio-tech? My cousin does that." (Focuses on the dry fact, leading to a dead end).
- **The Medium Hook:** "How are you liking the city so far?" (Better, but generic).
- **The Deep Hook:** "Chicago to here is a big jump. What's been the most 'culture shock' moment for you so far?" (Focuses on her internal experience and emotional transition).

By hooking the *emotion* (the jump/the shock) rather than the *fact* (the job), you signal that you are interested in *her*, not just her resume.

4. Tactical Empathy: Labeling and Mirroring

Borrowed from high-stakes hostage negotiation, these techniques are the most powerful tools for creating rapid connection. They bypass the logical mind and speak directly to the **Limbic System**.

Mirroring (The Isopraxism Effect)

In linguistics, this is repeating the last 1-3 critical words of what she just said, phrased as a question.

- **Her:** "I've had such a long day, my boss is being incredibly demanding."
- **You:** "Incredibly demanding?"
- **The Result:** This triggers a "biological requirement" for her to elaborate. She feels heard, and you didn't even have to come up with a new topic.

Labeling (Emotional Validation)

Labeling is a way of acknowledging her emotional state without being "therapist-y." You use the phrase "It seems like..." or "It sounds like..."

- **You:** "It sounds like you're the kind of person who takes a lot of pride in your work, and it's frustrating when it's not recognized."
- **The Result:** If you get it right, she will say, "Exactly!" This triggers a massive release of **Oxytocin** (the bonding hormone). You have just moved from "Stranger" to "Confidant."

5. The "Wait" Rule: The Power of the Silence

Anxious men fear silence. They treat a gap in conversation like a vacuum that must be filled with their own nervous energy. A confident man knows that **Silence is a Tool**.

After you ask a question or use a Mirror, *wait*. Count to three in your head. The **"Silence Gap"** puts a small amount of social pressure on her to fill the void. Often, the most interesting and personal information she shares will come *after* a pause. By not rushing to speak, you communicate that you are comfortable in your own skin and that you value her thoughts more than your own voice.

6. Eye Contact During Listening: The "Triangle" Method

As we discussed in Book 1, eye contact is vital, but staring can be aggressive. When listening, use the **Triangle Method** to keep the gaze soft and natural:

1. Look at her left eye.
2. Look at her right eye.
3. Look at her mouth (this signals attentive listening and, in romantic contexts, creates a subtle attraction).
4. Repeat.

This creates a "soft" gaze that is inviting rather than piercing. It signals to her **Fusiform Face Area** that you are fully present and processing her facial micro-expressions.

7. Avoiding the "Interview Mode" Trap

The most common conversation killer is asking too many questions in a row. This feels like an interrogation and puts the "work" of the conversation on her. To avoid this, use the **Statement-to-Question Ratio (2:1)**.

For every one question you ask, make two statements.

- **Question:** "What made you choose bio-tech?"
- **Statement 1 (Cold Read):** "You seem like someone who likes solving puzzles."
- **Statement 2 (Self-Disclosure):** "I've always been fascinated by how things work, though I went the engineering route instead."

Statements take the pressure off her and give *her* "Free Information" to hook into.

8. The Art of the Cold Read

A "Cold Read" is a statement about her personality based on your observations. It is far more engaging than a question because it shows you are paying attention to *who she is*.

- **Standard Question:** "Do you travel a lot?"
- **Cold Read:** "You have the energy of someone who's spent a lot of time exploring. I'm guessing you're not originally from around here."

Even if the cold read is wrong, it doesn't matter. She will correct you ("Actually, I've lived here my whole life!"), and you can follow up with, "Really? You have such a worldly vibe, what's your secret?" It keeps the energy high and the focus on her character.

9. The "Self-Disclosure" Bridge

To create a balanced connection, you cannot just be a "listening machine." You must also share of yourself. However, the timing is crucial.

The Rule: Share *after* she has shared. If she tells you about a struggle she had at work, listen, label it, and then share a brief (30-second) similar experience you've had. This creates **Reciprocity**.

Vulnerability vs. Weakness

- **Vulnerability:** Admitting to a challenge you faced and how you handled it. (Attractive/High Status).

- **Weakness:** Complaining about a situation you are refusing to change. (Unattractive/Low Status).

10. Summary: The Active Listening Checklist

1.   **Ditch the Script:** Stop rehearsing your next line. Be present in the now.

2. **Hunt for the Emotion:** Listen for the "Why," not just the "What." Find the values behind the nouns.

3. **Mirror & Label:** Use her own words and identify her feelings to show you're in her world.

4. **Embrace the Pause:** Let the silence do the heavy lifting.

5. **2:1 Ratio:** Balance your questions with observations, cold reads, and brief stories.

Action Steps: The "Deep Hook" Mission

The Task: In your next three conversations (even with friends or coworkers), identify at least two pieces of "Free Information" that are emotional, not factual.

- **Practice:** Use one Mirror ("...really stressful?") and one Label ("It seems like you're really passionate about that.")

- **Observe:** Watch how their body language relaxes and they lean in when you label their emotion correctly.

CHAPTER 4

HANDLE REJECTION WITH GRACE AND LOGIC

We have reached the most critical juncture in the social journey. You have mastered the "Open" and the "Flow," but now we must confront the ghost that haunts every man who dares to initiate: **Rejection.**

For many men, the fear of "No" is not just a social inconvenience; it is a perceived existential threat. This fear keeps millions of men silent, paralyzed in the corner of bars and coffee shops, watching opportunities pass them by. They view rejection as a definitive verdict on their value as a human being. They believe that if a woman is not interested, it means they are "not enough."

In this chapter, we are going to dismantle that delusion. We will look at the **Neurobiology of Social Pain**, the **Logic of Mating Variance**, and the **Strategy of the Graceful Exit**. You will learn that the ability to handle rejection with composure is actually one of the highest sub-

100

communications of value a man can possess. By the end of this chapter, you will not only stop fearing rejection; you will welcome it as a necessary data point on the path to success.

1. The Neurobiology of "No": Why it Hurts

To conquer the fear of rejection, you must first understand why your body reacts to it so violently. When you are socially rejected, your brain does not distinguish between a "bruised ego" and a "broken leg."

The Anterior Cingulate Cortex (ACC)

Functional MRI (fMRI) studies have shown that social rejection activates the **Anterior Cingulate Cortex**, the same region of the brain that processes physical pain. From an evolutionary perspective, this makes perfect sense. In the ancestral environment, being rejected by the "tribe" or a high-value mate meant death. You were less likely to survive, less likely to find food, and less likely to pass on your genes. Your brain developed a "Social Pain" signal to warn you to stay in the good graces of others.

The Amygdala Hijack

When you perceive a rejection—whether it's a cold shoulder or a polite "I have a boyfriend"—your **Amygdala** triggers a fight-or-flight response. Your heart rate spikes, your palms sweat, and your **Prefrontal Cortex (PFC)**—the center of logic—begins to shut down. This is why men often react to rejection in one of two low-value ways:

1. **The Supplicant:** He tries to "convince" her or apologizes profusely for existing.
2. **The Aggressor:** He becomes bitter, makes an insulting comment, or "sour grapes" the situation.

Both reactions are a sign that your brain has been hijacked by a primitive fear. Handling rejection with **Grace and Logic** is the act of using the **Ventrolateral Prefrontal Cortex (VLPFC)** to manually override that alarm system.

2. The Logic of Variance: It's Not About You

The greatest psychological shift you can make is moving from a "Personal" view of rejection to a "Statistical" view. This is the **Logic of Mating Variance**.

Imagine you are a world-class salesperson selling the highest-quality software on the market. If you call a company that just signed a five-year contract with a competitor yesterday, they will say "No." Does that "No" mean your software is bad? Does it mean you are a bad salesman? No. It simply means the **Timing** and **Circumstances** were not aligned.

The 90% Rule

In any given social environment, a woman's receptivity is determined by factors that have 0% to do with you:

- **The Boyfriend Factor:** She is in a committed, happy relationship.
- **The Emotional State:** She just had a fight with her mother or a bad day at work.
- **The Social Load:** She is out with a friend she hasn't seen in three years and wants a "girls' night" only.
- **The Logistics:** She is leaving in three minutes to catch a flight.

If you approach ten women and nine of them are "unavailable" for the reasons above, you haven't been "rejected" nine times; you have simply encountered **Statistical Variance**. The High-Value Man realizes that he is a "Price Tag" and she is the "Customer." If she doesn't buy, it doesn't change the value of the product; it just means she wasn't in the market today.

3. The "Status-Boost" of the Graceful Exit

Most men don't realize that **how you leave** is often more important than how you arrive. The moment a woman realizes she isn't interested, she is in a state of high social tension. She expects you to be awkward, angry, or clingy.

When you handle the "No" with total composure, warmth, and zero butt-hurt, you do something remarkable: **You prove your high status.**

Sub-communicating Abundance

By walking away with a smile and a "Hey, no worries, have a great night with your friends," you sub-communicate:

1. **Abundance:** You have so many options that her specific rejection doesn't affect your mood.
2. **Emotional Regulation:** You are a man who can control his own state.

3. **Respect:** You are a gentleman who respects her boundaries.

The Paradox: There are countless stories of men who handled a rejection so gracefully that the woman (or her friend) actually chased them down five minutes later because they were so impressed by his "Vibe" during the exit.

4. Categorizing the "No": Hard vs. Soft Rejection

Not all rejections are created equal. To handle them with logic, you must be able to categorize them in real-time.

Type A: The Hard No (Logistical/Fundamental)

- **Examples:** "I'm married," "I'm here for a private meeting," or total silence/turning the back.

- **The Logic:** This is a brick wall. There is no "game" that fixes this.

- **The Graceful Exit:** Immediate and clean. "Got it. I'll let you get back to it. Enjoy your evening!" Don't linger. Lingering turns you into a "creeper."

Type B: The Soft No (The "Test" or "Compliance Check")

- **Examples:** "I'm kind of busy right now," or "You're probably a player."

- **The Logic:** This is often a **Compliance Test**. Her brain is checking to see if you are easily rattled. She is checking for "Groundedness."

- **The Graceful Response:** Do not defend yourself. Acknowledge the comment and stay in the flow. "I get it, I look suspicious. I'll give you thirty seconds to realize I'm actually the best part of your Tuesday, and then I'll leave you alone."

5. Tactical De-Escalation: The "I Get It" Technique

If you feel the interaction is going south, the best way to handle it is to **De-Escalate** before she has to formally reject you. This is called "Taking it off the table."

If she looks uncomfortable or distracted, you say:

"Hey, it seems like you're really focused on [her book/her friend/her phone]. I'm going to go head back to my friends, but it was great meeting you for a second."

Why this works: You are the one who "ended" the interaction. You maintained the frame of the leader. You gave her the "Safety" she was looking for without making it a "big deal." This leaves the door open for future interactions (The "Call Back") if you see her again.

6. Managing the "Post-Rejection" Neurochemistry

Even if you handle it gracefully on the outside, your internal chemistry might still be reeling from the Amygdala spike. You must have a protocol for **Nervous System Regulation**.

The 5-Breath Reset

Immediately after walking away, do not go hide in the bathroom. Do not look at your phone. Stand tall, and take five "Box Breaths" (Inhale 4s, Hold 4s, Exhale 4s, Hold 4s). This stimulates the **Vagus Nerve** and tells your brain that the "threat" is over.

Re-Engagement (The Flywheel)

The biggest mistake is letting a rejection stop your **Social Momentum**. If you get rejected and then stop talking to everyone for an hour, the "pain" will calcify in your brain.

- **The Protocol:** Within 60 seconds of a rejection, make a small comment to someone else—the bartender, a guy at the table next to you, anyone. This proves to your brain that the "Social World" is still intact.

7. Reframing: Rejection as a "Filter," Not a "Verdict"

High-value men view rejection as a **Filtering Mechanism**. You are looking for a woman who is high-interest, available, and compatible with your energy. Every "No" is simply the universe helping you filter out the "Mismatches" faster.

If you want to find gold, you have to sift through a lot of dirt. If you get upset at the dirt for not being gold, you are the one being illogical. The "No" is the dirt. The "Yes" is the gold. Move through the dirt as fast as possible with a smile on your face.

8. Summary: The Graceful Logic Checklist

1. **Override the ACC:** Recognize the physical "sting" as a biological leftover, not a fact.
2. **Statistical Mindset:** It's about variance and timing, not your worth.
3. **Exit Early, Exit Clean:** The moment you see a "Red Light," leave with warmth.
4. **No "Sour Grapes":** Never be bitter. Bitter is low-status.
5. **Re-engage:** Keep the flywheel spinning by talking to the next person immediately.

Action Steps: The "Rejection Desensitization" Mission

To master this, you must experience the "stinging" sensation of the ACC until it no longer bothers you.

The Task: Go out and purposefully get "Rejected" five times.

- **How:** Ask for something slightly unreasonable or approach "Red Light" targets. Ask a barista for a 10% discount just because it's Tuesday.

- **The Goal:** Your goal is NOT to get the "Yes." Your goal is to get the "No" and practice the **Graceful Exit**. "No worries, had to ask! Have a great day."

- **Observe:** Notice how the "Pain" disappears after the third time. You are becoming **Antifragile**.

CHAPTER 5

MOVE FROM A GREETING TO REAL TALK

You have survived the initial approach, navigated the "open," and managed your internal state through the possibility of rejection. You are now in the "Green Zone." The conversation is happening, but there is a new danger on the horizon: **The Plateau.** This is the moment where "Small Talk" overstays its welcome. You've discussed the weather, your jobs, and how you both know the host. If you stay here too long, the energy will die, the "friend-zone" filters will activate, and you will become just another pleasant but forgettable stranger.

To build true attraction and a deep sense of connection, you must learn to bridge the gap from the superficial to the substantial. This requires engaging the **Orbitofrontal Cortex (OFC)**—the part of the brain involved in decision-making and reward processing—and the **Insular Cortex**, which processes emotional awareness. In this chapter, we will master the transition from "Safe Talk" to "Real Talk," using advanced techniques like the **Cold Read**, **Value-Based Branching**, and **Suggestive Playfulness**.

1. The Psychology of the Transition: Breaking the Formal Frame

Most people operate within a "Formal Frame" when meeting strangers. This is a protective social script designed to minimize risk. It is polite, predictable, and incredibly boring. To move to "Real Talk," you must be the one to break this frame.

The "Interrogation" vs. "Integration"

Small talk feels like an interrogation because it focuses on facts (The "What"). Real talk feels like integration because it focuses on motivations (The "Why").

- **Formal Frame:** "How long have you lived here?"
- **Substantial Frame:** "What was the specific moment you realized this city felt like home?"

When you ask about the *moment* or the *feeling*, you force her brain to move from the **Dorsolateral Prefrontal Cortex** (logical retrieval) to the **Hippocampus** (memory/emotion). You are literally changing the neural neighborhood of the conversation.

2. Value-Based Branching: Finding the "Hidden Why"

Every piece of "Free Information" she gives you is a branch. Most men follow the branch that leads to more facts. You are going to follow the branch that leads to **Values**.

The "Motivation Extraction" Technique

If she says she is a nurse, don't ask about her hours. Ask about the *drive*.

- **Her:** "I've been a pediatric nurse for three years."
- **You:** "That takes a specific kind of mental toughness. Were you the person in your family who always stepped up when things got chaotic, or did you have to learn that on the job?"

By making an assumption about her character (Value-Based), you invite her to talk about who she *is*, not just what she *does*. This triggers the **Ventromedial Prefrontal Cortex**, which is associated with self-referential thought and the "joy of self-disclosure."

A "Cold Read" is an observation presented as a statement rather than a question. It is the single most effective tool for moving into "Real Talk" because it demonstrates high social intuition.

Why Cold Reads Work

When you ask a question, you are taking value (information). When you offer a cold read, you are giving value (insight).

- **The Question:** "Are you a creative person?" (Low value, requires effort from her).

- **The Cold Read:** "You have the look of someone who is incredibly organized during the day, but probably has a very chaotic creative side that only comes out on the weekends." (High value, shows you are observing her).

The "Win-Win" of Being Wrong

If your cold read is right, she is amazed ("How did you know?"). If it's wrong, she will correct you with a high-energy explanation ("No, I'm actually organized 24/7 because..."). Either way, the conversation has moved to a deeper level of personality analysis.

4. Suggestive Playfulness: Managing the "Sexual Tension"

Real talk isn't just about "deep" topics; it's about **Vibe**. If the conversation is too serious, it becomes "The Interview." If it's too silly, it becomes "The Clown." You need **Suggestive Playfulness**.

The "Misinterpretation" Tool

This involves playfully "accusing" her of something based on a deliberate (and obvious) misinterpretation of her words.

- **Her:** "I really like the energy in this room."

- **You:** "Wait, are you trying to hit on me already? We just met. You have to at least buy me a drink first." (Said with a smirk/downward tonality).

This uses **Push-Pull** dynamics. You are "pushing" her away with the accusation, but "pulling" her in with the humor and eye contact. This spikes the **Adrenaline** and **Dopamine** levels in the interaction, moving it from "Friendly" to "Flirtatious."

5. The "Us" Frame: Creating an Instant Alliance

One of the most powerful ways to move into "Real Talk" is to shift the language from "I/You" to "We/Us." This creates a "Micro-Culture" between the two of you.

Narrative We-ing

Start including her in your future-tense observations.

- *"We should probably leave before they realize we're the most interesting people in here."*
- *"If we were stuck on a desert island, I feel like you'd be the one making the fire while I'd be trying to befriending the monkeys."*

This signals to her **Posterior Cingulate Cortex** that you are already viewing her as a partner or teammate. It bypasses the "Stranger" barrier and establishes a sense of familiarity.

6. Vulnerability Loops: The "Giver" Strategy

To get her to open up, you must be willing to show a "controlled" piece of vulnerability first. This is based on the **Law of Reciprocity**.

The "Minor Flaw" Disclosure

Don't share your deepest traumas. Share a minor, relatable flaw or an "embarrassing" passion.

- *"I'm going to lose all my 'cool points' here, but I actually spent three hours today researching the history of fountain pens."*

When you show that you are comfortable with your own "un-cool" parts, it signals that you are a "Safe Harbor." She will feel the sub-cortical urge to share something real about herself in return.

7. The Transition Checklist: From Small to Real

1. **Spot the Fact:** Listen for the "Noun" (Job, Location, Hobby).
2. **Dig for the Value:** Ask or state the *reason* behind the noun.
3. **Use a Cold Read:** Make a "You look like..." statement.
4. **Inject Playfulness:** Use misinterpretation to keep the energy light.
5. **Create the "Us" Frame:** Use "We" language to build an alliance.

6. **Check for "The Hook":** Is she leaning in? Is her pupil dilation increasing? These are signs the **Hypothalamus** is engaged.

Action Steps: The "Value Hunter" Mission

The Task: In your next conversation, forbid yourself from asking more than two "fact-based" questions.

- **The Goal:** Every time you want to ask "Where are you from?" or "What do you do?", replace it with a **Cold Read** or a **Value-Based Branch**.

- **Observe:** Watch the change in the other person's eyes when they realize they don't have to give the same "scripted" answer they've given a thousand times.

CONCLUSION

START EVERY INTERACTION STRONG

You have transitioned from the theoretical foundations of Book 1—building your internal value, regulating your nervous system, and understanding the evolutionary roots of attraction—into the active, kinetic world of Book 2. You have learned to read the invisible geometry of a room, to deploy situational openers that bypass social resistance, to listen with the precision of a high-stakes negotiator, and to handle the sting of rejection with the stoicism of a man who knows his worth is non-negotiable.

This conclusion is a **Synthesis**. We are going to integrate the mechanics of the "Open," the "Flow," and the "Transition" into a singular, cohesive philosophy of social dominance. To start every interaction strong is to operate from a position where the outcome is secondary to the process.

We must return to the brain one last time to understand why the "Start" is the most leveraged moment of any interaction. Your brain, and the brain of the woman you are approaching, is performing a massive "Data Dump" in the first ten seconds. This is governed by the **Thin-Slicing** capabilities of the **Adaptive Unconscious**.

The Amygdala's Safety Audit

Before she even hears your first word, her Amygdala is asking one question: *Threat or Opportunity?* If your body language is closed, your eyes are darting, or your approach is hesitant, you trigger a "Threat" response. The prefrontal cortex shuts down, and she enters a state of social avoidance.

To start strong, you must provide the "Safety Signal" immediately:

- **The "Smile Lag":** Don't approach with a plastered-on grin. Approach with a neutral, grounded face, and only when you make eye contact, let a genuine smile spread slowly. This signals that the smile is *earned* and authentic, rather than a nervous mask.

- **The Postural "Open":** Never approach "square on" (the "Predator Stance"). Approach at a slight angle, showing that your vital organs are unprotected. This is a biological signal of non-aggression and extreme confidence.

2. The Physics of Approach: Angles, Velocity, and Momentum

Most men fail because they move like a "Heat-Seeking Missile." They see a target, lock on, and move in a straight line. This creates an immediate spike in the woman's **Cortisol** levels.

The Parabolic Path

A High-Value Man utilizes "Ambient Movement." You do not walk *to* her; you walk *past* her.

- **The Tangent:** Your path should be a curve. You are walking toward the bar or the exit, and you happen to "notice" her as you pass through her social orbit.

- **The Vocal Bridge:** You deliver your opener while still moving or standing at a 45-degree angle. Only when she engages and "hooks" do you fully pivot your feet to face her. This creates a "Reward" system for her engagement.

3. The Philosophy of "Outcome Independence"

The strongest way to start any interaction is to not care how it ends. This is **Outcome Independence**. When you are "attached" to a specific result (getting a number, getting a laugh, getting a date), you create **Social Pressure**. This pressure is palpable; it acts like a repelling magnet.

The "Hunter" vs. "The King"

- **The Hunter** is lean and hungry. He is looking for something to "take" from the environment. His energy is desperate.
- **The King** already has everything he needs. He moves through his "kingdom" simply to see how his subjects are doing. He is a "Giver" of attention, not a "Taker" of validation.

Starting strong means adopting the "King" archetype. You are not approaching her because you *need* her; you are approaching her because you are a high-value man who noticed something interesting and decided to share that observation. If she responds, great. If she doesn't, you are still the King.

4. Mastering the "Vocal Lead" and the Resonance of Authority

Your voice is the bridge between your internal state and her perception. Most men start "weak" because their voice betrays their anxiety through pitch and pace.

The "Belly-to-Throat" Connection

When we are nervous, our breathing becomes shallow (chest breathing), which raises the pitch of our voice. This signals to the listener that we are in a "Submissive" or "Stressed" state. To start strong, you must utilize **Diaphragmatic Projection**.

- **The Resonance Check:** Before you open, take a deep breath into your belly. Speak from the "bottom" of your breath.
- **The Downward Inflection:** High-value men end their sentences with a "Period," not a "Question Mark."
  - *Weak Start:* "Hi, I'm Mark?" (Searching for approval).
  - *Strong Start:* "Hi. I'm Mark." (Stating a fact).

Starting strong does not always mean starting "Loud." A man who yells in a quiet library is not strong; he is socially uncalibrated.

The "Energy Match + 10%" Rule

To start strong, you must observe the "Energy Temperature" of the room and match it, plus about 10%.

- If the room is a high-energy nightclub, your start must be high-energy, physical, and loud.
- If the room is a quiet bookstore, your start must be low-energy, intellectual, and intimate.

The "+ 10%" is the crucial part. It positions you as the **Leader of the Interaction**. You are slightly more "vibrant" than the current environment, which naturally draws people toward your energy.

6. The "Social Warm-Up": Never Start from Zero

The biggest mistake men make is trying to "start strong" while they are "cold." If you have been sitting in the corner for an hour staring at your phone, and then you try to approach a beautiful woman, you will fail. Your brain is in **Internal Mode**.

The "Stirring the Pot" Technique

To ensure every interaction starts strong, you must be in a "Social State" before you even see your target.

- Talk to the doorman or the security guard.
- Talk to the person in line behind you about the wait.
- Compliment a stranger on their style or an accessory.
- Ask the bartender how their shift is going compared to last week.

By "stirring the pot" and engaging with everyone, you keep your **Mirror Neuron System** active and your vocal cords warmed up. When you finally see the woman you want to meet, you aren't "starting" a conversation—you are simply continuing a social flow that has been happening all night.

7. The "Us" Frame and Narrative Anchoring

As you move from the open to the flow, you must begin to create a "Micro-Culture." This is where you move from two strangers talking to an "Us" against the world.

The Narrative Anchor

Use your environment to create a shared secret or a shared enemy.

- *"We should probably leave before the DJ plays another 80s remix."*
- *"I feel like we're the only two people in this room who aren't pretending to enjoy the art."*

By using "We" and "Us," you are bypassing the **Posterior Cingulate Cortex's** stranger filters and moving directly into the "Social Group" neural pathways.

8. Handling the "Moment of Impact" and the Lean-Back

The "Moment of Impact" is the split second after you deliver your opener. This is where most starts crumble. There is often a "Micro-Pause" while her brain processes your presence.

The "Social Vacuum"

If you "Lean In" during this pause, you look needy. You are literally invading her personal space to "get" a response. To start strong, deliver your line and then **physically lean back** or shift your weight to your back foot. This creates a "Vacuum" that invites her to lean in and fill the space. It signals that you are not a threat and that you are not desperately waiting for her approval.

9. The Transition to Mastery: The "Hook" is the Goal

Remember, the "Start" is not the "Open"—it is the "Hook." You have started strong when the conversation moves from you *pushing* the energy to both of you *sharing* the energy.

The "Bridge" Mentality

Think of your start as a bridge. On one side is a stranger; on the other side is a connection. Your job in the first 60 seconds is to build that bridge as fast as possible using the tools we've covered:

1. **Situational Observation** (The Foundation).
2. **Active Listening** (The Support Beams).
3. **Vulnerability/Playfulness** (The Pavement).

Once the bridge is built, you stop being a "guy who approached" and you start being "a person she is talking to."

10. The 5,000-Foot View: Socializing as a Biological Process

To reach the level of mastery, you must stop seeing socializing as a series of "lines" and start seeing it as a **Biological Dance**.

- **Dopamine:** You provide this through humor, unpredictability, and cold reads.
- **Oxytocin:** You provide this through active listening, labeling her emotions, and vulnerability.
- **Serotonin:** You provide this through your status, your groundedness, and your ability to lead.

When you start an interaction strong, you are essentially "tuning" her neurochemistry to be receptive to you.

11. Final Summary: The "Start Strong" Manifesto

1. **Assume Attraction:** Approach as if she already likes you. This changes your micro-expressions to a "High-Status" default.
2. **Move on the Impulse:** Don't let the "Anxiety Loop" start. 3 seconds or less.
3. **Grounded Presence:** Feet shoulder-width apart, deep breaths, downward inflection.
4. **Be the Giver:** You are there to brighten her day with an observation, not to "get" her number.
5. **Calibrate the Energy:** Match the room, then lead the room.

Action Steps: The "Social Lead" Challenge

To wrap up Book 2, you are going to perform the **Social Lead Challenge**.

The Task: Go to a social venue. Your goal is to be the "Social Anchor" of that room for 30 minutes.

- **Step 1:** Speak to 5 people you are *not* attracted to (staff, guys, older people).

- **Step 2:** Once your "Social State" is high, approach one person you *are* attracted to.

- **Step 3:** Use a situational opener, a "Mirror," and a "Label."

- **Step 4:** Regardless of the outcome, exit with total grace and move immediately to talk to one more person.

The Goal: To prove to your brain that "Starting Strong" is a repeatable, mechanical process that you control.

REFLECTION QUESTIONS

CHECK YOUR PROGRESS

You have successfully navigated the tactical landscape of starting smooth conversations. You have moved from the theoretical "What" into the actionable "How." However, the transition from knowledge to mastery is not a straight line; it is a spiral. As you gain more experience in the field, you must return to your foundation to ensure that your internal architecture is not being eroded by old habits or the inevitable friction of social entropy.

This chapter is your **Metacognitive Audit**. Metacognition is the act of "thinking about thinking." For the high-value man, this means stepping outside of the emotional "heat" of a social interaction to objectively analyze the data points of your performance. We are going to look into the "Black Box" of your social interactions over the past few weeks to identify exactly where your "Social Software" is lagging.

Answer these sections with brutal, clinical honesty. The goal is not to feel good about your progress, but to identify the **Bottlenecks** that are preventing you from reaching Book 3.

1. The Internal State & The Pre-Approach Diagnostic

Before you ever speak a word, your physiology is communicating a message to the room. This section audits your **Bio-Feedback Loops**.

The Amygdala vs. The Prefrontal Cortex

When you see a woman or a group you want to approach, there is a split-second "War for the Brain." Your Amygdala triggers a fear response (Social Rejection = Death), while your Prefrontal Cortex attempts to rationalize the approach.

- **The 3-Second Rule Audit:** In your last three social outings, how many times did you observe an opportunity but fail to move within the first three seconds?

- **The Narrative Trap:** If you hesitated, what was the specific "Safety Narrative" your brain generated? (e.g., "She looks like she's leaving," "I don't want to be *that* guy.") Can you see now that these were actually biological defense mechanisms, not objective facts?

- **Heart Rate Variability (HRV):** During your last approach, was your breathing shallow (chest breathing) or deep (diaphragmatic)?
    - *The Diagnostic:* If you were chest breathing, you were in a "Sympathetic" state. This signals to her Mirror Neurons that you are anxious, which in turn makes *her* feel anxious.

2. The Mechanics of the "Open" & Vocal Tonality

The "Open" is the point of impact. It is where you establish your status and your intent.

The Vocal Authority Audit

Vocal tonality is the most honest sub-communication of status.

- **The Downward Inflection Test:** Record yourself saying, "Hi, I'm [Your Name]." Listen back. Does your voice rise at the end (the "Question Mark" tone)?
    - *The Diagnostic:* If your voice rises, you are sub-communicating a need for approval. If it stays flat or drops, you are communicating groundedness.

- **The Projection Audit:** Did the last three people you spoke to ask you to repeat yourself?
  - *The Logic:* If you have to repeat yourself, you are "reaching" for their attention. High-value projection comes from the diaphragm and demands that the other person "lean in" to you, rather than you leaning in to them.

The Angle of Attack

- **The "Predator" Check:** When you approached, did you walk directly at their face (Head-on)?
  - *The Logic:* A head-on approach triggers the **Periaqueductal Gray (PAG)** in the other person, signaling a threat.

- **The Parabolic Pivot:** Did you utilize a 45-degree angle? Did you "pivot" your body only after the verbal "hook" was established?

3. Active Listening & Neural Coupling Diagnostic

This is the transition from "Attracting" to "Connecting." It requires you to silence your internal monologue and engage with her "Global Narrative."

The "Interview Mode" Audit

- **The Question-to-Statement Ratio:** In your last conversation, what was the ratio? If you asked three questions for every one statement, you were in **Interrogation Mode**.

- **The Statement of Observation:** Did you use a **Cold Read** ("You look like someone who...")?
  - *The Diagnostic:* If you didn't, you are still playing it "safe." Safe is the enemy of attraction.

- **The Mirroring Effectiveness:** When you used the "Last Three Words" technique, did the other person expand on their story?
  - *The Logic:* If they just said "Yeah" and stopped, your mirror was likely too fast or lacked the "Curious Downward Inflection."

The "Free Information" Retrieval

- **The Memory Test:** From your last interaction, name one thing she is **passionate** about (Value) and one thing she **does** (Fact).
    - o *The Diagnostic:* If you can only remember the fact, you were not listening at Level 3. You were merely waiting for your turn to speak.

4. Rejection Handling & Emotional Antifragility

How you handle "No" is the ultimate proof of your status.

The "Social Pain" Response

- **The ACC Check:** When you were last rejected, did you feel a physical "pang" in your chest or stomach?
    - o *The Diagnostic:* That is your **Anterior Cingulate Cortex** firing. Acknowledge it as a biological leftover. Did you allow that feeling to dictate your next action?
- **The "Butt-Hurt" Index:** After the rejection, did you make a bitter comment, or did you offer a **Graceful Exit** ("No worries, have a great night!")?
    - o *The Logic:* The man who is bitter is a man who had his ego tied to the outcome. The man who is graceful is a man who knows his value is independent of her opinion.
- **The Recovery Velocity:** How many minutes passed between the rejection and your next social interaction?
    - o *The High-Value Target:* Under 60 seconds. If you went to your phone for 20 minutes, you allowed the rejection to become a "Verdict."

5. Transition to "Real Talk" & The "Us" Frame

This audits your ability to move the conversation from "Stranger" to "Alliance."

The Narrative Alliance

- **The "We/Us" Check:** How many times did you use the word "We" or "Us" during the interaction?
    - o *The Logic:* If you never used "We," you remained two separate individuals. "We" creates an instant **Micro-Culture.**

- **Playful Misinterpretation:** Did you purposefully "misunderstand" her in a way that allowed for a tease?
  - *The Diagnostic:* If the conversation was purely logical and factual, you failed to spike her **Dopamine** and **Adrenaline**.

6. Troubleshooting Your Social Bottlenecks

Based on your answers above, we can now categorize your current "Bottleneck." Every man has one primary area that holds him back.

Bottleneck A: The "Invisible" (Can't get the Open)

- **The Cause:** High Cortisol and over-active Amygdala.
- **The Fix:** You need **Desensitization**.
- **The Mission:** Go out and get 10 intentional rejections. Ask for things you know will get a "No." This proves to your brain that the "Social Pain" won't kill you.

Bottleneck B: The "Boring Nice Guy" (Can't get the Hook)

- **The Cause:** Fear of polarization and low "Vocal Authority."
- **The Fix:** You need to increase your **Risk Threshold**.
- **The Mission:** For the next three conversations, your goal is to say one thing that is purposefully "edgy" or observant. Use a **Cold Read** that might be wrong.

Bottleneck C: The "Interrogator" (Conversation dies in 3 minutes)

- **The Cause:** Lack of "Free Information" retrieval and statement-based flow.
- **The Fix:** You need to master **Labels and Mirrors**.
- **The Mission:** Have a 5-minute conversation where you are only allowed to ask **one** question. The rest must be mirrors, labels, or cold reads.

7. The 30-Day Neural Integration Plan

To ensure Book 2 becomes a permanent part of your personality, you must follow the **Rule of 100**.

1. **Open 100 Conversations:** Use situational observations. Do not seek numbers; seek "Hooks."
2. **Apply 100 Labels:** "It seems like you're..." This trains your brain to look for emotions instead of facts.

3. **Execute 100 Graceful Exits:** Leave every interaction (good or bad) with high posture and warmth.

By the time you reach 100, these skills will have moved from your **Prefrontal Cortex** (manual effort) to your **Basal Ganglia** (automatic habit).

8. Quantitative Progress Scorecard

Rate yourself on a scale of 1-10 (10 being Mastery) for the following:

Metric	Rating (1-10)	Priority for Book 3
Approach Consistency (The 3-Second Rule)		
Vocal Downward Inflection		
Active Listening (Labeling / Mirroring)		
Handling Rejection with Grace		
Transitioning to Real Talk / Teasing		
Self-Amusement & Outcome Independence		

Final Reflection: The Identity Shift

The final and most important question: **Do you still see yourself as a man who is "trying" to be social, or do you see yourself as a high-value man who is simply observing and leading his environment?**

In Book 1, we worked on your "Hardware" (Self-Worth). In Book 2, we worked on your "Software" (Social Tactics). If you are still "trying," you are still operating from a deficit. To move to Book 3, you must fully inhabit the identity of the **Calibrated Man**. You are the one who provides the value, the energy, and the leadership in the room.

BOOK THREE
NEVER RUN OUT OF THINGS TO SAY

INTRODUCTION
SPEAK WITHOUT CONSTANT PAUSES

You have successfully navigated the "Open" and survived the "Transition." You are now in the heat of the social exchange. Yet, for many men, this is where a new, more insidious enemy appears: **The Dead Air.** You have likely experienced that agonizing moment where a topic concludes, a silence stretches beyond the three-second mark, and you feel the "social weight" of the room crashing down on you. Your heart rate spikes, your internal "Editor" begins frantically scanning your mental archives for something—anything—to say, and you eventually blurt out a boring, logical question that effectively resets the attraction to zero.

This phenomenon is not a lack of personality; it is a **Neural Bottleneck**. In Book 3, we are going to dismantle the biological and psychological barriers that cause "Cognitive Social Stalling." You are not going to learn a list of "things to say." Instead, you are going to learn how to unlock your brain's natural **Associative Power**, allowing you to move from the clunky, manual labor of "thinking" to the effortless, high-status flow of "being."

1. The Anatomy of Social Stalling: Why the Brain Freezes

To solve the problem of running out of things to say, we must first diagnose the biological "Why" behind the awkward silence. Most men assume they are "boring" or "unimaginative," but the truth is usually found in your neurochemistry. Social stalling is almost always a result of **Brain Hijacking**, where the creative centers are suppressed by the survival centers.

The Amygdala-Broca Inhibition

When you feel social pressure, your **Amygdala**—the brain's threat-detection center—interprets a lull in conversation as a risk of social exclusion. In the environment of our ancestors, social exclusion often meant physical death. Consequently, the Amygdala triggers a "Freeze" response.

This sends a direct inhibitory signal to the **Broca's Area**, the region of the frontal lobe responsible for speech production. While your brain is frantically looking for words, the biological "switch" that produces them has been flipped to "Off." This is the "Mental Blank." It is not that you have no thoughts; it is that your brain has locked the door to the speech center to prevent you from saying something that might get you "exiled" from the tribe.

The Over-Active Internal Editor

The second cause of stalling is the **Prefrontal Cortex (PFC)** over-functioning as an editor. Most men have a very high "filter" for what they allow themselves to say. They believe every sentence must pass a rigorous vetting process:

- **The Status Filter:** "Does this make me look cool or successful?"
- **The Logic Filter:** "Does this follow perfectly from the last sentence?"
- **The Safety Filter:** "Is there any chance this could be misunderstood or offensive?"

When you run four or five filters simultaneously, your processing speed drops to zero. By the time a thought passes the vetting process, the moment has passed. High-value talkers do the opposite: they **Lower the Bar for Entry** to maintain **Conversational Momentum**. They understand that a "perfectly logical" boring sentence is far worse than a "random" high-energy observation.

2. The Philosophy of the "Infinite Thread"

The core methodology of Book 3 is the **Infinite Thread**. This is the realization that every single word, object, and emotion in an interaction is a "Hook" that leads to a dozen new directions.

Beyond Linear Dialogue

A conversation is not a straight line; it is a multidimensional web. Most men attempt to follow a linear path of logic, which is high-effort and low-reward.

- *Example:* "What do you do?" → "Marketing" → "Do you like it?" → "It's okay." → **Dead Air.**

This is **Vertical Thinking**. You are trying to dig deeper into a single hole that has already run dry. The "Infinite Talker" utilizes **Horizontal Branching**. He looks at the word "Marketing" and sees five distinct "Threads":

1. **The Emotional Thread:** "Marketing is basically just professional storytelling. Were you the kid who was always making up elaborate stories to get out of trouble?"

2. **The Observational Thread:** "You have a very 'creative' energy, but marketing can be quite corporate. How do you keep your soul alive in that environment?"

3. **The Associative Thread:** "Marketing makes me think of *Mad Men*—whiskey and high-stakes pitches. Is your office more like that, or more like a bunch of people staring at spreadsheets?"

4. **The Value-Based Thread:** "Most people do marketing because they like influence. What's the one thing you'd convince the whole world to do if you had the perfect ad campaign?"

In the following chapters, you will learn to see these threads instantly. You will stop "searching" for topics because you will realize the topic is already in front of you. The world is not empty; it is overflowing with data points waiting to be connected.

A major paradigm shift in Book 3 is the realization that **what you say matters far less than the state from which you say it.** #### The 90/10 Rule of Attraction In social interactions, approximately 90% of the impact comes from your **Vocal Tonality, Body Language, and Emotional Presence**, while only 10% comes from the literal meaning of your words. When you "run out of things to say," you are over-prioritizing the 10% (the data) and neglecting the 90% (the delivery).

When you speak with a **Downward Inflection** and a relaxed, unhurried tempo, you sub-communicate high status. This allows you to say almost anything—even something mundane—and have it be perceived as captivating. The silence only becomes "awkward" when you look at it as a problem to be solved. If you remain comfortable in the silence, she will feel the need to fill it, or she will simply enjoy the "Grounded Presence" you provide.

Lowering the Social Stakes

To speak without pauses, you must treat the conversation as a **Playground**, not a **Performance**. In a performance, you are judged on your accuracy. In a playground, you are judged on your engagement. By shifting your mindset to "Self-Amusement," you unlock the **Default Mode Network (DMN)**—the part of the brain that produces creative, spontaneous thought. This is where "wit" lives.

4. The Neural Roadmap to Fluency: From Manual to Automatic

Moving from "Stalling" to "Flowing" is a journey of neural reorganization. We are moving the task of conversation from the "Slow" part of the brain to the "Fast" part.

1. **Conscious Competence (The Manual Phase):** At first, you will have to "manually" look for threads and "manually" remember to use open-ended questions. This requires effort and might feel clunky. This is where most men give up, but this is exactly where the neural pathways are being built.

2. **The Basal Ganglia Shift:** With repetition, these skills move into the **Basal Ganglia**—the seat of procedural memory (the same part of the brain that allows you to drive a car without thinking about the pedals).

3. **Unconscious Mastery (The Social Flow State):** Eventually, you enter the "Flow State." Words appear in your mouth before you have even fully "thought" them. You are no longer "trying" to talk; you are simply witnessing the conversation happen through you.

5. Bridging the Gap: What This Book Will Give You

Throughout the next seven chapters, we will install the specific "software" required for this level of fluency.

- **Chapter 1 (Free Association):** Training your **Associative Cortex** to link any two unrelated concepts, ensuring a mental "blank" is physically impossible.

- **Chapter 2 (High-Value Questions):** Moving away from "Interrogation" and toward "Inspiration" by asking questions that trigger the **Ventromedial Prefrontal Cortex** (the brain's reward center).

- **Chapter 3 (Storytelling):** Learning how to package your life experiences into narrative arcs that build **Oxytocin** and genuine rapport.

- **Chapter 4 (The Echo Effect):** Using linguistic recycling to keep the conversation moving with zero cognitive effort on your part.

- **Chapter 5 (Observation):** Learning to use the physical environment as an "External Hard Drive" for conversational topics.

Final Summary: The Manifesto of the Natural Talker

1. **Trust the Association:** Your brain is a supercomputer of connections. Stop trying to "think" and start trying to "notice."

2. **Maintain the Rhythm:** It is better to say something "random" and keep the vibe going than to be silent while searching for the "perfect" line.

3. **Surrender the Ego:** The fear of saying something "stupid" is the primary cause of being "boring." High-status men are comfortable being misunderstood.

4. **Embrace the Association:** Trust your brain's ability to find connections without manual effort.

By the time you finish this volume, you will realize that "running out of things to say" was never a lack of content—it was a lack of **Permission**. You are about to give yourself permission to be the most fluid, engaging, and captivating version of yourself.

CHAPTER 1

USE FREE ASSOCIATION TO FIND TOPICS

In the previous book, we discussed the "Open" and the "Transition." You have successfully broken the ice, but now you face the most common bottleneck in social dynamics: the fear of the **Mental Blank**. You are standing there, the initial momentum is fading, and your brain feels like a hard drive that has suddenly crashed. You are searching for a "topic," but the harder you search, the more elusive the words become.

This happens because you are treating conversation as a **Search Retrieval Task** rather than an **Associative Process**. You are looking for a "correct" thing to say in your memory banks, which engages the slow, logical **Dorsolateral Prefrontal Cortex**. This part of the brain is excellent for solving math problems or filing taxes, but it is the enemy of charisma. High-value conversationalists operate in the **Associative Cortex**. They don't "find" topics; they "generate" them by linking the present moment to an infinite web of mental connections.

1. The Neurobiology of the Associative Web

Your brain does not store information in linear, isolated files. It is not a library of books; it is a **Neural Forest**. Every concept you have ever learned is a tree with roots that entangle with a thousand other trees. When you hear the word "Ocean," your brain doesn't just think of $H_{2}O$. In a fraction of a millisecond, your **Hippocampus** and **Temporal Lobes** activate a cluster of related data points: the smell of sunblock, the feeling of salt on skin, a movie you saw about a shipwreck, a seafood restaurant in Lisbon, and the abstract concept of "The Unknown."

The "Mental Blank" occurs when you put a **Gating Mechanism** on this forest. You tell your brain: *"Don't give me the shipwreck or the sunblock; give me something 'cool' that will make her like me."* This gate creates **Cognitive Friction**. By the time your brain filters through the possibilities to find the "perfect" thought, the social window has slammed shut.

To use Free Association effectively, you must remove the gate. You must allow the **Default Mode Network (DMN)**—the brain's creative, "idle" state—to offer up the raw data it finds. You must trust the first three things that come to mind.

2. The "Word-Chain" Technique: Training the Muscle

Fluency is a muscle, and most men have allowed it to atrophy through years of "polite," logical, and filtered conversation. The "Word-Chain" is the foundational drill designed to bypass the **Internal Editor** and force your brain to find "Horizontal" connections.

The Mechanics of the Drill

Look at any object in the room. Let's take a mundane stimulus: a **Chair**.

1. **Chair** → Wood (Material)
2. **Wood** → Forest (Origin/Nature)
3. **Forest** → Camping (Activity/Memory)
4. **Camping** → Ghost stories (Emotion/Mystery)
5. **Ghost Stories** → That time I stayed in a "haunted" hotel in New Orleans (Personal Narrative)

In less than five seconds, you have moved from a piece of furniture to a high-value travel story. The chair was never the topic; it was the **Launchpad**.

Field Application: The "Noun-to-Narrative" Shift

When she speaks, she is giving you "Nouns." If she says she works in **Finance**, a low-value man performs a "Vertical Search": *"Do you like it?"* or *"How long have you done that?"* This is boring because it requires zero associative effort.

The high-value man performs a **Horizontal Association**:

- **Finance** → Money → Power → *The Wolf of Wall Street* → Adrenaline.

- **The Association:** *"Finance? You have a very calm vibe for someone in that world. I'm picturing you as the only person in the office who isn't throwing phones at the wall when the market dips. How do you maintain that Zen?"*

3. The Three Vectors of Association

To prevent your associations from becoming "random" or "weird," you must calibrate them. There are three primary directions you can pull a conversation thread.

Vector A: The Sensory & Atmospheric Association

This focuses on the "Vibe" or the aesthetic of a word. It bypasses logic and goes straight to the **Primary Somatosensory Cortex**.

- *Stimulus:* "I just moved here from London."

- *Association:* Fog, rain on cobblestones, the sound of the Underground, the feeling of "history" everywhere.

- *Output:* *"London has this specific heavy, historical energy—like every street corner has a secret from three hundred years ago. Do you miss that 'old world' mystery, or is the modern sun here a relief?"*

Vector B: The Thematic & Philosophical Association

This focuses on the "Why" behind a statement. It engages the **Medial Prefrontal Cortex**, which handles social and self-referential thought.

- *Stimulus:* "I spent my weekend volunteering at an animal shelter."

- *Association:* Compassion, non-verbal connection, the "unfiltered" nature of animals.

- *Output: "There's something very grounding about hanging out with dogs. They don't care about your social status; they just want to know if you're a good person. It's like a soul-reset from the city grind."*

Vector C: The Self-Referential & Narrative Association

This is the bridge to **Vulnerability**. It uses her stimulus to reveal something about your own history.

- *Stimulus: "I love old black-and-white movies."*
- *Association: Nostalgia, your grandfather's living room, the "simpler" glamour of the past.*
- *Output: "My grandfather used to watch those old noir films every Sunday. There's a specific ritual to that kind of storytelling that makes modern movies feel a bit 'noisy' by comparison. What started the obsession for you?"*

4. Overcoming "The Filter" (The Perfectionist Trap)

The primary reason men run out of things to say is not a lack of content; it is a **Surplus of Judgment**. You are judging your own thoughts before they reach your tongue. This creates a "stutter" in your social energy.

The "Anti-Logic" Principle

In a high-value interaction, **Logic is a secondary concern.** If you associate from "Marketing" to "The time I tried to sell lemonade when I was six," the logical leap is huge, but the **Emotional Leap** is perfect. High-status men do not apologize for their thoughts. They state their associations as if they are the most natural thing in the world.

When you trust your associations, you sub-communicate that your internal world is so vast and interesting that you don't need to "vet" it for anyone else. This is the definition of **Self-Amusement**.

5. The "Looping" Strategy: Engineering Reciprocity

A "Dead-End" occurs when both people stop associating. This usually happens after a "Fact-Exchange." To prevent this, every association you produce must end with a **"Loop"**—an invitation for her to associate back.

The "Statement-Question" Hybrid

Instead of just stating your association, you tie it back to her experience.

- *Example: "That reminds me of [Your Association]... were you more like [Option A] or [Option B] when you were experiencing that?"*

By providing two options, you lower the **Cognitive Load** for her. You are doing the work of building the "Bridge," and she simply has to walk across it.

6. The "Environment as an External Drive"

If you ever truly find your internal associative web is "dry" (usually due to high Cortisol), you must turn to the environment. This is **Contextual Association**.

Look at the lighting, the music, a weird painting, or the way the bartender is shaking a drink. Apply the same Word-Chain logic to these external stimuli.

- **Music** → 90s Grunge → Flannel shirts → My older brother's garage band → Smelling like gasoline and cigarettes.

- **The Output:** *"This song takes me back to my brother's garage band days. The whole house smelled like gasoline and teenage angst. Did you have a rebellious music phase, or were you a 'choir girl'?"*

7. Action Steps: The Neural Integration Drills

To reach mastery, you must move these drills from your **Prefrontal Cortex** (effort) to your **Basal Ganglia** (habit).

1. **The 30-Second Object Sprint:** Set a timer. Pick an object. Associate five steps away from it. Do this ten times a day.

2. **The "Podcast Shadow":** Listen to a podcast. Every time the guest says a "Noun," pause it and come up with three associations (Sensory, Thematic, Self-Referential).

3. **The "Yes, And" Solo Drill:** Start a sentence. Associationally link the next sentence to the previous one, regardless of how weird it gets. Do this for two minutes straight.

Summary: The Mastery of Association

1. **Remove the Filter:** Your first thought is usually the most authentic. Say it.

2. **Move Horizontally:** Don't dig deeper into facts; jump to related emotions and themes.

3. **Use the Three Vectors:** Sensory, Thematic, and Self-Referential paths ensure you are never stuck.

4. **Loop Back:** Always give her a hook to join your associative journey.

By the end of this chapter, you should realize that "running out of things to say" is a physical impossibility. The world is an infinite library of topics for the man who has learned to pull on the threads of association.

CHAPTER 2

ASK HIGH-VALUE OPEN-ENDED QUESTIONS

A High-Value Question is not an interrogation; it is an invitation to a world she rarely gets to share.

In Chapter 1, you learned how to unlock your **Associative Cortex**, ensuring that your mental reservoir of topics is never dry. You now have the "What"—the infinite threads of conversation. However, possessing raw material is only the first step. To transition from a "capable talker" to a "high-value leader," you must master the art of directing that material. You must move from **Data Collection** to **Emotional Exploration**.

The most prevalent failure in modern social dynamics is the **Interview Trap**. This occurs when a man, fearing silence, defaults to a series of "Low-Value" questions that force the woman to do the heavy lifting of logical retrieval. In this chapter, we will dismantle that habit and install the **High-Value Open-Ended Question** framework. These are queries specifically engineered to bypass the logical filters and trigger a massive dopamine response by engaging the **Self-Referential Processing** centers of the brain.

1. The Neuro-Economics of Conversation: Cognitive Cost vs. Reward

Every interaction you engage in is governed by an invisible economy. Every question you ask carries a "Cognitive Cost." When you speak to a stranger, you are essentially asking them to spend their limited mental energy on you.

Low-Value Questions: The Energy Tax

"What do you do for work?" "Where are you from?" "How long have you lived here?" These questions are the "taxes" of conversation. They require the brain to access the **Lateral Prefrontal Cortex** to retrieve cold, dry, factual data.

This is "Search Engine" work. It is repetitive, uninspired, and exhausting. If a woman is high-value and attractive, she has likely been asked these questions five times already tonight. When you ask them, her brain begins to categorize you as "Work"—another person she has to "process" rather than "experience."

High-Value Questions: The Dopamine Gift

Conversely, a High-Value Question—such as "What's the most unexpected thing that's happened to you this week?"—triggers the **Ventromedial Prefrontal Cortex (vmPFC)**. This is the hub for self-value, ambition, and reward.

Neurological studies show that talking about oneself in an evaluative or emotional way activates the same reward centers as eating gourmet food or receiving a financial windfall. When you ask a High-Value Question, you aren't "taking" information; you are "giving" a dopamine spike. You are providing her with a platform to feel creative, seen, and expansive.

2. The Anatomy of an "Open-Ended" Question

An open-ended question is technically any query that cannot be answered with a simple "Yes" or "No." However, in the architecture of social power, we must distinguish between "Open" and "Expansive."

The "Closed" Dead-End

- *Query:* "Do you like your job?"
- *Response:* "Yeah, it's fine."
- *Result:* The momentum dies. You are now forced to "re-start" the engine from zero.

The "Open" Expansion

- *Query:* "What's the one thing about your job that makes you feel like you're actually making an impact, rather than just filling a seat?"
- *Result:* She cannot give a one-word answer. She has to search her **Episodic Memory**, identify a value or a feeling, and articulate it. You have effectively "Hooked" her into the dialogue.

The Hierarchy of Inquiry: What, How, and Why

1. **"What" (The Observational Layer):** This is your best tool for gathering sensory data and "Free Information." *"What was the energy like in that city compared to here?"*
2. **"How" (The Process Layer):** This focuses on her internal mechanics and mindset. *"How did you manage to stay so grounded when everything was falling apart?"*
3. **"Why" (The Core Layer):** Use this with extreme caution. "Why" can often sound like an interrogation, a judgment, or a challenge to her logic. Instead of asking "Why did you move?", use a "What" frame: *"What was the specific catalyst that made you realize it was time for a new chapter?"*

3. The "Cold Read" Question: The High-Status Shortcut

As we established in Book 2, a High-Value man rarely "asks" for permission or information—he **Assumes** it. This is the **Assumptive Frame**. By turning a question into a statement, you remove the "burden" of the interview and position yourself as a man of intuition.

- **The Formula:** [Observation] + [Assumption] + [Check-In]
- **Low-Value Question:** "What kind of hobbies are you into?"
- **High-Value Cold Read:** "You have a very 'kinetic' energy about you. I'm guessing you're the type of person who can't sit still in an office—you probably have some adventurous hobby like rock climbing or boxing that people wouldn't expect. Am I close?"

The Biological Effect: This triggers the **Self-Verification** process. Humans have an innate drive to be understood and "seen." If your cold read is accurate, she is impressed by your social acuity. If you are wrong, she will move heaven and earth to "correct" you and reveal who she *actually* is. Either way, you receive a flood of "Free Information" without ever sounding like an interrogator.

4. Directing the Association: The "Value-Probe"

In Chapter 1, you mastered **Free Association**. Now, you will use High-Value Questions to "Probe" the underlying values behind those associations. This is how you move from "Small Talk" to "Deep Connection."

- **Stimulus:** She mentions she just started a new yoga teacher training.

- **Association (from Chapter 1):** Discipline, inner peace, physical mastery, escaping the noise.

- **The Value-Probe:** *"Most people do yoga just to stretch, but a teacher training is a different level of commitment. What's the internal 'noise' you're trying to silence when you're on the mat?"*

By asking about the **Internal Noise**, you have bypassed the "Yoga" (the fact) and targeted the **Reward** (the emotional motivation). You are no longer talking about her schedule; you are talking about her soul.

5. Avoiding the "Logic Loop" and the "Fact-Trap"

The "Logic Loop" is the primary reason conversations become boring. It is the habit of asking follow-up questions based on linear data rather than emotional resonance.

- **The Fact-Trap:**
    - *Her:* "I just got back from a month in Italy."
    - *You:* "Oh, where did you go? Rome? How was the weather? Was it expensive?"
    - *Result:* You have become a travel agent. Her brain is in "Logistics Mode."

- **The High-Value Exit:**
  - *Her:* "I just got back from a month in Italy."
  - *You:* "Italy has a way of making you realize that the way we live here is slightly insane. If you could have bottled up the 'vibe' of a Tuesday afternoon in Rome and brought it back to your daily life here, what would that look like?"

This question requires her to compare cultures, evaluate her personal lifestyle, and share a desire. It is cognitively stimulating and positions you as a man who thinks about the **Quality of Life**, not just the **Location of Life**.

6. The "Two-Sided" Question: The Choice Frame

Sometimes, a question is *too* open. If she is in a "low-energy" state, a massive, expansive question might feel like "too much work." To lead effectively, you must provide a **Choice Frame**. This offers the structure of a closed question with the reward of an open one.

- **The Formula:** [Open Question] + [Option A] or [Option B]?
- **Example:** *"How do you usually navigate big social events like this? Are you the 'Social Architect' who wants to meet everyone in the room, or the 'Selective Observer' who picks one interesting person and ignores everyone else?"*

This provides her with two "Neural Anchors." She can pick one, or she can say "Actually, I'm a mix of both." Either way, you have made it **Easy** for her to succeed. High-value men make social success easy for those around them.

7. The "Prospection" Frame: Thinking in Possibilities

High-value men do not dwell in the past or the mundane present. They operate in the **Possibility Frame**. This shifts the conversation from "What is" to "What could be."

- **The "Possibility" Probe:** "If you woke up tomorrow and realized you didn't have to answer to anyone—no boss, no family obligations—what would be the very first thing you'd do that you've been putting off?"

This engages the **Prefrontal Cortex's** capacity for **Prospection**—the ability to simulate future states. This is an inherently optimistic and "high-vibe" mental state. By being the catalyst for this simulation, you become associated with her highest aspirations and her sense of freedom.

8. The "Vulnerability Loop" in Inquiry

A High-Value Question can sometimes feel "too heavy" if you haven't provided a baseline of trust. To balance this, you must use the **Vulnerability Loop**.

- **The Technique:** Share a small, non-needy vulnerability *before* asking the high-value question.

- **Example:** *"I've always struggled with staying present when I'm working on a big project. I tend to live three months in the future. How do you find that balance between being ambitious and actually enjoying the moment you're in right now?"*

By sharing your struggle first, you give her "Permission" to be honest. You are setting the **Standard of Depth** for the interaction.

9. Action Steps: The "Inquiry Master" Field Audit

You must move these concepts from your "Intellectual Map" to your "Actionable Reality."

1. **The Stranger Audit:** Today, interact with three people in low-stakes environments (baristas, gym staff). Ask one "How" or "What" question that focuses on an emotion. Note the difference in their facial expressions and engagement.

2. **The "No-Fact" Challenge:** Attempt to have a 10-minute conversation with a friend or colleague where you are forbidden from asking about "Names, Dates, or Titles." Focus entirely on "Drivers, Feelings, and Possibilities."

3. **The Assumption Drill:** Replace three questions today with **Cold Reads**. Instead of asking "Where are you going?", say "You look like someone who is heading toward something exciting/relaxing."

1. **Lower the Cognitive Cost:** Make it effortless and rewarding for her to speak.

2. **Target the vmPFC:** Aim your questions at the reward centers, not the storage centers.

3. **Use Cold Reads:** Assumptions sub-communicate status and trigger deeper "Free Information."

4. **Avoid the Logic Loop:** Stay in the realm of possibility, value, and emotion.

By the end of this chapter, you should realize that the "Right Question" is the steering wheel of the interaction. You don't need to talk the most; you simply need to be the man who asks the questions that lead to the most interesting, dopamine-rich places.

CHAPTER 3

SHARE STORIES THAT BUILD GENUINE RAPPORT

In Chapter 2, you learned how to steer an interaction using High-Value Questions—how to pull a woman out of "Fact Mode" and into "Meaning Mode." But if questions are the steering wheel, stories are the engine. A great question opens a door. A great story walks both of you through it.

Most men sabotage rapport because they treat storytelling like a performance. They either:

- Tell a long, unstructured "life update" that drains the energy.
- Try to impress with achievements, which triggers resistance.
- Overshare pain too early, which creates emotional pressure.
- Or avoid stories entirely, and stay trapped in interview-style conversation.

The goal of this chapter is simple: install a storytelling framework that makes you feel natural, makes her feel safe, and makes the interaction feel like it has depth—even if you've only known each other for ten minutes.

Because here is the truth: rapport is not built through information. It is built through shared emotion. And nothing transports emotion faster than a story.

1. The Biology of Story: Why Narratives Create Instant Bonding

Humans are not wired for data. We are wired for narrative. When you speak in facts, you activate logic circuits. When you speak in story, you activate simulation circuits.

A story causes the listener's brain to "run" your experience as if it were happening to them. This is known as Neural Coupling. Your words stop being "information" and become a shared internal movie.

That is why a woman can forget your job title five minutes after you say it—but remember the story about you getting lost in a foreign city, or the time your friend accidentally ruined a birthday surprise.

Storytelling creates rapport because it triggers three key effects:

The "Shared Reality" Effect

A story is not a statement; it's an experience. Experiences create the feeling of "we," even before you've earned the right to say "we."

The Oxytocin Effect

When a story contains warmth, humor, vulnerability, or meaningful emotion, the brain releases oxytocin, the bonding hormone. Oxytocin is the chemical signature of "I trust this person."

The Status Without Bragging Effect

A story shows your character indirectly. It demonstrates social intelligence, courage, humor, taste, and self-awareness—without you ever claiming those traits.

This is how high-value men communicate value. Not through declarations. Through narrative proof.

Most men think they need "big stories." They don't. You need small stories told well.

The most effective social story is a Micro-Arc: a 20-to-60 second narrative with a clear emotional shape.

The Three-Act Micro-Arc:

Act 1: Setup (Context + Hook)

Where were you? What was the situation? Give just enough detail to orient her brain.

Act 2: Tension (Conflict or Surprise)

Something goes wrong. Something unexpected happens. This is the emotional ignition.

Act 3: Release (Outcome + Meaning)

What happened next? What did you learn? What was funny about it? This is the payoff.

Example: The "Wrong Place" Story

Act 1 (Setup): "Last month I tried to be spontaneous and go to this 'secret' restaurant a friend recommended."

Act 2 (Tension): "I walked into the place confident... and realized it was a couples' salsa class. And they were already in a circle."

Act 3 (Release): "I froze for two seconds like a malfunctioning robot, then I just committed. I did one awkward step, apologized to everyone's eyeballs, and escaped. Now I'm apparently the guy who almost became a salsa instructor against his will."

Notice what makes it work:

- It's short.
- It has a clear pivot moment.
- It ends with humor and self-awareness.
- It doesn't make you look perfect. It makes you look human.

Perfection creates distance. A controlled imperfection creates connection.

3. The "Rapport Triangle": What a Good Story Must Signal

A story is not random entertainment. It is a social signal.

To build genuine rapport, your stories should communicate one (or more) of these three traits:

A. Warmth (Safety + Humanity)

Stories about family, friendships, small kindness, loyalty, self-reflection, gratitude, or sincere curiosity.

B. Competence (Capability + Standards)

Stories about solving a problem, learning a skill, taking initiative, leading a group, building something, or making a hard decision.

C. Playfulness (Lightness + Social Ease)

Stories that show humor, spontaneity, mischief, charm, or your ability to laugh at yourself.

This is the Rapport Triangle: Warmth, Competence, Playfulness.

Most men lean too hard on Competence (to impress) and forget Warmth and Playfulness (to connect).

The paradox: the more you try to "prove" yourself, the less safe you feel to be around. Storytelling is where you must demonstrate value without needing her approval.

A high-value story feels like: "This is my world. You're welcome here." A low-value story feels like: "Please validate me for having a world."

4. The Story Bridge: How to Pull Stories from Her Words

You do not "insert" stories. You bridge into them.

A woman will constantly give you Story Seeds—small details that can become a doorway.

She mentions: "I love hiking."

Story Seed: Adventure, nature, discomfort, challenge, calm, freedom.

Instead of asking ten more logistical questions, you bridge:

The Story Bridge Formula:

[Her seed] → [Your association] → [Your micro-arc] → [Loop back to her]

Example:

Her: "I love hiking."

You: "That's dangerous. Hiking creates this illusion that you're a disciplined outdoors person... and then it humbles you immediately. I once went on what I thought was a 'light trail'—" (Micro-arc story) "—Do you hike for the peace, or do you like the challenge of it?"

Now you've done four things:

- You validated her interest without praise-bombing.
- You created shared emotion through narrative.
- You showcased personality.
- You looped it back so she can re-enter.

Stories without a loop become monologues. The loop turns it into rapport.

This is also how you avoid the "I'm talking too much" fear. You're not dumping a story. You're building a bridge.

5. The "Vulnerability Calibration": How to Be Real Without Oversharing

Vulnerability is not trauma. Vulnerability is controlled honesty.

Most men get this wrong in two opposite ways:

- They are a stone wall. No depth. No humanity. No emotional access.
- Or they become a confession booth. Too much, too soon.

The correct approach is Calibration: you share a "small truth" that signals depth, then you watch how she responds.

The Spectrum of Vulnerability (Low → High):

Level 1: Light self-awareness

"I used to be terrible at social stuff. I had to learn it the hard way."

Level 2: A real struggle, framed with strength

"I'm ambitious, but I've had to learn how to actually enjoy my life instead of always chasing the next thing."

Level 3: Deep personal pain

This level is reserved for later, once trust is real—not just "vibes."

Early rapport is built with Level 1 and Level 2 vulnerability.

The rule: Vulnerability must include a stable frame.

If you share something heavy, it must end in grounded meaning, humor, or growth.

Bad vulnerability sounds like: "Here is my wound. Please hold it."

Good vulnerability sounds like: "Here is what shaped me. I'm strong enough to talk about it."

Women don't bond with a man who is bleeding on them. They bond with a man who is honest, self-aware, and regulated.

6. The Anti-Brag Protocol: How to Show Value Without Triggering Resistance

Bragging fails because it forces her to evaluate you. Evaluation creates distance.

The solution is narrative framing.

Three ways to communicate competence without bragging:

A. The "Problem → Lesson" Frame

Instead of: "I'm really successful."

Tell: "I made a mistake, learned the lesson, and adjusted."

This signals maturity and competence—without arrogance.

B. The "Third-Party Spotlight" Frame

Instead of making yourself the hero, make someone else the hero. You can still show your standards and taste.

Example: "My friend is absurdly disciplined. He'll wake up at 5 a.m. for fun. Watching him made me realize how much 'motivation' is actually just environment."

C. The "Understatement" Frame

High-status men do not hype themselves. They state things calmly.

Low-status: "It was insane, everyone loved it, it was crazy."

High-status: "Yeah, it went well. I was relieved. I put a lot into it."

Understatement communicates inner security.

The goal is not to look impressive. The goal is to feel real—and let the right traits leak through naturally.

Storytelling is not talent. It is preparation + repetition.

A. The Story Bank Exercise (10 Minutes)

Write down five short stories from your life. One for each category:

- A funny social mistake
- A moment you took a risk
- A time you learned a hard lesson
- A moment of warmth or loyalty
- A strange or unexpected experience

Do not write novels. Write bullet points: Setup, Tension, Release.

B. The 60-Second Micro-Arc Drill

Set a timer for 60 seconds. Practice telling one story out loud, using the three-act structure. Record yourself once. Remove excess detail. Keep the pivot moment.

C. The "One Story Per Interaction" Rule

In your next three conversations, tell one micro-arc story each time. Not three. One.

Your nervous system must learn that storytelling is safe, natural, and welcome.

D. The Loop Practice

After every story, ask a loop question that invites her story.

Examples:

"Have you ever had something like that happen?"

"Are you more the [Option A] type or [Option B] type in those situations?"

"What's your version of that?"

This turns story into reciprocity, which turns conversation into rapport.

Summary: The Mastery of Rapport Through Story

Stories create Neural Coupling: she experiences your world, not just your facts.

Use the Three-Act Micro-Arc: Setup, Tension, Release—short and emotionally shaped. Aim for the Rapport Triangle: Warmth, Competence, and Playfulness. Bridge from her words: Story Seeds → Micro-arc → Loop back.

Calibrate vulnerability: share truth with a stable frame, not emotional neediness. Avoid bragging: let value leak through narrative proof, not self-praise.

By the end of this chapter, you should understand that the purpose of conversation is not to "keep talking." The purpose is to create shared emotional reality. High-value stories do exactly that—and they make a woman feel like she's not speaking to a stranger, but to a man with a real inner world she wants to explore.

CHAPTER 4

USE THE ECHO EFFECT TO DEEPEN DIALOGUE

In the preceding chapters, we have focused on the "Active" generation of conversation: how to associate threads from thin air, how to ask high-value questions, and how to package your own life into compelling narratives. These techniques are powerful, but they require a significant amount of **Cognitive Load**. There will be moments in your social life—whether due to fatigue, a high-pressure environment, or a partner who is particularly shy—where "pushing" the conversation feels like a monumental task.

In this chapter, we introduce the most powerful "Low-Effort, High-Impact" tool in the social arsenal: **The Echo Effect**. Known in clinical psychology as "Mirroring" and in negotiation circles as "Linguistic Recycling," the Echo Effect allows you to keep a conversation moving forward indefinitely while doing only 10% of the verbal work. It is the art of using the other person's own words as a mirror to draw out deeper emotional data, effectively turning them into the primary driver of the dialogue while you maintain the frame of the leader.

1. The Neuroscience of Mirroring and Social Cohesion

The Echo Effect is not just a conversational "trick"; it is rooted in the fundamental biology of human connection. Our brains are hardwired with **Mirror Neurons**—specialized cells that fire both when we perform an action and when we observe someone else performing that same action.

The "Same Tribe" Signal

When you repeat a person's words back to them, their **Superior Temporal Sulcus** and **Inferior Frontal Gyrus** (the centers for empathy and social perception) receive a powerful signal of safety. On a subconscious level, the brain interprets an "Echo" as: *"This person is like me. They understand my frequency. I am safe to disclose more."*

Triggering the Self-Disclosure Reward

As we discussed in Chapter 2, talking about oneself triggers the **Ventromedial Prefrontal Cortex**, releasing dopamine. The Echo Effect is the ultimate catalyst for this process. By "Echoing" the last few words of her sentence, you are essentially giving her a "permission slip" to continue her dopamine-rich self-exploration. You aren't just listening; you are facilitating her own discovery of her thoughts.

2. The Mechanics of the Echo: How to Recycle Energy

The technical execution of the Echo is deceptively simple: you take the last one to three words of what the other person just said and repeat them back as a question or a "labeling statement."

The Anatomy of the Echo

- **The Stimulus:** "I really love my job, but lately the management has been so restrictive."
- **The Echo:** "So restrictive?" (Inflected with a downward, curious tone).
- **The Result:** She will almost certainly expand: "Yeah, they started this new micromanagement policy where we have to log every fifteen minutes of our day..."

Why This Is Better Than a Question

If you had asked, *"Why are they restrictive?"*, it would have felt like an interrogation. It requires her to switch into "Logical Retrieval" mode. By simply Echoing, you are staying in the "Emotional Flow." You are a mirror, not a prosecutor. You are inviting her to explain the *feeling* of being restricted, rather than the *mechanics* of the restriction.

3. Calibrating the Inflection: Downward vs. Upward

The "Magic" of the Echo Effect lives in your **Vocal Tonality**. The same words can have two completely different impacts depending on the "Curve" of your voice.

The "Inquisitive" Upward Inflection

This is the standard question tone (where the pitch rises at the end). Use this when you want her to clarify a specific fact or when the energy is high and playful.

- *"New York?"* (Rising pitch = "Tell me more about the city.")

The "Late-Night FM DJ" Downward Inflection

This is the high-status, grounded tone (where the pitch drops at the end). This is the "Negotiator's Echo." It sounds like a statement of fact rather than a question. It is incredibly soothing and encourages deep emotional vulnerability.

- *"New York."* (Falling pitch = "I hear you, and I sense there's a deeper feeling there.")

By using the downward inflection, you sub-communicate that you are "Grounded" and "Unreactive." This allows her to feel that she can share more complex or even "darker" emotions without you judging her or becoming overwhelmed.

4. Moving from "Simple Echoing" to "Emotional Labeling"

Once you have mastered the 1-to-3 word Echo, you can upgrade to **Emotional Labeling.** This is the process of echoing the *feeling* behind the words rather than the words themselves. This is a primary tool used by FBI hostage negotiators to build instant rapport in high-stakes situations.

The "It Seems Like ..." Formula

Instead of repeating words, you label the subtext.

- **Her:** *"I've been working twelve-hour days trying to get this project finished, and no one has even noticed."*
- **The Label:** *"It seems like you feel your effort is being taken for granted."*

The Result: This triggers a "That's Right" response. When someone says "That's Right," their brain experiences a massive surge of **Oxytocin**. They feel profoundly "seen." At this point, the rapport is no longer just "good"—it is "intimate." You have bypassed the superficial layer and touched the core of her experience.

5. The "Silence as a Tool" Technique

A critical component of the Echo Effect is what you do *after* the Echo: **Nothing.**

In our "Open" and "Transition" phases, we feared silence. In the "Echo" phase, silence is your ally. After you deliver an Echo or a Label, you must wait. This is known as **The Effective Pause**.

Most men feel the need to fill the silence, which often cuts off the woman's thought process just as she was about to go deeper. By Echoing and then remaining silent for 3 to 5 seconds, you are creating a "Vacuum." Humans are biologically programmed to fill vacuums. She will fill that space with more information, more emotion, and more investment.

6. When to Use the Echo: Strategy and Calibration

While the Echo Effect is powerful, it is not a "one-size-fits-all" solution. Using it too frequently can make you sound like a "Social Parrot" or a therapist. You must calibrate its use based on the **Energy Level** of the interaction.

Scenario A: The "High-Energy" Echo

If she is excited and talking fast, use short, upward-inflected echoes to "fan the flames" of her excitement.

- *"The best trip ever?"*
- *"Totally spontaneous?"*

Scenario B: The "Stalling" Echo

If the conversation is hitting a wall and she is giving short answers, use the downward-inflected Echo to dig under the surface.

- **You:** *"How was your weekend?"*
- **Her:** *"It was okay, just visited some family."*
- **You (Echo):** *"Just family."* (Falling pitch).
- **Her:** *"Well, my sister is going through a lot right now, so it was actually pretty intense..."*

7. Avoid the "Parrot Trap": Paraphrasing for Variety

To keep the technique invisible, you must occasionally switch from a literal "Echo" to a "Paraphrase." This shows that you aren't just repeating sounds, but that you are actively processing her meaning.

- **Literal Echo:** "Management is restrictive?"
- **Paraphrase:** "So you feel like you've lost your autonomy at work."

The paraphrase is slightly higher "Cognitive Load" for you, but it builds even higher rapport because it demonstrates high-level **Empathy** and **Intelligence**.

8. Action Steps: The "Echo" Field Mission

To integrate the Echo Effect into your subconscious (moving it to the **Basal Ganglia**), you must practice it in low-stakes environments.

1. **The "Barista Challenge":** During your next coffee order or grocery checkout, use exactly two Echoes. Notice how the person usually stops their "autopilot" script and engages with you more authentically.

2. **The "Downward Drill":** Record yourself saying three words with an upward inflection and then a downward inflection. Listen to the difference. Focus on making the downward tone sound "Grounded" and "Comforting."

3. **The "Three-Second Rule":** In your next conversation, after you ask a question or use an Echo, count to three in your head before saying another word. Watch how much "Free Information" the other person provides in that gap.

Summary: The Mastery of Linguistic Recycling

1. **Recycle, Don't Invent:** Use her words to do the work for you.

2. **Inflection is Everything:** Use downward tones to build deep, "Late-Night" rapport.

3. **Label the Emotion:** Go beneath the words to identify the feeling.

4. **Embrace the Pause:** Let the silence pull the information out of her.

By the end of this chapter, you should feel a sense of relief. You no longer need to be a "Conversation Machine." You simply need to be a high-quality "Social Mirror." When you master the Echo, you will find that people describe you as "the most interesting person they've talked to all night," even if you barely said a word of your own.

CHAPTER 5

BRIDGE SILENCE USING SIMPLE OBSERVATIONS

Up to this point, we have treated conversation as an internal process—something happening between your mind and hers. We have explored the **Associative Cortex** for topics, the **vmPFC** for reward-based questions, and the **Limbic System** for narrative rapport. But there is a final, often overlooked source of conversational energy that requires zero memory retrieval and zero creative "work."

That source is the **Immediate Environment**.

When a conversation stalls, most men make the mistake of looking "inward" to find a solution. They scan their mental archives for a joke, a fact, or a story. This inward focus increases **Social Anxiety** because it creates a "Performance Gap." In this chapter, we will master the art of **External Observation**. We are going to turn the room, the people, the music, and the physical objects around you into an "External Hard Drive" for conversational fuel. This technique ensures that even if your mind goes completely blank, the world around you will provide the next thread.

1. The Psychology of Shared Reality

In social psychology, there is a concept known as **Joint Attention**. This occurs when two people are not just looking at each other, but are looking at a third object together.

The "Triadic" Interaction

Most high-pressure interactions are "Dyadic"—just you and her, face-to-face. This creates a "staring contest" dynamic that can feel confrontational. By shifting the focus to an external observation, you create a **Triadic Interaction**. This lowers the tension immediately. You are no longer "examining" her; you and she are now a "team" examining the world together.

Grounding the Nervous System

When you make a simple observation about the environment, you trigger your **Parietal Lobe**, which handles spatial awareness. This shift from the "Internal/Abstract" (thinking of what to say) to the "External/Concrete" (noticing a weird painting) actually lowers your heart rate. It grounds you in the present moment, which is the hallmark of a high-value, unreactive man.

2. The "Notice-Label-Link" Framework

To bridge a silence using an observation, you cannot just point at something and name it. That's what a toddler does. A high-value man uses the **Notice-Label-Link (NLL)** framework to turn a random sight into a conversational bridge.

Step 1: Notice (The Stimulus)

Identify a unique or "weird" element in the environment. It could be the lighting, a song, the way someone is dressed, or a specific drink at the bar.

- *Example:* You notice the music is an obscure 80s synth-wave track.

Step 2: Label (The Vibe)

Add an emotional or aesthetic label to the observation. Don't just say what it is; say what it *feels* like.

- *Example: "This music feels like the soundtrack to a movie about a heist that's definitely going to fail."*

Step 3: Link (The Bridge)

Connect that label back to her or a shared experience.

- *Example: "...It gives me 'main character' energy. Are you the type of person who needs a specific soundtrack to get through the day, or do you prefer total silence?"*

3. The Three Levels of Observation

Not all observations are created equal. To maintain a high-value frame, you must calibrate the "depth" of your observation to the current level of rapport.

Level 1: The Ambient Observation (Low Stakes)

This is about the "Physics" of the room. Use this during the "Transition" phase or when a topic has just died.

- *"The lighting in here makes everyone look like they're in a 1940s spy novel. I feel like I should be handing you a secret briefcase."*

Level 2: The Social Observation (Medium Stakes)

This is about the "Energy" of the people around you. It shows you are socially intuitive and aware.

- *"Have you noticed that couple in the corner? They've been on their phones for twenty minutes. I can't tell if they're profoundly bored or if they're actually having a really intense argument over text."*

Level 3: The Micro-Observation (High Stakes/Intimacy)

This is a specific, "Cold Read" observation about *her*—specifically something she has chosen or a gesture she has made. This builds massive attraction because it shows you are paying a level of attention most men lack.

- *"I noticed you keep twisting that ring whenever you talk about your trip. It's like you're trying to physically hold onto the memory. Is that the most significant piece of jewelry you own?"*

4. Turning "Negative" Situations into "High-Vibe" Bridges

One of the most powerful uses of observation is when something goes **wrong**. A spill, a loud noise, a bad song, or a long wait for a drink.

A low-value man complains about these things. He becomes a victim of the environment. A high-value man uses them as **"Shared Adversity."**

- *Example:* The music suddenly cuts out.
- *High-Value Observation: "Well, I guess the DJ decided it was time for us to have a private moment. How are you handling the sudden pressure of being the only entertainment in the room?"*

By "Leaning In" to the awkwardness, you prove that your state is not dependent on external circumstances. This is the definition of **Self-Amusement**.

5. The "External Hard Drive" Drill

To ensure you never run out of things to say, you must train your brain to constantly "buffer" environmental data.

The Mission: When you are walking down the street or sitting in a coffee shop, practice the "Five-Senses Scan."

1. **Sight:** What is the most "out of place" object in your field of vision?
2. **Sound:** What is the "sub-layer" of noise? (The hum of the fridge, the distant traffic).
3. **Smell:** What is the dominant scent? (Old paper, expensive perfume, burnt coffee).
4. **Touch:** What is the temperature or the texture of your seat?
5. **Vibe:** If this room were a person, what would their personality be?

By practicing this, you ensure that when a silence occurs in the field, your "Notice" trigger is already primed. You won't have to search for something to say; you will simply "report" on what you have already noticed.

6. The "Assumptive Observation" (Advanced)

This combines Chapter 4 (The Echo) and Chapter 5. You observe an environmental fact and make an **Assumption** about how she relates to it.

- *"I see you went for the Tequila. That usually means one of two things: either you had a very long day and need to delete it, or you're celebrating something and want to accelerate it. Which version of you am I talking to?"*

This is high-value because it takes a "boring" observation (she is drinking tequila) and turns it into a "High-Value Question" (what is her current state?).

7. Managing the "Visual Scan"

A warning: When you are looking for observations, you must avoid the **"Predatory Scan."** If your eyes are darting around the room frantically looking for a topic, you will look anxious.

The "Grounded Look"

Your eyes should move slowly. When you notice something, let your gaze linger for a half-second before you speak. This sub-communicates that you are "taking in" the world at your own pace. You are not a "Scanning Computer"; you are a "Connoisseur" of the environment.

8. Action Steps: The Environmental Integration Audit

1. **The "Three-Observation" Rule:** In your next social interaction, commit to making at least three observations using the NLL framework (Notice-Label-Link).

2. **The "People Watching" Drill:** Go to a public place for 15 minutes. Pick three couples and come up with a "Narrative Observation" for each (e.g., "They look like they've been married for 40 years but still have a secret handshake").

3. **The "Sensory Shift":** When you feel a silence becoming "Awkward," consciously shift your focus from your own thoughts to your **Peripheral Vision**. Name three things in your head before you speak.

Summary: The Mastery of the Physical World

1. **Shift to Triadic Interaction:** Use objects to lower the pressure between you and her.

2. **Notice, Label, Link:** Turn a sight into a story and then into a question.

3. **Use the Three Levels:** Calibrate your observations to the level of rapport.

4. **Embrace the "Wrong":** Use environmental mishaps to show your unreactive nature.

By the end of this chapter, you should realize that you are never truly "alone" in a conversation. You have an entire room full of props, characters, and soundtracks waiting to be used. When you master observation, the world becomes your co-host.

CONCLUSION

BECOME A NATURAL TALKER

We have reached the final pillar of Book 3. You have moved through the **Associative Cortex** to find infinite threads, mastered the **Neuro-Economics** of high-value questions, learned to trigger **Neural Coupling** through storytelling, utilized the **Echo Effect** to recycle energy, and turned the **Physical World** into an external hard drive for conversation.

But there is a final, vital shift that must occur for these techniques to transition from "tools you use" to "who you are." This is the transition from **Conscious Competence**—where you are still "calculating" your next move—to **Unconscious Mastery**. To become a "Natural Talker," you must stop trying to "do" conversation and start allowing yourself to "be" the conversation.

1. The Neural Shift: From the Prefrontal Cortex to the Basal Ganglia

When you first started this journey, your social interactions likely felt like "manual labor." You were over-relying on your **Dorsolateral Prefrontal Cortex (dlPFC)**—the area of the brain responsible for complex

166

planning, monitoring, and error detection. This is the "high-energy" part of the brain. It is excellent for solving math problems, but it is the enemy of charisma. When the dlPFC is over-active, you feel "stiff," "stuck," or "in your head."

Becoming a natural talker requires shifting the task of conversation to the **Basal Ganglia** and the **Cerebellum**. These regions handle "procedural memory"—the same parts of the brain that allow you to ride a bike, tie your shoes, or drive a car without consciously thinking about the intricate physics of the movements.

The "Flow State" of Dialogue

Natural talkers operate in what psychologists call the **Social Flow State**. In this state, the "Internal Editor" (the dlPFC) is effectively deactivated. This allows for **Spontaneous Self-Expression**. When you stop monitoring your output for "correctness," your humor becomes sharper, your associations become more daring, and your tonality becomes naturally more grounded. You are no longer "performing" for an audience; you are simply reacting to the immediate sensory data of the moment.

2. The Philosophy of "Outcome Independence"

The greatest barrier to becoming a natural talker is the **Fear of Social Loss**. When you are attached to a specific outcome—making her like you, getting her number, appearing "cool"—your brain enters a state of high-alert. This triggers the **Amygdala**, which sends inhibitory signals to your speech centers.

The "Self-Amusement" Frame

A Natural Talker prioritizes **Self-Amusement** over **Social Approval**. He says things because *he* finds them interesting, funny, or curious.

- **The Neurochemistry:** When you find yourself funny or interesting, your brain releases **Endorphins** and **Dopamine**.
- **The Mirror Effect:** Because of **Mirror Neurons**, the person you are talking to will subconsciously "catch" your state of amusement.

You do not seek to entertain her; you seek to entertain yourself, and you simply invite her to join the party. This is the ultimate "High-Value" sub-communication. It tells her that your "State" is internal and self-generated, not dependent on her reaction.

3. Embracing the "Social Messiness": The End of Perfectionism

A common trap for men is the "Perfectionist Bottleneck." They wait to speak until they have a "perfect" thing to say. This leads to long, agonizing pauses and a lack of social momentum.

Natural conversation is inherently messy. It involves "umms," "ahhs," mid-sentence pivots, and associations that don't always land perfectly. A Natural Talker accepts this messiness as a feature, not a bug. He understands that **Momentum is more important than Accuracy.** #### The "Recovery" Muscle High-value social skill is not the absence of awkward moments; it is the ability to recover from them with unreactive grace. If an association falls flat, a Natural Talker doesn't panic. He simply uses the **Notice-Label-Link** framework from Chapter 5 to comment on the failure:

- *"Well, that story went absolutely nowhere. I think I just bored myself. How are you coping with being trapped in this conversation?"*

By calling out the "fail," you prove that you are unreactive and high-status. You are comfortable in the "Social Mess," which makes her feel safe to be "imperfect" around you as well.

4. The Power of "Micro-Presence" and the TPN/DMN Balance

To never run out of things to say, you must be a master of **Temporal Presence**. Most men "run out" of things to say because they are living in the "Future" (worrying about what to say next) or in the "Past" (worrying about what they just said).

Task Positive vs. Default Mode

When you are in the **Task Positive Network (TPN)**—the "doing" mode—you are focused on the "goal" of the conversation. This makes you sound like an interviewer. When you shift to a state of **Presence**, you allow the **Default Mode Network (DMN)** to function. The DMN is where creativity and "daydreaming" live.

When you are 100% present, the DMN offers up quirky, personal, and daring associations that you could never "plan" for. You notice the specific way she tilts her head, the rhythm of the background music, or the strange texture of the napkins. These "Micro-Observations" are the raw fuel for infinite dialogue.

5. Final Integration: The Three Laws of the Natural Talker

As you move out of Book 3 and into the field, you must internalize these three laws. They are the "Operating System" for your new social life.

Law I: Trust the First Association

In 90% of social situations, your first thought is the most authentic. Stop the "Two-Second Audit" where you check your thought for "coolness." If your brain links her career in "Dentistry" to "That scene in *Finding Nemo*," say it. The "weirdness" of the association is what makes it charismatic.

Law II: The World is the Script

You are never responsible for 100% of the content. Use the environment, use her words (The Echo), and use the shared "Vibe." You are a co-author of the interaction, not a solo novelist trying to write a script in real-time.

Law III: State Over Content

The literal meaning of your words is only 10% of the interaction. Your **Unshakable State**—your comfort in silence, your warmth in speech, and your playful energy—is what she will remember. If your "State" is high-value, the words could be about anything.

6. The Habit of Expression: Moving Beyond the "Dating" Frame

Becoming a Natural Talker is not just about attracting women; it is a way of moving through the world. To truly master these skills, you must move beyond the "Dating" frame and realize that every interaction is a chance to practice your **Associative Muscle**.

The "All-Day" Practice

Don't wait for "High Stakes" moments to use these tools. Use them with the barista, the Uber driver, your boss, and your family. The more you practice "Free Association" and "Echoing" in zero-stakes environments, the more these neural pathways will be "hot-wired" when you are talking to a woman you are deeply attracted to. You are building a **Social Superpower** that will affect every area of your life, from your romantic success to your professional influence.

Ultimately, the ability to talk effortlessly is an **Evolutionary Signal**. It tells the world that your nervous system is regulated, your status is high, and your "social intelligence" is vast. In the environment of our ancestors, the "Natural Talker" was the one who could negotiate peace between tribes, attract the highest-quality mates, and lead through the power of narrative.

By mastering the "Flow" of conversation, you are reclaiming your ancestral right to be a leader of men and a pursuer of high-value women. You are no longer a "student" of social skills; you are a man who understands the very fabric of human connection.

REFLECTION QUESTIONS

CHECK YOUR PROGRESS

Congratulations on completing the tactical core of Book 3. You have moved through the high-level mechanics of conversational flow, from the neurological roots of association to the subtle art of environmental observation. However, as we discussed in the Conclusion, knowledge is not mastery. Mastery is the result of **Directed Reflection**.

This chapter is designed to act as a **Social Diagnostic**. It is not a test to pass or fail; it is a mirror for your current neurological habits. To get the most value from this section, answer each question with brutal honesty. If you find yourself wanting to say "I know how to do that," ask yourself instead: **"Did I actually do that in my last three interactions?"**

Part 1: Auditing the Associative Muscle

Focus: Chapter 1 – Free Association

The goal of Chapter 1 was to dismantle the "Internal Editor" and allow your brain to branch horizontally rather than digging vertically into dry facts.

1. The "Mental Blank" Frequency Audit Think back to your last three conversations with someone new. Did you experience a moment of "Brain Freeze"?

- **If Yes:** Was the blank caused by a lack of ideas, or by your brain rejecting the ideas it found because they weren't "good enough"?

- **The Neuro-Diagnostic:** If you found ideas but rejected them, your **Dorsolateral Prefrontal Cortex** is still over-policing your output. You are prioritizing "Safety" over "Flow."

2. The Velocity of Branching When a new topic is introduced (e.g., "I just started a new job"), how many seconds does it take for your brain to find three distinct associations (Sensory, Thematic, Self-Referential)?

- **Self-Correction:** If it takes more than three seconds, you are likely still using "Vertical Search" (searching for facts about the job) rather than "Horizontal Association" (thinking about the feeling of a first day, the concept of ambition, or the smell of a new office).

3. The Logic-to-Energy Ratio In your recent conversations, have you caught yourself apologizing for a "weird" transition? (e.g., "This is random, but ...")

- **High-Value Insight:** A natural talker never apologizes for his associations. If you are still using "disclaimers," you are seeking permission to be yourself. Are you ready to trust that your internal world is inherently interesting enough to share without a preamble?

Part 2: The Inquiry Architect

Focus: Chapter 2 – High-Value Open-Ended Questions

In Chapter 2, we analyzed the "Cognitive Cost" of your questions. You learned to move from the Lateral Prefrontal Cortex (Fact-Finding) to the Ventromedial Prefrontal Cortex (Reward-Seeking).

4. The "Interview Trap" Diagnostic Review the last five questions you asked a woman. How many of them could be answered with a single word or a short, factual sentence?

- **The Audit:** If more than two were factual (Where? How long? What?), you are still taxing her cognitive load without providing a dopamine reward. How can you rephrase those "Search Engine" questions into "Possibility" frames?

5. The Cold Read Challenge How many times in the last week have you used a **Cold Read Statement** instead of a question?

- **Example Audit:** Instead of asking "Are you an artist?", did you say "You have a very creative energy; I'm guessing you spend your weekends making something with your hands"?
- **The Metric:** A high-value man should aim for a 1:3 ratio—one cold read for every three questions. Statements build more attraction than inquiries.

6. The "Why" vs. "What" Calibration When you wanted to understand someone's motivation, did you use the word "Why" (which can trigger defensiveness) or a "What/How" frame?

- **Reflection:** Did the person lean in when you asked, or did they lean back to "explain" themselves? If they leaned back, your inquiry was likely too logical or interrogative.

Part 3: The Narrative Bond

Focus: Chapter 3 – Storytelling and Neural Coupling

Chapter 3 taught you to package your life into three-act micro-arcs that trigger **Oxytocin** and **Neural Coupling**.

7. The Conflict Audit Think of the last story you told. Was there a clear "Pivot" or "Conflict"?

- **The Analysis:** If your story was just a series of positive events, it was likely a "Brag." Did you include a **Vulnerability Loop**? Did you show a moment where you were confused, intimidated, or wrong? If not, you missed the chance to trigger the "Me Too" effect.

8. The Sensory Anchor Count In your last story, did you use at least two sensory details (smell, texture, sound) that were *not* visual?

- **The Neuro-Diagnostic:** Visual details are processed logically. Smells and textures go straight to the **Amygdala** and **Hippocampus**. If you aren't using "Sensory Anchors," you aren't achieving "Neural Coupling"—she is just hearing you, not *feeling* you.

9. The "Bridge Back" Verification After you finished your story, did you immediately ask a question that linked the *theme* of your story to *her* life?

- **Reflection:** Did the conversation flow seamlessly back to her, or was there a "clapping moment" where she just said "Oh, wow, cool story"? If there was a pause, you failed to build the bridge.

Part 4: The Social Mirror

Focus: Chapter 4 – The Echo Effect

The Echo Effect is your "Low-Energy" superpower. It allows you to maintain depth without inventing new content.

10. The Tonality Test When you use the Echo Effect (repeating the last 1-3 words), are you using an **Upward Inflection** (questioning) or a **Downward Inflection** (grounded)?

- **The Audit:** If you use upward inflections too much, you sound like a curious child. If you use downward inflections, you sound like a powerful man who understands her. Which one did you project in your last interaction?

11. The "Effective Pause" Audit After you delivered an Echo or an Emotional Label, did you remain silent for at least three seconds to let her fill the vacuum?

- **The Diagnostic:** If you rushed to speak because the silence felt "awkward," you are still uncomfortable with the vacuum. Silence is where the most valuable "Free Information" is revealed. Can you sit in that silence without fidgeting?

12. The Emotional Labeling Accuracy Have you successfully used the "It seems like..." formula to name an emotion she was feeling but hadn't stated?

- **Reflection:** If she replied "Exactly!" or "That's right!", you hit the **Oxytocin Jackpot**. If she corrected you, did you handle the correction with unreactive grace, or did you get defensive?

Focus: Chapter 5 – Bridging Silence Using Observations

Chapter 5 moved the focus from your internal world to the "External Hard Drive" of the environment.

13. The Triadic Shift In your last interaction, did you shift the focus from "Me and You" to "Us and the Room"?

- **The Audit:** Did you use a **Notice-Label-Link** to comment on a third object (a person, a song, a weird drink)? If not, were you stuck in a "staring contest" dynamic?

14. The "Negative-to-Positive" Flip When something went wrong in the environment (a spill, a loud noise, a long line), did you complain, or did you use it as a "Shared Adversity" joke?

- **High-Value Metric:** Complaining is low-value. Using a mishap to demonstrate your **Unreactive State** is high-value. Which one did you do?

15. The Grounded Scan When you looked around the room for a topic, were your eyes moving frantically (Predatory Scan) or slowly and deliberately (The Connoisseur)?

- **Reflection:** Did the person you were with feel like you were "leaving" the conversation to find a topic, or that you were "including" them in your observation?

Part 6: The Natural State

Focus: Conclusion – Becoming a Natural Talker

The Conclusion focused on the shift from Conscious Competence to Unconscious Mastery.

16. The Self-Amusement Audit In your last conversation, what percentage of your jokes or comments were said specifically because *you* found them funny or interesting?

- **The Metric:** If that number is less than 50%, you are still "performing" for her approval. A natural talker is his own primary audience.

17. The Recovery Diagnostic When a joke didn't land or a story fell flat, did you feel a "spike" of Cortisol (panic), or did you laugh and call out the awkwardness?

- **The Neuro-Diagnostic:** Your comfort with failure is the ultimate signal of high status. If you are still hiding your mistakes, your **Amygdala** is still in charge of your social identity.

18. The "All-Day" Practice Habit How many "Zero-Stakes" interactions did you have today (barista, cashier, coworker) where you practiced at least one technique from this book?

- **The Final Audit:** If you only use these tools when you "have to" (on a date), they will never become part of your **Basal Ganglia**. Mastery is a 24/7 habit.

Scoring Your Progress: The Integration Scale

For each section above, give yourself a score from 1 to 10 based on how often you **actually embodied** the principle in the field.

- **15-40: The Technician.** You are still "calculating." You have the tools, but the gears are grinding. You need more "Zero-Stakes" practice to move the skills from your Prefrontal Cortex to your Basal Ganglia.

- **41-75: The Charismatic.** You are starting to hit "Social Flow." You have moments of effortless brilliance followed by moments of over-thinking. Focus on the **Self-Amusement** and **Presence** drills.

- **76-100: The Natural.** You are no longer "doing" social skills; you are a social presence. The world has become your script. Your primary focus should now be on **Leadership** and **Influence** (which we will cover in Book 4).

BOOK FOUR
FLIRT NATURALLY AND RESPECTFULLY

INTRODUCTION

EXPRESS ROMANTIC INTEREST CLEARLY

In Book 3, you mastered the **Social Flow**. You learned to unlock your associative cortex, utilize the environment as an external hard drive, and maintain a conversation indefinitely. You have become a man who is "easy to talk to." However, as many men discover to their peril, being easy to talk to is a double-edged sword. Without the psychological and biological shifts contained in Book 4, you risk becoming the "Professional Best Friend"—the man who provides immense emotional value but never triggers the visceral, romantic tension necessary for a relationship.

This introduction marks the most critical transition in your journey. We are moving from **Social Connection** to **Romantic Polarity**. The difference between a "pleasant chat" and a "flirtatious interaction" is not necessarily the topic of conversation; it is the **Clarity of Intent**.

To understand why expressing interest clearly is high-value, we must look back at our evolutionary history. In the realm of biology, flirting serves as an **Honest Signal**—a concept in evolutionary biology that refers to a trait or behavior that is difficult to fake and signals an individual's underlying fitness.

The Risk of the Expression

When you express romantic interest, you are taking a **Social Risk**. You are putting your ego on the line and potentially facing rejection. In the tribal environment of our ancestors, a man who could take such a risk without being crushed by the outcome sub-communicated a high level of **Emotional Resilience** and **Social Status**.

A man who "sneaks" his interest—who acts as a friend for months hoping she eventually notices him—is sending a "Dishonest Signal." He is attempting to bypass the risk of rejection. This lack of transparency is perceived by the female nervous system as a sign of low status and potential instability. Clarity, therefore, is not just about being "direct"; it is a biological proof of strength.

2. The Neurobiology of Attraction: From Oxytocin to PEA

In Book 3, we focused heavily on **Oxytocin** (the bonding hormone) and **Dopamine** (the reward chemical). These are essential for rapport. However, romantic attraction requires a different chemical cocktail. To move from "Friend" to "Romantic Interest," you must trigger the release of **Phenylethylamine (PEA)** and **Noradrenaline**.

The PEA Spike: "The Molecular Love Secretion"

PEA is a natural amphetamine produced by the brain. It is responsible for the "butterflies," the racing heart, and the heightened sensory awareness that occurs when you are attracted to someone.

- **Rapport (Book 3):** Focuses on **Comfort**. It lowers the heart rate and creates a sense of safety.

- **Attraction (Book 4):** Focuses on **Tension**. It raises the heart rate and introduces a sense of "Exciting Uncertainty."

If you provide only comfort, her brain categorizes you as "Family/Friend." To trigger attraction, you must introduce the "Edge" of romantic intent. Expressing interest clearly is the catalyst that shifts the brain from the **Platonic Circuit** to the **Sexual Circuit**.

3. The Anterior Cingulate Cortex: The Incongruence Filter

One of the most common reasons men are labeled "creepy" is not because they expressed interest, but because they were **Incongruent**.

The **Anterior Cingulate Cortex (ACC)** is the part of the brain involved in error detection and social evaluation. It is highly developed in women. If you are feeling deep attraction for a woman but are acting like a "polite acquaintance," her ACC registers a massive mismatch between your body language (dilated pupils, leaning in, micro-expressions) and your words.

The "Creepiness" Equation

Creepiness = (Perceived Interest) - (Transparent Intent)

When she senses your interest but you are not being honest about it, her nervous system enters a state of "High Alert." She doesn't know what your true motives are. However, when you say, *"I have to tell you, you have a very distracting smile. It's making it quite difficult for me to remember what we were talking about,"* you have closed the gap. Your words now match your energy. The ACC relaxes, trust is built, and the "creepiness" disappears.

4. The "Friend Zone" Paradox: Why Flow is Not Enough

Many men believe that if they just "build enough rapport," a woman will eventually fall for them. This is the **Rapport Fallacy**. Rapport builds a foundation, but **Polarity** builds the house.

Feature	The Platonic Frame (Book 3)	The Romantic Frame (Book 4)
Primary Goal	Connection & Understanding	Tension & Attraction
Key Chemical	Oxytocin (Bonding)	PEA (Excitement)
Vibe	"We are the same."	"We are different but drawn together."

Feature	The Platonic Frame (Book 3)	The Romantic Frame (Book 4)
Communication	Deep, Logical, Cooperative	Playful, Teasing, Polarizing

Sexual Polarity

Polarity is the "pull" between two opposites. Think of it like magnetism. Two North poles (or two people acting exactly the same) repel each other. For attraction to exist, there must be a "Positive" and a "Negative" charge. By expressing your masculine intent clearly, you provide the "Charge" that allows her to relax into her feminine response.

5. The Intention-Clarity Framework: The Three Pillars

To express interest "Naturally and Respectfully," we utilize a three-pillar framework. This ensures your intent is felt without being overwhelming.

Pillar 1: Verbal Vulnerability (The "Truth" Statement)

This is the act of stating your appreciation for her character or energy without expecting anything in return.

- *Weak Expression:* "You're really pretty." (Low value, focused on surface).
- *High-Value Expression:* "There is a specific kind of 'spark' in the way you see the world that I find really captivating. It's rare to find that."

Pillar 2: Sub-textual Tension (The "Gaze")

This involves using the techniques we will master in Chapter 4 (Eye Contact) and Chapter 5 (The Shift). It is the ability to look at a woman and let her see that you find her attractive. This communicates intent through the **Visual-Spatial** centers of her brain, bypassing the logical filters.

Pillar 3: The Playful Frame (The "Tease")

This is the "safety valve" of flirting. It allows you to express interest while keeping the mood light. If tension gets too high, a well-placed tease (Chapter 2) "breaks" the tension and makes the interaction feel like a game rather than a high-pressure interview.

6. The High-Value Ethics: Outcome Independence

The word "Respectful" in this book's title is not a suggestion—it is a requirement for high-status behavior. A man who flirts respectfully is a man who is **Outcome Independent**.

The "Gift" Mindset

Most men flirt with a "Taking" mindset. They give a compliment because they want a specific reaction (a smile, a phone number, validation). This creates **Social Pressure**. A high-value man flirts with a "Giving" mindset. He expresses his appreciation as a gift.

- *"I'm telling you this because it's true, not because I need you to do anything about it."*

When you are truly outcome-independent, you cannot be "rejected." If you tell a woman you find her fascinating and she doesn't feel the same way, your reality doesn't change. You still found her fascinating. By expressing your truth and being okay with any result, you prove that your "State" is internal. This is the ultimate aphrodisiac.

7. Overcoming the Amygdala Hijack: The Courage to be Bold

The reason most men don't express interest clearly is simple: **Fear**. Specifically, the fear that the social connection will be "broken" if they make a move. This is your **Amygdala** attempting to protect you from the "death" of social exclusion.

To become a natural talker and a natural flirter, you must realize that the "safe" path—the path of the friend—is actually the most dangerous path. It leads to the slow death of attraction. The "bold" path—expressing interest—is the only path that leads to romantic success. In this book, we will learn "exposure therapy" techniques to dampen the Amygdala's fear response, allowing you to remain calm and grounded while expressing your desire.

8. Why Clarity is the Ultimate Form of Respect

We live in a culture that is increasingly confused about social boundaries. Because of this, many men have retreated into a shell of "neutrality," fearing they will be seen as "creepy" if they show interest.

However, high-value women find "neutral" men exhausting. They want to be with a man who has the **Social Intelligence** to read the room and the **Courage** to lead the interaction. Clarity is respect because it saves her time and energy. It removes the "Ambiguity Tax" from the conversation.

When you are clear about your intent, you give her the agency to decide if she wants to move forward with you. You are treating her as an equal, capable of handling your desire. That is true respect.

9. Action Steps: The "Intent" Audit and Practice

Before moving to Chapter 1, you must perform a psychological audit of your current social habits.

1. **The "Vague" Audit:** Review your last three interactions with women you were attracted to. Did you say or do *anything* that made your romantic intent clear? If the answer is "No," you were operating in the "Friend Zone" by default.

2. **The "Compliment Cleanse":** For the next 48 hours, stop giving surface-level compliments. If you feel the urge to say "You look nice," stop and look deeper. What about her *character* or *energy* is actually drawing you in? Write these down.

3. **The "Risk" Drill:** In a low-stakes environment (e.g., with a coworker or a friend), practice stating a "vulnerable truth" about something you appreciate about them. Get comfortable with the feeling of your heart rate rising as you express an honest opinion.

Summary: The Gateway to Polarity

- **Flirting is an Honest Signal:** Clarity communicates status and emotional resilience.

- **Trigger the PEA Spike:** Move from comfort (Oxytocin) to tension (Phenylethylamine).

- **Close the Incongruence Gap:** Use the ACC to your advantage by making your words match your energy.

- **The Gift Mindset:** Express interest because it's your truth, not because you need a reaction.

By the end of Book 4, you will no longer be "the guy who is nice to talk to." You will be the man who transforms a room's energy simply by being honest about his desires. You will learn to flirt not as a "technique," but as a natural extension of your high-value identity.

CHAPTER 1

RECOGNIZE ATTRACTION CUES AND PSYCHOLOGY

In the Introduction, we established the "Internal Shift"—the necessity of owning your romantic intent to avoid the "Friend Zone" and build genuine polarity. However, for intent to be high-value, it must be **calibrated**. Blindly expressing desire without reading the room is socially unintelligent. To be a "Natural," you must develop a sophisticated "Biological Radar" that allows you to detect the subtle, often involuntary, signals of interest emitted by the female nervous system.

This chapter is a deep dive into the **Invisible Language of Attraction**. We will move past superficial "body language tips" and deconstruct the evolutionary psychology and neurobiology that drive attraction cues. By the end of this chapter, you will be able to read the room with the precision of a social scientist, knowing exactly when to "push" the tension and when to maintain the "flow."

1. The Psychology of "Plausible Deniability"

To recognize attraction cues, you must first understand why they are so subtle. In evolutionary terms, directly stating sexual interest carried immense social risk for women (risk of social stigma, physical safety, or commitment without investment). Consequently, the female brain evolved to utilize **Plausible Deniability**.

Attraction cues are designed to be "semi-opaque." They are strong enough for a socially calibrated man to notice, but subtle enough that if he turns out to be low-value or aggressive, she can "deny" the intent.

> **The Rule of the Natural:** A high-value man doesn't wait for a verbal "green light." He looks for the biological "yellow lights" that signal it is safe to proceed.

2. The Autonomic Nervous System: The Involuntary Signals

True attraction is a physiological event managed by the **Autonomic Nervous System (ANS)**. Because the ANS is involuntary, these cues are nearly impossible to fake. When a woman is attracted to you, her brain shifts from the "Social/Platonic" state to a state of "Arousal" (in the clinical sense—heightened alertness).

Pupil Dilation (Mydriasis)

When the brain's **Hypothalamus** identifies a high-value stimulus (you), it triggers the sympathetic nervous system. This causes the pupils to dilate to let in more light, allowing the brain to process more information about the "target."

The "Vibe" of Skin Conductance

Attraction causes "Micro-sweating" or increased skin conductance. You might notice her hands looking slightly damp or a slight "flush" on her cheeks or chest (the "Sex Flush"). This is a result of increased blood flow and heart rate. It is a biological "Honest Signal" that her body is preparing for a high-energy interaction.

3. The Facial "Micro-Map" of Interest

The face is the most densely packed area for social signaling. While people can fake a "polite" expression, the **Limbic System** often leaks the truth through micro-expressions.

The Duchenne Smile vs. The Social Smile

A "Social Smile" only involves the **Zygomatic Major** muscles (the mouth). A "Duchenne Smile"—a genuine expression of pleasure—involves the **Orbicularis Oculi** (the muscles around the eyes). If she is attracted to you, her eyes will "crinkle" even during brief laughter.

The Triadic Gaze

This is a specific eye-movement pattern that signals romantic interest. Her gaze will move in a triangle: **Eye -> Eye -> Lips -> Eye.**

- If she looks at your lips while you are speaking, her brain is subconsciously simulating physical intimacy. This is a massive "Green Light."

Lip Moistening and Biting

The tissues of the lips are highly sensitive to blood flow. When the nervous system is aroused, the lips can feel dry or tingly. Fiddling with the lips or biting them is an unconscious attempt to soothe that sensation. It also serves the secondary evolutionary purpose of drawing your attention to her mouth.

4. Proxemics: The Geography of the Body

Proxemics is the study of human use of space and the effects that population density has on behavior, communication, and social interaction. In flirting, space is the ultimate currency.

The "Lean In" and the "Torso Pivot"

The **Ventral Side** (the front of the body) contains our most vulnerable organs. We instinctively turn our torsos away from threats and toward rewards.

- **The High-Value Cue:** Even if she is talking to someone else, if her feet and torso are angled toward you, her "Intent" is with you.

- **The "Lean":** If she decreases the distance between your faces by even two inches, she is testing your "Personal Space" boundary.

The Direction of the Feet

The feet are often the most honest part of the body because we rarely consciously control them. If her feet are pointed directly at you, her "Internal Compass" is locked on. If one foot is pointed toward the exit, she is looking for an "out," regardless of how much she is smiling.

5. Displacement Activities and "Preening"

When a person feels a mix of excitement and social anxiety (the hallmark of attraction), the brain experiences "Excess Energy." This energy is discharged through **Displacement Activities** or **Preening**.

Hair Manipulation

Exposing the underside of the wrist or the neck while playing with hair is an ancient biological signal. The neck is a high-vulnerability area; exposing it signals **Trust**. The scent glands in the hair and neck also release pheromones.

- **The Cue:** Tucking hair behind the ear or "flipping" it to one side to expose the neck.

Fiddling with Jewelry or Glassware

If she is rotating a ring or stroking the stem of her wine glass while looking at you, she is displacing the "PEA Spike" (Phenylethylamine) energy. It is a sign of nervous excitement.

6. Verbal Cues and "Linguistic Mirroring"

As we learned in Book 3, the brain uses **Mirror Neurons** to build rapport. In attraction, this mirroring becomes "Romantic Calibration."

Vocal Pitch Changes

Studies in evolutionary psychology show that women often slightly raise the pitch of their voice when speaking to a man they find attractive (sub-communicating youth/fertility), or conversely, drop to a "husky" lower register if they are attempting to build intimacy.

- **The "Laughter" Cue:** If she laughs at your jokes—even the ones you *know* aren't that funny—she is signaling **Social Compliance**. She is more interested in the "Bond" than the "Content."

The "We" Frame

Listen for the shift from "I/You" to "We."

- *"We should go to that coffee shop sometime."*
- "We would be such a disaster on a road trip."

    This signals that her brain has already begun "Future-Pacing" a reality where the two of you are a unit.

7. The IOI vs. IOD Scale (Calibration)

In the field, you must categorize these cues into **Indicators of Interest (IOIs)** and **Indicators of Disinterest (IODs)**.

Indicator of Interest (IOI)	Indicator of Disinterest (IOD)
Prolonged eye contact (>3 seconds)	Looking around the room / checking phone
Touching your arm or shoulder	Crossing arms tightly over the chest
Re-initiating conversation when it stalls	Giving short, "dead-end" answers
Mirroring your posture or drinking rhythm	Leaning away or creating physical barriers
Exposing "vulnerable" skin (wrists, neck)	Pointing feet toward the exit

The "Rule of Three"

One IOI could be an accident. Two could be a coincidence. **Three is a Pattern.** Once you identify three IOIs within a five-minute window, the "Social Contract" has been signed. You are now expected to move the interaction forward (Book 4, Chapter 3 & 4).

8. Tactical Calibration: What to do with the Data?

Recognizing a cue is useless if you don't act on it. However, the action must match the cue's intensity.

- **If you see "Yellow Lights" (Subtle IOIs):** Increase your eye contact and introduce a **Playful Tease** (Chapter 2). Test the waters.

- **If you see "Green Lights" (Strong IOIs):** Introduce **Physical Touch** (Chapter 3) or move to a more intimate "Romantic Shift" in conversation (Chapter 5).

- **If you see "Red Lights" (IODs):** Do not "Push." Return to **Book 3: Flow & Rapport**. Re-establish safety before attempting to build tension again.

9. Action Steps: The "Field Radar" Drill

To master this, you must move from "Analyzing" to "Intuition."

1. **The "Silent Observation" Exercise:** Go to a public place (lounge, cafe, mall) and observe couples. Identify three "Preening" behaviors and three "Ventral Side" pivots. Do not listen to their words; only watch their "Biological Dance."

2. **The "IOI Search":** In your next three conversations with women, your primary goal is not to be "funny"—it is to spot **Three IOIs**. Once you spot them, make a mental note. Did her pupils dilate? Did she touch her hair?

3. **The "Feet Check":** During any interaction (social or professional), glance at the person's feet. Are they pointed at you? Practice noticing this without breaking eye contact for more than a split second.

Summary: The Mastery of Perception

- **Attraction is Involuntary:** It is driven by the Autonomic Nervous System.

- **Look for Plausible Deniability:** Cues are meant to be subtle.

- **Trust Biology over Words:** A "No" in words but a "Yes" in body language (proxemics/pupils) means she is feeling tension but is socially hesitant.

- **The Rule of Three:** Wait for a pattern before escalating.

By mastering the recognition of these cues, you remove the "Guesswork" from dating. You no longer wonder if she likes you; you *know* because her biology is telling you. This knowledge gives you the **Grounded Confidence** to lead the interaction with absolute respect and zero hesitation.

CHAPTER 2

APPLY PLAYFUL TEASING AND BANTER

In Chapter 1, you learned to calibrate your "Biological Radar." You now know how to look for the **Autonomic Nervous System** signals—the dilated pupils, the ventral pivots, and the preening—that signal a woman is ready for more than just a polite conversation. But knowing she is interested is only half the battle. To catalyze that interest into a genuine romantic connection, you must introduce **Playful Friction**.

Many men believe that being "nice" and "agreeable" is the safest path to attraction. This is a neurological fallacy. While agreeableness builds **Oxytocin (Bonding)**, it rarely builds **Phenylethylamine (Excitement)**. Banter is the art of testing boundaries and challenging her in a way that signals you are not intimidated by her beauty or status. In this chapter, we will deconstruct the "Physics of Wit" and learn how to use teasing to build an addictive dopamine loop.

Banter is essentially a "Play Fight" for the adult human brain. Just as lion cubs play-fight to build coordination and assess strength, humans use banter to assess **Emotional Resilience** and **Cognitive Flexibility**.

The Temporoparietal Junction (TPJ) and Incongruity

Humor is the result of **Incongruity Resolution**. When you tease a woman, you present her brain with a statement that is "technically" a challenge or a criticism, but your tonality and context signal "play." The **Temporoparietal Junction (TPJ)** and the **Medial Prefrontal Cortex (mPFC)** work together to resolve this mismatch.

When her brain realizes you aren't actually attacking her, but are playing a game, it releases a sudden burst of **Dopamine** and **Endorphins**. This is the "Relief" response. By repeating this cycle—**Tension (The Tease) followed by Relief (The Smile)**—you create a chemical roller coaster that is far more memorable than a static, polite conversation.

The "Pre-Frontal Cortex" Test

A woman of high value is subconsciously looking for a man whose "Frame" is stronger than her own. If you agree with everything she says, her brain interprets you as "Lower Status" or "Compliant." If you can playfully disagree or tease her, you demonstrate that your internal state is not dependent on her approval. This signals **Genomic Fitness**—the strength of your nervous system to handle social pressure.

2. The Golden Rule of Banter: Warmth-to-Friction Ratio

Before we learn the specific techniques, we must master **The Calibration of the Heart**. Banter without warmth is just bullying. Banter without friction is just a compliment.

To stay in the "High-Value Flirting" zone, you must maintain an **80/20 Ratio**:

- **80% Warmth & Rapport:** You are present, listening, and genuinely appreciating her (Book 3).

- **20% Playful Friction:** You are teasing, challenging, and "Pushing" her away (Book 4).

The "Smiling Eyes" Check

The most important part of a tease is not the words; it's the **Non-Verbal Subtext**. If your face is serious when you tease her, her **Amygdala** will interpret it as a threat. If your eyes are "smiling" (the Duchenne smile we discussed in Chapter 1) and your body is relaxed, she knows it's a game.

> **Note:** A tease should never be about something a person cannot change (like their height or a permanent physical feature). A high-value tease is always about a **choice**, a **personality quirk**, or a **momentary behavior**.

3. High-Value Banter Technique #1: The False Assumption

The "False Assumption" is the most effective way to transition from a boring factual conversation to a playful one. Instead of asking her a question, you make a "wildly inaccurate" assumption about her character.

- **The Scenario:** She tells you she's an accountant.
- **The Low-Value Response:** "Oh, that's cool. Do you like math?" (Boring/Logical).
- **The High-Value False Assumption:** "An accountant? I knew it. You have that 'secretly dangerous' look. I bet you're the one who cooks the books for the local mafia on the weekends, aren't you?"

Why it Works:
1. **It's a Challenge:** She now has to "defend" her honor in a fun way.
2. **It's Creative:** It shows you have an active imagination (DMN activation).
3. **It's Polarizing:** You are projecting a "character" onto her, which is inherently more interesting than the truth.

4. High-Value Banter Technique #2: The Reluctant Disqualification

This is the art of "Pushing" her away playfully. It sub-communicates that you have high standards and aren't just trying to "win" her over. It turns the dynamic around: instead of you trying to impress her, she starts trying to impress you.

- **The Scenario:** She admits she doesn't like your favorite movie or food.
- **The Technique:** "Wow. And I thought we were actually getting along. This is a disaster. I think we're going to have to see other people. I'll send you the paperwork for the social divorce tomorrow."

Key Components:
- **The Hyperbole:** Use words like "disaster," "heartbreaking," or "unacceptable."
- **The "Social Divorce":** Treat the "breakup" as if it's a high-stakes legal event.
- **The Immediate Return:** After the tease, give her a half-smile to show the "Pull" is still there.

5. High-Value Banter Technique #3: The Roleplay

Roleplaying is the ultimate "Dopamine Hack." It allows you to create a fictional world where you and she have a pre-existing relationship. This bypasses the awkward "getting to know you" phase and moves straight into shared intimacy.

Examples of Micro-Roleplays:
- **"The Couple on the Brink":** "Stop looking at me like that, we are in public. People will think we're actually having a nice time, and I have a reputation for being difficult to uphold."
- **"The Bodyguard":** "You're doing great with this drink, but I'm going to need to see some identification. You look like the type of person who causes trouble in quiet lounges."
- **"The Bad Influence":** "I can see it in your eyes. You're the bad influence in your friend group. I need to keep a safe five-foot distance from you for my own protection."

6. The "Push-Pull" Dynamic: The Physics of Tension

Attraction is like a rubber band. If you only "Pull" (compliment/agree), the band goes limp. If you only "Push" (tease/disqualify), the band breaks. **Push-Pull** is the act of doing both in rapid succession.

The Push-Pull Formula:

1. **The Pull (Validation):** "You actually have a really amazing perspective on that..."

2. **The Push (Tease):** "...it's just a shame your taste in music is so tragic. I was almost impressed."

3. **The Pull (Physical/Visual):** (Maintain warm eye contact and a slight smile).

By doing this, you are effectively "poking" her nervous system. She gets the dopamine hit of the compliment, followed by the cortisol "challenge" of the tease, followed by the relief of your warm smile. This cycle is incredibly addictive to the human brain.

7. Calibrating the "Bite": When is it Too Much?

Banter requires a high level of **Social Intelligence**. You must monitor her **Micro-Expressions** (Book 4, Chapter 1) to ensure the tease is landing as a game, not an insult.

Signs the Tease is Working:

- She laughs or hits you playfully on the arm.

- She teases you back (this is a massive IOI).

- Her body language remains open and she leans in.

Signs the Tease has "Bitten" Too Hard:

- Her smile doesn't reach her eyes (fake smile).

- She looks away or crosses her arms.

- She starts giving one-word answers (Book 3: Transition/Red Light).

The "Quick Recovery" Move:

If you feel a tease has gone too far, do not apologize profusely. That is low-value. Instead, "Pivot to Warmth":

- *"I'm just teasing you. I actually think it's pretty bold that you [insert something you teased her about]. Seriously, it's refreshing."*

- Use the **Echo Effect** (Book 3) to get her talking again and re-establish safety.

In Book 3, we encouraged "Me Too" moments to build rapport. In Book 4, we avoid "Me Too" in favor of **"Oh, Really?"**

- **Rapport (Me Too):** "You like hiking? Me too! I love the outdoors."
- **Attraction (The Challenge):** "You like hiking? Are you the 'I have all the professional gear and a GPS' hiker, or the 'I get lost and have to be rescued by a helicopter' hiker? Because I need to know what I'm getting into here."

The Challenge Frame forces her to **Qualify** herself to you. When a woman qualifies herself to a man ("No, really, I'm actually quite good at it!"), her brain registers him as a high-value individual. We only qualify ourselves to people we respect or want to impress.

9. Developing Your "Banter Archive"

Banter should feel spontaneous, but like the "Associative Threads" in Book 3, you can prepare "Banter Archetypes" that fit your personality.

The Archetype	The Vibe	Example
The Arrogant / Playful	You are "too good" for her in a funny way.	"I'd tell you my secret, but you'd probably just go and tell everyone. You look like a gossip."
The Accusatory	You accuse her of trying to "seduce" or "trick" you.	"Are you only being this nice to me because you want me to buy you another drink? I'm not that easy."
The Reluctant Mentor	You treat her like a "troubled student."	"You're doing okay at this 'socializing' thing, but we really need to work on your high-fives. That was weak."

10. The Ethics of Teasing: The "Punching Up" Rule

To remain respectful, always **"Punch Up."**

- **Punching Up:** Teasing someone about their strengths or their "power." (e.g., Teasing a very smart woman about her "nerdy" obsession with science). This is a compliment disguised as a tease.
- **Punching Down:** Teasing someone about an insecurity or a weakness. This is just being a jerk.

High-value flirting is about making her feel **seen and challenged**, not diminished. Your goal is to be the "fun obstacle" in her night, not a source of stress.

11. Action Steps: The "Playful Friction" Integration

1. **The "False Assumption" Challenge:** In your next three interactions, replace one "What do you do?" question with a "False Assumption." Note the difference in the energy of her response.
2. **The "Disqualification" Practice:** Next time a woman says something she's proud of, give her 2 seconds of a "skeptical look," then smile and say, "Okay, that's actually kind of impressive. Don't let it go to your head."
3. **The "Smiling Eyes" Drill:** Practice in the mirror. Say a teasing line like "You're a total troublemaker" while maintaining a cold, serious face. Then say it again while letting your eyes crinkle. Feel the difference in the "energy" of the words.

Summary: The Mastery of Social Friction

- **Agreeability is for Friends; Banter is for Lovers:** You must transition from building comfort to building tension.
- **Incongruity triggers Dopamine:** Use the "Tension and Relief" cycle to keep her engaged.
- **The Roleplay bypasses small talk:** Create shared fictional worlds to build instant intimacy.
- **Push-Pull is the Engine:** Constant movement between validation and disqualification is the secret to attraction.

By mastering banter, you move from being a "passive observer" of the conversation to the "Director" of the interaction. You aren't just talking; you are playing. And when you play with a woman's nervous system in a respectful, calibrated way, you become an unforgettable presence in her life.

CHAPTER 3

USE PHYSICAL TOUCH APPROPRIATELY

In the previous chapters, we mastered the **Invisible Language of Attraction** and the **Neurobiology of Banter**. You have learned to read her cues and create a playful, high-dopamine environment through wit. However, there remains a final barrier that separates a "great conversation" from a "romantic connection." That barrier is the **Physical Threshold**.

Many men, even those who are socially gifted, suffer from a profound "Touch Hesitation." They fear that initiating physical contact will be seen as aggressive, creepy, or disrespectful. This fear is often rooted in a lack of **Calibration**. In this chapter, we will deconstruct the science of human touch (Haptics) and master the **Escalation Ladder**. You will learn how to bridge the physical gap in a way that is consensual, calibrated, and deeply grounding for her nervous system.

1. The Neurobiology of Haptics: Beyond Words

Touch is our first language. Long before a human infant understands syntax or logic, it understands the world through the **Somatosensory System**. When you touch a woman appropriately, you are bypassing her **Prefrontal Cortex** (the logical, judging brain) and speaking directly to her **Limbic System** and **Insular Cortex**.

C-Tactile Afferents: The "Social Touch" Fibers

Human skin contains specialized nerve endings called **C-tactile (CT) afferents**. Unlike the nerves that detect pain or temperature, CT fibers are specifically tuned to "low-force, slow-velocity" stroking—the kind of touch used in grooming, hugging, and flirting.

When these fibers are activated, they trigger a cascade of neurochemicals:

- **Oxytocin:** The "bonding hormone" that lowers defensive barriers and creates a sense of trust.

- **Reduction in Cortisol:** Physical touch lowers the "stress hormone," making her feel safer and more relaxed in your presence.

- **Endorphins:** Creating a mild analgesic and euphoric effect.

The "Vagal Brake" and Safety

Appropriate touch signals to the **Vagus Nerve** that the environment is safe. A woman's nervous system is constantly scanning for "threat vs. safety." A man who never touches her is an enigma; a man who touches her poorly is a threat; but a man who touches her with **Calibrated Intent** is a partner.

2. The Psychology of the "Touch Gap"

Why do men hesitate? Usually, it is a fear of the **Social Cost** of a negative reaction. However, from a psychological perspective, **Hesitation is often more "creepy" than the touch itself.**

The "Hover Hand" and Incongruence

If you want to touch her but your hand hovers or you pull back quickly in fear, her **Amygdala** registers "Incongruence." As we discussed in the Introduction, incongruence triggers an alarm. She senses you want something but are afraid to own it, which makes you seem untrustworthy.

The "Anchor" Effect

In Neuro-Linguistic Programming (NLP), "Anchoring" is the process of associating a physical stimulus with an emotional state. If you touch her arm exactly when she is laughing at a joke, her brain will subconsciously link your physical presence to the feeling of joy. Over time, your touch becomes a "trigger" for her to feel good.

3. The Escalation Ladder: A Step-by-Step Framework

Physical intimacy is a ladder, not a leap. You must "test" each rung before moving to the next. If you get a "negative" response on any rung, you simply move back down one step. This is the essence of **Consent-Based Calibration**.

Level 1: The Social/Functional Touch (Safe Zone)

This touch is brief, purposeful, and occurs in "neutral" zones (shoulders, outer arms, hands).

- **The High-Five/Fist Bump:** A low-stakes way to test her "touch receptivity."
- **The "Guide" Touch:** Placing a hand on the small of her back or her outer arm to guide her through a crowded room. This is seen as "Protective/Masculine" and is highly calibrated.
- **The Emphasis Touch:** Briefly touching her forearm to emphasize a point in a story.

Level 2: The Playful/Friendly Touch (Banter Zone)

This occurs once you have established the "Banter Loop" (Chapter 2). It is more intentional but still "plausibly deniable."

- **The "Playful Push":** Pushing her shoulder slightly when she teases you ("You are such a troublemaker").
- **The "Compliance Test":** Grabbing her hand to "show her something" (e.g., "Look at this ring," or "Your hands are freezing").
- **The Shoulder-to-Shoulder:** Sitting close enough that your shoulders or thighs occasionally brush.

Level 3: The Intentional/Romantic Touch (Intimacy Zone)

This is where the "Shift" (Chapter 5) occurs. This touch is prolonged and enters her "Intimate Space" (0–18 inches).

- **The "Hair Sweep":** Gently moving a stray hair from her face or behind her ear. This is a massive "Signal of Intent."
- **The Hand-on-Knee/Thigh:** Used when sitting down, usually accompanied by deep eye contact.
- **The Prolonged Hand Hold:** Moving from a "lead" to a "hold."

4. Calibration: Reading the "Pullback" vs. the "Lean-In"

You must be a master of **Micro-Feedback**. Every time you touch her, you are looking for one of three reactions:

The Reaction	Meaning	The Next Move
The Lean-In / Stay	Positive. She is comfortable and enjoys the contact.	Maintain the contact or move up a rung on the ladder.
The Freeze	Neutral / Uncertain. She isn't sure how she feels yet.	**Withdraw.** Give her space, return to verbal rapport, and try again later.
The Pullback / Flinch	Negative. You have moved too fast or the context is wrong.	**Withdraw immediately.** Do not make it awkward. Re-establish verbal safety.

The "Test and Withdraw" Method

A high-value man never "clings." The most powerful way to build tension is to touch her briefly and then be the first one to pull away. This creates a **"Vacuum"** (as discussed in Book 3). It makes her subconsciously want to close the gap you just created.

5. Contextual Calibration: Where are you?

The "Appropriate" in this chapter's title refers to the environment. Your **Somatosensory Cortex** must be aware of social "Staging."

- **High-Stakes/Public (Work/Formal Event):** Keep touch to Level 1. Anything more can create "Social Anxiety" for her, as she is worried about being judged by others.
- **Medium-Stakes (Cafe/Lounge):** Move into Level 2. The environment is relaxed enough for playful friction.
- **Low-Stakes/Private (Date/Park/Late Night):** This is where Level 3 becomes appropriate. The lack of an "Audience" allows her to relax her "Social Filter" and follow her biological impulses.

6. The "Power" of the Hand: Guiding vs. Grabbing

There is a major difference in how your hand feels to her.

- **Low-Value Touch (The "Claw"):** Tense fingers, gripping too hard, or "clinging." This signals anxiety and a "Taking" energy.
- **High-Value Touch (The "Warm Weight"):** Your hand should be relaxed, warm, and firm but not "gripping." This signals **Grounded Confidence**.

Pro-Tip: If your hands are cold, warm them up on your drink or in your pockets before initiating touch. Cold touch triggers a "Startle Response" in the skin, which is the opposite of the "Oxytocin Response" we want.

7. Common Mistakes and How to Avoid Them

Mistake #1: The "Ask for Permission" Trap

Asking "Can I hold your hand?" or "Can I put my arm around you?" sounds polite, but it often kills the mood. Why? Because it forces her into her **Logical Brain** to make a "Contractual Decision."

- **The High-Value Way:** Use the **Escalation Ladder**. Start with a "Social Touch." If she responds well, move up. Your "permission" is her body language.

Mistake #2: Touching Too Late

Waiting until the very end of a 3-hour date to make your first move. This creates massive pressure (The "Big Move" Anxiety).

- **The High-Value Way:** Start with Level 1 touch within the first 15 minutes. This makes physical contact a "Normal" part of your interaction rather than a "Special Event."

Mistake #3: Ignoring the "Micro-Flinch"

If you touch her and she slightly stiffens, and you *keep* your hand there, you have just crossed the line into being "Creepy."

- **The High-Value Way:** Be hypersensitive. If you feel even a tiny bit of resistance, withdraw immediately and go back to being a "Great Conversationalist."

8. The "Physical Anchor" Exercise

To practice this, you can use a "Functional" excuse to touch.

1. **The "Reading the Palm" (Playful):** "I'm not a psychic, but I bet I can tell your future." Take her hand, look at it, and give her a **Cold Read** (Chapter 2). This is a Level 2 touch with a verbal "Banter" frame.

2. **The "Check the Fabric" (Playful):** "Is this silk? It looks like it would be incredibly soft." Briefly touch the sleeve of her jacket. This is a Level 1 "Curiosity" touch.

3. **The "Jewelry Check":** "That's a unique bracelet. Is there a story behind it?" Take her wrist gently to look at the jewelry. This combines Level 1 touch with a "High-Value Question."

9. Action Steps: The Haptic Integration Drill

1. **The "Social Touch" Quota:** In your next three social interactions (could be with friends or colleagues), practice giving three "Emphasis Touches" on the arm or shoulder during a story. Note how it changes the "Warmth" of the interaction.

2. **The "Guide" Practice:** Next time you are walking through a door or a crowd with a woman, practice placing your hand on the small of her back for exactly two seconds to guide her. Note her reaction.

3. **The "Withdrawal" Drill:** Practice touching someone's arm during a laugh and being the **first** to pull away. Notice how they often lean closer to you after you withdraw.

- **Touch is a Biological Bridge:** It lowers cortisol and builds oxytocin.

- **Use the Escalation Ladder:** Move from social to intimate in calibrated steps.

- **Test and Withdraw:** Never "cling." Be the first to break the contact to build tension.

- **Context is King:** Calibrate your touch to the "Social Pressure" of the environment.

By mastering the Escalation Ladder, you remove the fear and "clumsiness" from physical intimacy. You become a man who is comfortable in his own skin and, by extension, makes a woman feel comfortable in hers. Physical touch is the "Grounded" companion to your "Flowing" conversation. When they work together, the result is irresistible attraction.

CHAPTER 4

BUILD CONNECTION THROUGH EYE CONTACT

We have progressed from the **Invisible Language** of cues to the **Social Friction** of banter and the **Haptic Escalation** of touch. You now have the verbal and physical tools to build attraction. But there remains one sensory channel that is more powerful, more primal, and more direct than any other: **The Gaze.**

In human evolution, eye contact is the ultimate "Intent Detector." It is the only part of our nervous system that is physically visible to another person. When you look into a woman's eyes, you aren't just "seeing" her; you are performing a high-speed data exchange between your **Limbic Systems**. In this chapter, we will move beyond the basic advice of "look people in the eye" and deconstruct the sophisticated neurobiology of the romantic gaze. You will learn how to use eye contact to build unbearable tension, communicate "Grounded

Certainty," and create a sense of intimacy that feels like it has lasted for years, even if you just met.

1. The Neurobiology of the Gaze: The STS and Social Salience

When you lock eyes with someone, a specific region of your brain—the **Superior Temporal Sulcus (STS)**—immediately ignites. The STS is responsible for processing social cues and, specifically, the direction of another person's attention.

The "Intent Detector"

The human eye is unique among primates because of our large, white **Sclera**. Evolution designed our eyes this way so that we could easily track where others are looking.

- **Direct Gaze:** Signals high "Social Salience." It tells the other person's brain, "You are the most important thing in my environment right now."
- **Averted Gaze:** Signals low status, fear, or lack of interest.

The Oxytocin Spike

Studies in the *Journal of Research in Personality* have shown that prolonged, mutual gaze (looking at each other for 2 minutes or more) triggers a massive release of **Oxytocin** and **Phenylethylamine (PEA)**. This occurs even between total strangers. By holding a woman's gaze for just a few seconds longer than "socially required," you are chemically forcing her brain to categorize the interaction as "Significant" and "Romantic."

2. The Psychology of the "Gaze Break"

Most men fail at eye contact not because they don't look, but because of *how they stop looking*. The way you break eye contact is a definitive signal of your **Social Rank**.

The Downward Break (Low Value)

When you lock eyes and then quickly look down at the floor, your brain is signaling submission. In the animal kingdom, looking down is how a subordinate de-escalates a conflict with an alpha. In dating, it sub-communicates that you are intimidated by her beauty or presence.

The Horizontal/Side Break (Neutral/High Value)

Breaking gaze to the side suggests that you are "processing" a thought or simply checking your surroundings. It is a neutral, relaxed movement that doesn't signal fear.

The "Slow-Fade" Break (High Value)

A natural talker doesn't "snap" his eyes away. He holds the gaze until he has finished his point, lingers for a split second of silence, and then slowly lets his eyes drift away as if he's contemplating his next thought. This communicates that you are the "Source" of the interaction's pace.

3. The "Triangle Gaze": Communicating Romantic Intent

In Book 3, we focused on "The Social Gaze"—looking eye-to-eye to build rapport. In Book 4, we introduce the **Triangle Gaze**. This is the specific movement pattern that signals sexual interest without you having to say a word.

The Pattern:

1. **Look at her Left Eye.**
2. **Shift to her Right Eye.**
3. **Drop to her Lips.**
4. **Return to the Eyes.**

The Premotor Cortex Activation

When you look at a woman's lips, her **Premotor Cortex**—the area of the brain that plans movements—actually begins to simulate the act of kissing. You are effectively "poking" her brain's physical desire center.

- **Calibration Note:** Do not stare at the lips for too long. A "micro-drop" to the lips (lasting about 0.5 seconds) is enough to send the signal. If you stare, it becomes "Predatory." If you "flicker," it becomes "Flirtatious."

4. The 70/30 Rule of Connection

To maintain a high-value frame, you must balance **Intimacy** with **Independence**. If you stare at her 100% of the time, you look like a "Fan" or a "Predator." If you look at her less than 50% of the time, you look disinterested or distracted.

The Calibration:

- **When You Are Speaking:** Aim for **50–60%** eye contact. You should look away occasionally to "find your words" (this shows you are thinking and not just performing).
- **When She Is Speaking:** Aim for **70–80%** eye contact. This signals "Active Presence" and high status. It shows you are strong enough to take in everything she is "throwing" at you.

The "Silent Demand"

If she stops talking and you maintain the gaze without speaking, you are creating a **Social Vacuum**. Because silence + eye contact = high tension, her brain will feel a biological urge to "fill the space" by sharing deeper, more personal information. This is how you move from small talk to deep connection.

5. Reading the "Window to the Soul": Pupil Dilation and Blink Rates

Because eye contact is managed by the **Autonomic Nervous System**, the eyes provide "Honest Signals" that she cannot consciously control.

Pupil Dilation (Mydriasis)

As we touched on in Chapter 1, pupils dilate when the brain identifies a "High-Value Stimulus." In a dimly lit bar or lounge, pupils will naturally dilate, but if hers are significantly larger than yours, she is experiencing a **Dopamine Spike**. Her body is literally trying to "take in more of you."

The Blink Rate

- **High Blink Rate (30+ per minute):** Signals high arousal, nervousness, or attraction. Her nervous system is "revving."
- **Low Blink Rate:** Signals "Predatory" focus or extreme comfort.

The "Slow Blink" (Intimacy)

When a woman feels safe and deeply connected to a man, she may perform a "Slow Blink"—closing her eyes for a fraction of a second longer than usual. This is a sign of high trust (Limbic safety), similar to how cats signal affection.

6. The "Eye-Smile" (The Duchenne Gaze)

Charisma isn't just about where you look; it's about the **Muscular Vibe** around your eyes.

- **The "Predator Stare":** Wide eyes, no crinkling, high tension. This triggers her **Amygdala** (Fear).
- **The "High-Value Smirk":** Relaxed eyes, slight squinting (activating the **Orbicularis Oculi**), and a "warm" gaze. This triggers her **Pre-Frontal Cortex** (Safety & Pleasure).

  The "Squinch" Technique: Slightly narrowing your eyes (as if you are looking at something in the distance or finding her "amusing") makes you look more dominant and certain. It removes the "wide-eyed" look of surprise or anxiety.

7. Managing the "Visual Pressure"

There will be moments when the eye contact becomes so intense that she will be the one to break it. This is a good thing. It means you have successfully built **Romantic Tension**.

The "Re-entry"

When she breaks the gaze and looks away, do not follow her eyes. Keep your head looking forward and wait for her to "Return." When she looks back and finds you still looking at her with a calm, unbothered smile, you have "Won" the frame. You have proven that you are the more grounded individual in the interaction.

Walking and Eye Contact

One of the most powerful moves is "The Side-Look." While walking side-by-side, turn your head completely to look at her while she is talking. This shows a level of **Dedicated Presence** that most men are too "busy" or "distracted" to give.

8. Advanced Drills: Mastering the Gaze

1. **The "Stranger Gaze" (Confidence Builder):** When walking down the street, make eye contact with every person you pass. Your goal is not to stare them down, but to be the **last** one to look away. When you can do this with men and women of all ages, your "Social Anxiety" will plummet.

2. **The "Triangle Drill" (Mirror Work):** Practice the Eye-Eye-Lips-Eye pattern in the mirror. Time it. It should take about 2 seconds total. Learn to do it with a slight, knowing smirk.

3. **The "3-Second Linger":** In your next conversation, every time she finishes a sentence, count "one-one-thousand, two-one-thousand" in your head while maintaining eye contact before you respond. This creates a "Vacuum" of tension that is incredibly magnetic.

9. Action Steps: The Visual Connection Audit

1. **The "Downward Break" Correction:** For the next 24 hours, consciously ensure that every time you break eye contact, you look **Left, Right, or Up**, never Down.

2. **The "70/30" Challenge:** In your next interaction, try to "out-listen" the other person visually. See if you can maintain 80% eye contact while they are speaking without blinking excessively.

3. **The "Lip-Drop" Test:** Once you identify 3 IOIs (Chapter 1), perform one **Triangle Gaze**. Note her reaction. Does she bite her lip? Does she look away and smile? Does she lean in?

Summary: The Power of the Unspoken

- **Eye Contact is Direct Nervous System Communication:** It bypasses logic and speaks to the Limbic System.

- **The Way You Break Gaze Defines Your Status:** Always break horizontally or slowly; never look down in submission.

- **The Triangle Gaze Signals Intent:** It activates her Premotor Cortex and simulates intimacy.

- **Silence + Eye Contact = Tension:** Use the "Silent Demand" to draw her into deeper levels of sharing.

By mastering your gaze, you become a man who is "Seen" as powerful before he even speaks. Eye contact is the "Laser" that focuses all the rapport and banter you've built into a single point of romantic intensity. When you look at a woman with **Grounded Intent**, you aren't just looking at her—you are showing her a glimpse of the man you truly are.

CHAPTER 5

SHIFT FROM FRIENDLY TO ROMANTIC

We have reached the most critical tactical junction in your social development. You have the **Flow** (Book 3), you can read **Attraction Cues** (Ch. 1), you've mastered **Playful Friction** (Ch. 2), you understand the **Escalation Ladder of Touch** (Ch. 3), and your **Gaze** is grounded and intentional (Ch. 4).

However, many men possess all these tools yet still find themselves stuck in a "High-Quality Platonic Loop." They are having a great time, she is laughing, the eye contact is good, but the "Vibe" remains "Friendly." To move from a "great talk" to a "romantic encounter," you must perform a **State Shift**. You must consciously flip the switch from the "Social/Cooperative" frame to the "Intimate/Polarizing" frame.

This chapter is about the **"Bridge"**—the verbal and sub-textual techniques that signal to her nervous system that you are not just a charming conversationalist, but a man who is actively pursuing her.

1. The Neurobiology of the Shift: Moving to the "Reward Circuit"

In social bonding (Book 3), we relied heavily on the **Temporoparietal Junction (TPJ)** for empathy and the **Dorsal Striatum** for cooperative habits. When we shift to a romantic frame, we are looking to activate the **Ventromedial Prefrontal Cortex (vmPFC)** and the **Ventral Tegmental Area (VTA)**—the core of the brain's "Reward and Intimacy" circuit.

The Intimacy Circuit

The vmPFC is involved in "Self-Referential Processing" and "Emotional Valuation." When an interaction shifts from friendly to romantic, her brain stops asking "Is this person interesting?" and starts asking "How do I feel about myself when I am with this person?" and "What is the romantic value of this man?"

The Cortisol-Dopamine Paradox

A successful romantic shift requires a small, temporary spike in **Cortisol** (tension/uncertainty) followed immediately by a massive flood of **Dopamine** and **Oxytocin**. The "Shift" is inherently a risky social move. By taking that risk, you trigger her **Hypothalamus** to release the chemicals of attraction. If there is no risk, there is no "Shift."

2. The "Us" Frame: Isolating the Connection

The first step in shifting from friendly to romantic is changing the **Geography of the Conversation**. Most "friendly" conversations are about the external world (The "Third Object"). Romantic conversations are about **The Two People in the Interaction.**

The Transition from "The World" to "Us"

- **Friendly:** "Have you seen that new exhibit? The art is fascinating."
- **Romantic:** "I noticed the way you were looking at that painting. You have this very quiet, intense way of focusing that I'm finding really interesting."

The "Social Penetration Theory" (Altman & Taylor)

According to this psychological framework, intimacy develops as communication moves from relatively shallow, non-intimate layers to deeper, personal layers.

1. **Orientation Phase:** "Small talk" (Book 3).
2. **Exploratory Affective Phase:** Shared opinions and personality (Book 4, Ch. 1-2).
3. **Affective Phase:** (THE SHIFT) Discussion of private matters, feelings, and **Direct Attraction**.
4. **Stable Phase:** Deep intimacy and commitment.

To "Shift," you must lead the interaction from Phase 2 into Phase 3. You do this by making her the **Primary Subject** of the conversation.

3. The Verbal Bridge: Stating the Truth

The most direct way to shift the frame is to use a **"Truth Statement."** This is where you stop "playing the game" for a moment and speak with absolute, grounded sincerity.

The "I Noticed" Formula:

1. **Observation:** A specific, non-physical trait you've noticed.
2. **Feeling:** How it makes you feel or what it makes you think.
3. **Intensity:** A grounded look that communicates intent.

   Example: *"You know, I've been sitting here trying to focus on what you're saying about your job, but I keep getting distracted by how much 'fire' you have when you talk about things you love. It's a very rare quality, and I'm finding it incredibly attractive."*

Why This Works:

- **Congruence:** It matches your internal state (attraction) with your external words.
- **Vulnerability:** You are admitting you are "distracted" or "finding it attractive," which takes social courage.
- **Polarity:** It forces her to acknowledge you as a man, not just a "friend."

4. Sub-textual Anchoring: The "Romantic Pause"

If the verbal bridge is the "Engine" of the shift, the **Romantic Pause** is the "Transmission."

In Chapter 4, we discussed the power of eye contact. To shift the frame, you use a specific type of pause. During a high-energy moment of laughter or rapport, you **suddenly go quiet and still.**

1. **The Laughter:** You are both laughing at a joke.

2. **The Cut:** You stop laughing, maintain deep eye contact, and let your smile fade into a "knowing smirk" or a grounded, neutral expression.

3. **The Linger:** You hold this for 3–5 seconds without saying a word.

The "Silent Demand" (Again)

In this silence, her **Insular Cortex** (which processes internal bodily states) will spike. She will feel her heart rate, her breathing, and the physical tension in the air. By not "breaking" the silence, you are sub-communicating: *"I am comfortable with this tension. Are you?"* This is often the moment where a woman realizes, "Oh, this is not just a friendly chat anymore."

5. Moving the Content: From Logic to Desire

To maintain the romantic frame after the "Shift," you must change the **Nature of your Questions**. Move away from "What/How" questions (Book 3) and toward **"Desire/Motivation"** questions.

The Logic Question (Friendly)	The Desire Question (Romantic)
"What do you do for fun?"	"What is the one thing that makes you feel most alive?"
"Where did you grow up?"	"What was the moment in your childhood that shaped who you are today?"
"What kind of guys do you like?"	"What is a 'secret' quality in a man that instantly wins you over?"

The "Vulnerability Loop"

When you ask a desire-based question, you must be prepared to share your own answer first. This is a "Vulnerability Loop." By sharing a piece of your "Internal Map," you give her "Neural Permission" to share hers.

- *"I've always been driven by this need to build something that lasts. I think that's why I'm so drawn to people who have that same 'restless' ambition. Do you have that, or are you more of the 'peaceful' type?"*

6. Physical Convergence: The "Leading" Hand

As you shift the verbal and emotional frame, your physical contact (Chapter 3) must move from "Playful" to "Intentional."

The "Anchor" Touch

During the "Romantic Pause" or the "Truth Statement," you should establish a steady, non-moving touch.

- **The Hand on the Arm:** Not a "tap," but a steady, warm pressure.
- **The "Lean In":** Moving your face into her "Intimate Zone" (approx. 12 inches away).

The "Compliance Check" for the Kiss

If you have shifted the frame successfully, you are now leading toward physical intimacy. You can "test" her readiness with a **Subtle Proximity Shift**:

1. While talking, slowly move your face closer to hers.
2. If she maintains eye contact and doesn't pull back, she is "Complying" with the intimacy.
3. If she looks down at your lips (The Triangle Gaze from Ch. 4), the "Green Light" is 100% active.

7. The "Pull-Back" Strategy: Managing the Intensity

A "Natural" knows that too much intensity too fast can trigger the **Amygdala's "Safety Filter."** If you feel the tension getting "too heavy" or if she seems slightly overwhelmed, you must **"Break the Frame"** momentarily.

- **Technique:** After a very intense, romantic moment, lean back, take a sip of your drink, and say something playful/banter-heavy.
- *"Okay, we need to stop being so serious. You're far too good at this 'soul-searching' thing. Tell me something completely shallow and unimportant about yourself."*

This is the **"Pressure Release Valve."** It proves that you are in control of the interaction's emotional temperature. It makes her feel safe because she knows you won't let the intensity spiral out of control.

8. Handling the "Shift Resistance"

Sometimes, you will attempt a "Shift," and she will try to move back to the "Friendly" zone. This usually happens if she is nervous or if her "Social Filter" is high.

- **The Resistance:** You give a Truth Statement, and she laughs it off or changes the subject back to work.

- **The High-Value Response:** Do not get frustrated or "chase." Simply smile, agree with her "friendly" topic for a moment, and then **"Wait and Re-try."** * **The Diagnostic:** If she resists the shift three times, she likely only views you as a friend, or she isn't ready for romance in this environment. In either case, your high-value move is to stay in "Flow" (Book 3) and remain the coolest guy in the room without "needing" the romance to happen.

9. Action Steps: The "Shift" Integration

1. **The "Us" Transition Drill:** In your next conversation, consciously notice when you are talking about the "World." Force yourself to pivot to an observation about "Her" or "The Connection."

2. **The "3-Second Silence" Practice:** During a moment of high rapport, practice the "Romantic Pause." Look at her with grounded intent and count to three in your head before speaking. Note the change in her "State."

3. **The "Truth Statement" Challenge:** Prepare one "Truth Statement" that is authentic to you. Practice saying it out loud until it feels "Heavy" and "Grounded," not "Needy."

Summary: The Architect of Intimacy

- **Romantic Interest is a State Shift:** You must move from the TPJ (Social) to the vmPFC (Intimacy).

- **Use the "Us" Frame:** Stop talking about the world and start talking about the two people in it.

- **The Verbal Bridge is Courage:** Stating your truth is the ultimate high-status signal.

- **Silence and Gaze are the Catalysts:** Use the "Romantic Pause" to let the tension settle in her body.

- **The Pressure Release Valve:** Manage the intensity by alternating between "Deep Truths" and "Playful Banter."

By mastering the "Shift," you ensure that you never again leave a conversation wondering, "Does she know I like her?" You become the man who can lead a woman from a crowded, noisy room into a private, intimate world of your own making.

CONCLUSION

FLIRT WITHOUT PRESSURE

We have traveled through the dense architecture of human attraction. You have learned to decode the involuntary signals of the **Autonomic Nervous System**, to dance on the edge of social friction with **Banter**, to bridge the physical gap through the **Escalation Ladder**, and to weaponize the "Laser" of your **Gaze**. In Chapter 5, you learned the "Shift"—the moment where you lead the interaction into the intimate, romantic realm.

However, there is a final, overarching philosophy that governs all these techniques. Without it, the skills you've learned can become heavy, manipulative, or "try-hard." This philosophy is **Outcome Independence**, practiced through the art of **Flirting Without Pressure**.

To truly master Book 4, you must become a man who can express intense romantic desire while simultaneously communicating that he is perfectly okay if that desire is not reciprocated. This is the ultimate paradox of the high-value man: **High Intent, Zero Need.**

1. The Neurobiology of Relaxation: The Vagus Nerve and Co-Regulation

When you flirt with "Pressure," your nervous system is in a state of "High Alert." Your **Amygdala** is scanning for signs of rejection, and your **Sympathetic Nervous System** is flooding your body with adrenaline.

The problem is that humans are biologically wired for **Neural Mirroring**. If you are tense and "needing" a specific result, her nervous system will mirror that tension. Her **Vagus Nerve**—the "Brake" of the nervous system—will fail to engage. Instead of feeling the "Butterflies" of attraction, she will feel the "Static" of social anxiety.

The High-Value Relaxation

When you flirt without pressure, you are operating from your **Parasympathetic Nervous System**. You are relaxed, grounded, and "at home" in your own skin. This allows for **Co-Regulation**. Your calm state signals to her brain that this interaction is safe. When the brain feels safe, it can afford to release **Dopamine** and **Phenylethylamine (PEA)**.

> **The Rule of Ease:** If you aren't relaxed, she can't be attracted. Pressure is the "Oxytocin-Killer."

2. The Psychology of "Outcome Independence"

Most social conditioning teaches us that flirting is a "transaction." You give a compliment; you expect a smile. You ask for a number; you expect a "Yes." This is "Outcome-Dependent" behavior.

The Scarcity Mindset (The "Thirsty" Brain)

When you are dependent on the outcome, your brain is operating from a state of **Scarcity**. This activates the **Dorsolateral Prefrontal Cortex (dlPFC)** in a way that makes you over-analyze every micro-movement. You become a "Social Accountant," constantly checking the "balance" of the interaction.

The Abundance Mindset (The "Flow" Brain)

A high-value man flirts because he enjoys the process of expressing his appreciation for beauty and character. He sees himself as a "Wealthy" individual—emotionally and socially. He has so much "value" to give that it doesn't matter if one specific person doesn't "deposit" it back.

By removing the "Need" for a result, you remove the "Pressure" from her. You become a man who is easy to be with because you don't require her to "do" anything to maintain your emotional state.

3. The "Hunted" vs. "Desired" Distinction

There is a profound difference between a woman feeling "Hunted" and feeling "Desired."

- **The Hunted Feeling:** This occurs when a man flirts with "Taking" energy. He is trying to "get" her number, "get" her attention, or "get" her to like him. It feels like an invasion. Her **Amygdala** triggers a "Flight" response.

- **The Desired Feeling:** This occurs when a man flirts with "Giving" energy. He is sharing his appreciation. He is "gifting" her his attention and his masculine presence. It feels like an invitation. Her **Reward Centers** trigger an "Approach" response.

Flirting as a Gift

Imagine you give a friend a birthday present. If you stand there staring at them, waiting for them to tell you how great the gift is, you've created pressure. If you hand them the gift, smile, and go back to your drink, you've given a true gift.

High-value flirting is the same. You state your intent ("I think you're incredibly charming"), and then you **Withdraw slightly** (The Push-Pull from Ch. 2). You give her the space to "open the gift" in her own time.

4. The "Rubber Band" Theory of Pacing

The key to flirting without pressure is **Calibration of Pacing**. Think of the connection between you as a rubber band.

- If you move toward her too fast (overwhelming interest), the band goes limp; there is no tension.

- If you pull away too fast and never show interest, the band snaps.

- **The Sweet Spot:** You create a "stretch" by showing interest (The Shift, Ch. 5), and then you wait for her to move toward you to close the gap.

The "Social Vacuum"

If you have expressed your interest clearly (as we learned in the Intro and Chapter 5), you have created a "Vacuum." A woman of high value will feel the urge to fill that vacuum with her own effort. If you don't give her the "Space" to do that—because you are too busy "Pressuring" her with more compliments or more questions—she will never feel the "Pull" of attraction.

5. The Ethics of the "Clean Withdrawal"

One of the most respectful things a man can do is know how to **End an Interaction** when the romantic chemistry isn't there.

Many men, upon realizing a woman isn't reciprocating their interest, either become aggressive or "mopey." Both are low-value responses. A high-value man performs a **Clean Withdrawal**.

The Logic of the "Graceful Exit":

1. **Identify the "Red Light":** You've attempted the "Shift" (Ch. 5), and she has remained in the "Friendly" zone.

2. **Accept the Data:** Her nervous system isn't matching yours. This is not a "rejection" of your soul; it's a lack of chemical alignment.

3. **The High-Status Move:** *"It's been a total pleasure meeting you. I love your energy, but I've got to get back to my friends. Have a great night."*

By leaving while the "Vibe" is still good, you preserve your value. You show that you are a man with a full life and other options. Ironically, this "Clean Withdrawal" often triggers a "Dopamine Spike" in the woman— she wonders why you left so easily, which can sometimes "Flip the Switch" of attraction in her mind.

6. The "Safety First" Protocol: Respecting Boundaries

Respect is not just a moral choice; it is a **Tactical Advantage**. A woman who feels 100% safe with you will allow herself to be 100% more "adventurous" with you.

The Consent of Body Language

As we learned in Chapter 3 (Touch), your "Consent" comes from her body language.

- If you lean in and she leans in: **Safe.**

- If you touch her arm and she relaxes: **Safe.**

- If she breaks eye contact and looks away: **Give Space.**

Pressure occurs when a man ignores these "Micro-IODs" (Indicators of Disinterest) and continues to "Push." By being the man who **Notices and Respects** the smallest sign of hesitation, you become "The Safest Man in the Room." In the world of dating, the "Safest Man" is often the one who gets to be the "Most Intimate."

7. Integrating the Book 4 Skillset: The "Natural" Routine

To move these skills from your "Logical Brain" to your "Muscle Memory," you must practice them as a single, fluid motion.

The High-Value Flirting Flow:

1. **Entry (Book 3):** Use the environment or a high-value question to start the "Flow."

2. **Calibration (Book 4, Ch. 1):** Scan for IOIs. Is she "Ventrally" aligned? Are her pupils dilating?

3. **Friction (Book 4, Ch. 2):** Introduce a "False Assumption" or a "Playful Disqualification" to build dopamine.

4. **Escalation (Book 4, Ch. 3 & 4):** Use "Emphasis Touches" and "Triangle Gaze" to bridge the physical gap.

5. **The Shift (Book 4, Ch. 5):** Drop into a "Truth Statement." Make the conversation about "Us."

6. **The Release (Conclusion):** Lean back, relax, and let her "come to you."

8. Flirting as a Lifestyle, Not a Tactic

The final lesson of Book 4 is that flirting should not be something you "do" to a woman you like. It should be an expression of your **Natural State**.

The "Social Scientist" Practice

Practice being "Playfully Flirtatious" with everyone you meet—the barista, the elderly man at the park, your colleagues. Not in a "sexual" way, but in a **"High-Energy/Challenging"** way.

- Use "Banter" with your friends.
- Use "Grounded Eye Contact" with your boss.
- Use "Warmth and Truth" with your family.

When you live your life this way, "Flirting" with a woman you find attractive doesn't feel like a "Performance." It's just you being yourself. The "Pressure" vanishes because there is nothing to "win"—you are simply living your truth.

9. The Philosophy of the "Grounded Masculine"

In the modern world, many men are afraid of their own desire. They have been told that "Wanting" is "Harmful." Book 4 has hopefully shown you that **Masculine Desire is a Gift**, provided it is wrapped in **Social Intelligence and Respect.**

A man who knows how to flirt is a man who can bring color, excitement, and "Life" into a woman's world. He is the "Dopamine Catalyst." By mastering these skills, you aren't just "picking up girls"; you are becoming a man who has the power to create "Magic Moments" in an otherwise mundane world.

10. Action Steps: The "Ease" Protocol

1. **The "Check-In" Drill:** In your next interaction, pause for a split second and ask yourself: "Am I leaning in more than she is?" If yes, lean back. **Match her physical effort.**

2. **The "No-Result" Night:** Go out with friends with the explicit goal of "Flirting with three people and then leaving before the conversation ends." This trains your brain that the **Interaction is the Reward**, not the number or the kiss.

3. **The "Vulnerability" Practice:** Tell someone (friend or date) one thing you genuinely appreciate about them that has nothing to do with their looks. Notice how it feels to share a "Truth" without needing a reaction.

- **Outcome Independence is Power:** Needing nothing makes you the most powerful person in the room.

- **Co-Regulation is the Secret:** Your relaxation allows her to feel attraction.

- **Desired, Not Hunted:** Flirt as a "Giver" of value, not a "Taker."

- **The Clean Withdrawal:** Respect yourself and her enough to leave when the chemistry is absent.

- **Lifestyle Integration:** Be the man who brings "Playful Friction" to every area of his life.

You have now completed the tactical and philosophical core of Book 4. You are no longer just a "good talker." You are a man who can navigate the complex, beautiful landscape of human attraction with grace, courage, and absolute respect.

REFLECTION QUESTIONS

CHECK YOUR PROGRESS

You have navigated the foundational mechanics of **Book 4**. We have moved from the biological "Why" of attraction to the tactical "How" of banter, touch, eye contact, and the romantic shift. However, as any master of the social arts will tell you, information without integration is merely a burden on the intellect. To become a "Natural," these concepts must migrate from your **Prefrontal Cortex** (logical processing) to your **Basal Ganglia** (habitual/procedural memory).

This final chapter of Book 4 is designed as a **Neuro-Somatic Audit**. It is a series of deep-dive reflection questions and mental simulations intended to reveal your sticking points, calibrate your internal "Social Radar," and solidify your identity as a high-value man.

To get the most out of this chapter, do not simply skim these questions. Your brain processes information more deeply when you engage in **Self-Referential Encoding**. This is the process where the **Medial Prefrontal Cortex (mPFC)** links new information to your personal experience, making it "stick" permanently.

Before you can lead another person's nervous system, you must be the master of your own. These questions focus on your **Internal State** and **Outcome Independence**.

1. **The Transparency Test**
   - **The Question:** "When I feel a spark of attraction for someone, do I attempt to hide it behind a 'mask' of neutrality, or do I allow my energy to match my internal reality?"
   - **The Science:** Recall the **Anterior Cingulate Cortex (ACC)** from the Introduction. If you are feeling attraction but acting like a platonic friend, you are creating **Social Incongruence**.
   - **Reflection:** Think of the last time you liked someone but "played it safe." What was the physical sensation in your body? Was it a tightening in the chest (anxiety) or a grounded warmth? How might the interaction have changed if you had simply acknowledged the "distracting" nature of her smile?

2. **The "Neediness" Audit**
   - **The Question:** "Am I flirting to *get* a reaction, or am I flirting to *give* appreciation?"
   - **The Science:** "Taking" energy activates the **Amygdala** in the other person, signaling a threat to their autonomy. "Giving" energy activates the **Ventral Tegmental Area (VTA)**, signaling a reward.
   - **Reflection:** If you were to give a compliment and the woman responded with a simple "Thank you" before walking away, would your mood drop? If yes, you are outcome-dependent. How can you shift your perspective so that the act of *expressing* your truth is the reward itself?

3. **The "State" Ownership**
   - **The Question:** "Who is the 'Atmospheric Director' of my social interactions?"
   - **The Science:** Through **Neural Mirroring**, the person with the most stable and grounded nervous system eventually "entrains" the other person to their state.

- o **Reflection:** Do you wait for a woman to show interest before you turn on your "charm," or do you enter the room with a pre-set state of playful warmth?

Section 2: Reading the Invisible Language (Calibration)

This section audits your ability to utilize the **Biological Radar** discussed in Chapter 1.

4. The Micro-Cue Recognition

- o **The Question:** "Can I identify the exact moment an interaction shifts from 'Social' to 'Receptive'?"

- o **The Science:** Attraction is a series of involuntary "Yellow Lights" from the **Autonomic Nervous System**.

- o **Reflection:** Recall a recent conversation. Did you notice her **Ventral Alignment** (torso toward you)? Did you see any **Preening** (hair adjustments)? If you missed these at the time, what prevented you from seeing them? Was it "Internal Dialogue" (the voice in your head) blocking your external perception?

5. The Proximity Comfort

- o **The Question:** "How do I react when someone enters my 'Intimate Zone' (within 18 inches)?"

- o **The Science:** Your **Proxemic Threshold** is a mirror of your social status. High-value individuals are comfortable with physical closeness.

- o **Reflection:** When a woman leans in toward you, is your first instinct to lean back to "restore" space, or do you hold your ground and enjoy the tension? Practice the "Grounded Pillar" visualization—remaining still as the world moves around you.

Section 3: The Physics of Wit (Banter & Friction)

Banter is the "Stress Test" of attraction. These questions evaluate your ability to manage **Dopamine Loops**.

6. The "Nice Guy" Residue

- o **The Question:** "Do I feel a 'pang' of guilt or fear when I playfully tease a woman?"

- o **The Science:** This is often a result of **Social Conditioning** that equates "politeness" with "value." In reality, the **Temporoparietal Junction (TPJ)** craves the incongruity of humor to build a bond.
  - o **Reflection:** What is the difference between an insult and a tease? (Hint: It's the **Warmth-to-Friction Ratio**). Can you think of a time when a tease felt like a "Gift" because it showed you were paying attention to her unique quirks?

7. The Qualifying Frame

- o **The Question:** "In my conversations, am I the one asking for 'approval,' or am I the one 'evaluating' the connection?"
- o **The Science:** This is about **Frame Control**. Whoever is being "qualified" is the one seeking the other's value.
- o **Reflection:** When a woman tells you something impressive about herself, do you immediately say "Wow, that's amazing!" (Low-value/Submissive) or do you say "That's actually quite cool... I didn't realize you were so [Trait]" (High-value/Evaluating)?

Section 4: Haptics and the Gaze (The Physical Bridge)

This section focuses on Chapters 3 and 4—the most visceral elements of Book 4.

8. The "Touch Hesitation" Barrier

- o **The Question:** "What is the specific thought that stops me from initiating a Level 1 'Social Touch'?"
- o **The Science:** This is an **Amygdala Hijack**. Your brain is predicting a "Social Death" (rejection) that isn't actually a threat.
- o **Reflection:** If you knew for 100% certainty that she would respond positively to a hand on the arm, would you do it? If the answer is yes, then your barrier is fear, not a lack of technique. How can you use the "Test and Withdraw" method to lower the stakes of your physical escalation?

9. The Gaze Endurance

- **The Question:** "Can I hold eye contact during a moment of silence without feeling the need to 'break the tension' with a joke or a question?"

- **The Science:** Silence + Gaze = **Maximized Phenylethylamine (PEA).**

- **Reflection:** Next time you are in a conversation, try to let a silence linger for 3 seconds longer than usual while maintaining a warm, grounded gaze. Does it feel like an eternity? If so, your "Tension Tolerance" needs work.

Section 5: The Architect of Intimacy (The Shift)

This section audits your ability to lead the interaction into the **Romantic Zone** (Chapter 5).

10. The Truth Statement Proficiency

- **The Question:** "How comfortable am I stating a 'Vulnerable Truth' without a punchline?"

- **The Science:** Truth statements activate the **Ventromedial Prefrontal Cortex (vmPFC)**, the seat of emotional intimacy.

- **Reflection:** Can you recall the last time you told a woman exactly *why* you found her interesting? Not just "you're pretty," but a deep observation of her character. If you haven't done this, what are you protecting yourself from?

11. The Leadership Mandate

- **The Question:** "Am I waiting for her to 'make it romantic,' or do I accept the responsibility of leading the interaction there?"

- **The Science:** In the dance of polarity, the **Masculine Lead** provides the "Container" in which the **Feminine Response** can flourish.

- **Reflection:** Many men wait for a "clear signal" that never comes because the woman is waiting for the man to lead. How would your dating life change if you assumed interest until proven otherwise?

Finally, we audit the **Philosophy of Ease** from the Conclusion.

12. The "Creepiness" Calibration

- o **The Question:** "Am I hyper-aware of 'Micro-Withdrawals,' and do I respect them immediately?"
- o **The Science:** Respecting a "No" (verbal or non-verbal) actually increases your **Social Value** and trust-rating in her **Insular Cortex**.
- o **Reflection:** Have you ever stayed in a conversation or kept a hand on someone when they were clearly "checking out"? If so, what was the "Need" that blinded you to their cues? How can you become more "Externalized" (focused on her) rather than "Internalized" (focused on your desire)?

13. The "Clean Withdrawal" Skill

- o **The Question:** "Can I walk away from an interaction where there is no chemistry while still leaving her feeling better than I found her?"
- o **The Science:** This is the ultimate test of **Outcome Independence**.
- o **Reflection:** Think of a time you were "rejected." Did you leave with a smile and a "Have a great night," or did you leave with a "Bruised Ego"? The man who can be rejected and stay grounded is the man who eventually becomes "Un-rejectable."

The Final Simulation: The "Perfect" Calibration

Imagine you are at a crowded social event. You see someone you are genuinely attracted to. Walk through the following mental rehearsal, checking your internal reactions at each stage:

1. **The Approach:** You enter the interaction with no goal other than to see if she is as interesting as she looks (Book 3).
2. **The Hook:** Within 3 minutes, you've noticed her pupils dilate as you tell a story using "Associative Threads."

3. **The Friction:** She mentions she loves a certain city. You say, "Oh no, I was starting to like you, but that city is for people who have no sense of adventure. We're going to have to fix your taste in travel." (Book 4, Ch. 2).

4. **The Linger:** You hold the gaze for 2 seconds after she laughs at your tease. You notice she doesn't look away (Book 4, Ch. 4).

5. **The Shift:** You lower your voice slightly, lean in, and say, "In all seriousness, I really love the way your eyes light up when you're defending your terrible travel choices. It's very distracting." (Book 4, Ch. 5).

6. **The Result:** She blushes and looks down at your lips.

Now, the Reflection: In this simulation, where did you feel the most "Resistance"? Was it the tease? The silence? The truth statement? That point of resistance is your **Growth Edge**.

Summary of Progress

If you have answered these questions honestly, you should now have a "Heat Map" of your social skills.

- **If you struggle with the "Shift":** Re-read Chapter 5 and practice "Truth Statements" with friends.

- **If you struggle with "Banter":** Re-read Chapter 2 and practice "False Assumptions" with everyone you meet.

- **If you struggle with "Touch":** Re-read Chapter 3 and focus on "Level 1" social touches until they are second nature.

Book 4 is not about "tricks"; it is about **Transforming your nervous system.** You are moving from a man who *waits* for life to happen to a man who *creates* the life he wants through clear intent and respectful leadership.

BOOK FIVE

KEEP HER INTERESTED FOR THE LONG TERM

INTRODUCTION

BUILD A BOND THAT LASTS

You have mastered the art of the "Spark." Through Books 1 through 4, you transformed from someone who might have felt social anxiety or uncertainty into a man capable of navigating the complex architecture of human attraction. You've learned to unlock your social potential, read the silent language of the nervous system, weave conversational flow, and calibrate the delicate tension of romantic desire. But as any man who has experienced the "burnout" of a short-lived fling knows, **creating attraction is a sprint; maintaining it is a marathon.**

We now enter the territory of **Sustainability**.

In the modern dating landscape, the "initial hook" is common, but depth is rare. We live in an era of "disposable" connections, driven by the paradox of choice and the dopamine-heavy nature of digital dating. However, the high-value man seeks something more profound: a relationship (whether short-term or life-long) that doesn't just "survive" but *thrives*. Book 5 is dedicated to the **Neurobiology of Long-Term**

Polarity. We are moving away from the "PEA Spikes" (the rush of new love) and into the world of **Enduring Attachment, Emotional Safety, and Purposeful Leadership.**

1. The Neurochemical Transition: From PEA to Oxytocin and Vasopressin

To build a bond that lasts, you must understand that the human brain undergoes a massive chemical shift as a relationship moves past the first few months.

The "Lust" Phase (The Dopamine/PEA Surge)

In the beginning, the brain is flooded with **Phenylethylamine (PEA)** and **Dopamine**. This is a state of "positive stress." It is why you can stay up all night talking and feel no exhaustion. It is the "Spark" we cultivated in Book 4. However, the brain cannot sustain this level of arousal indefinitely; the receptors eventually down-regulate to protect the nervous system.

The "Attachment" Phase (The Oxytocin/Vasopressin Era)

As the relationship matures, the primary drivers shift to the **Hypothalamus**, which releases **Oxytocin** (the "Cuddle Hormone") and **Vasopressin**.

- **Oxytocin** facilitates trust, relaxation, and psychological safety. It lowers the reactivity of the **Amygdala**, making her feel "at home" in your presence.

- **Vasopressin** is linked to "Mate Guarding" and long-term commitment behaviors in the male brain. It is the chemical of "Protective Stability."

The challenge of Book 5 is learning how to cultivate these "Binding" chemicals without losing the "Excitement" chemicals. A bond that lasts is one where she feels **Safe** (Oxytocin) but still **Intrigued** (Dopamine).

2. The Concept of "The Emotional Bank Account"

In long-term dynamics, we must apply the work of **Dr. John Gottman** and the concept of the "Emotional Bank Account." Every interaction you have is either a **Deposit** or a **Withdrawal**.

- **Deposits:** Acts of reliability, active listening, supporting her goals (Chapter 2), and maintaining mystery (Chapter 4).

- **Withdrawals:** Broken promises, emotional volatility, stagnation, or failing to lead (Chapter 5).

A relationship becomes "unstable" when the balance nears zero. In Book 5, we will learn how to make high-value deposits that build a "buffer" against the inevitable conflicts of life (Chapter 3). We are moving from "Game" to "Character."

3. The Paradox of Polarity: Why Most Long-Term Bonds Fail

The most common reason a woman loses interest in a "good man" is the loss of **Polarity**. Polarity is the "Magnetic Tension" between masculine and feminine energies.

In the beginning, this tension is high. But as comfort grows, many men become "Nice Guys" who seek only to please, or "Stagnant Partners" who stop growing. When the masculine "Pole" becomes soft and indecisive, the feminine "Pole" is forced to move into a masculine, "doing/deciding" role to keep the relationship moving. This kills attraction.

The "Static" vs. "Dynamic" Bond

- **Static Bond:** You become "Best Friends." You are comfortable, predictable, and eventually... bored. The sexual tension evaporates because there is no "distance" to bridge.

- **Dynamic Bond:** You are partners and allies, but you maintain your own "Purpose" (Chapter 5) and "Boundaries" (Chapter 1). You remain an "Individual" even within the "Couple."

Book 5 will teach you how to be her "Rock" while remaining a "Moving Target"—someone who continues to evolve and surprise her.

4. The Four Pillars of Long-Term Interest

To build a bond that lasts, we will focus on four psychological pillars that will be deconstructed throughout this book:

Pillar I: The Framework of Respect (Boundaries)

Without boundaries, there is no respect. Without respect, there is no attraction. You will learn to set the "Rules of Engagement" early, ensuring that the relationship is built on a foundation of mutual high-value behavior rather than "people-pleasing."

Pillar II: The Architecture of Growth (Support)

A high-value man doesn't just "have" a woman; he **elevates** her. By supporting her ambitions and understanding her "Neuro-Somatic" needs, you become an indispensable part of her success. You become the "Secure Base" from which she can explore the world.

Pillar III: The Mastery of Conflict (Emotional Intelligence)

Conflict is not the enemy of a relationship; **poorly managed conflict** is. You will learn how to use the "Vagal Brake" to stay calm during arguments and how to resolve issues without damaging the "Sexual Frame."

Pillar IV: The Spirit of Adventure (Mystery & Spontaneity)

The brain is wired for **Novelty Detection**. To keep her interested, you must battle the "Habituation Effect." You will learn how to keep the "Spark" alive through purposeful unpredictability.

5. Transitioning from "Flirting" to "Leadership"

In Book 4, you were a "Flirt." In Book 5, you become a **"Leader."** Leadership in a relationship is not about dominance or "Alpha" posturing; it is about **Responsibility**. It is about being the man who has a vision for his life and invites her to join him in that vision.

- A flirt asks, "What do you want to do tonight?"
- A leader says, "I've planned something for us tonight; be ready at seven."

This subtle shift in the **Prefrontal Cortex**—moving from "seeking approval" to "providing direction"—is what sustains a woman's interest over years instead of weeks. It provides her with the "Limbic Ease" of knowing she is with a man who can handle the world.

6. The "Somatic Safety" of the Long-Term Bond

For a woman to remain deeply interested, her body must feel "Somatic Safety" in your presence. This means her **Parasympathetic Nervous System** is dominant when she is with you.

However, safety without "Edge" leads to the "Friend Zone." In this book, we will explore the **"Safe-Danger" Balance**. You are the man who can protect her and listen to her (Safe), but you are also the man who challenges her and maintains his own "Primal Edge" (Danger). This balance is the "Secret Sauce" of the long-term spark.

7. Action Steps: Preparing for the Long-Term Shift

As we begin Book 5, perform this "Audit" of your current or past long-term interactions:

1. **The Predictability Audit:** In your last relationship, did you become so predictable that she could guess exactly what you would say or do? How can you introduce 10% more "unpredictability" into your social presence?

2. **The Purpose Audit:** Do you have a goal in life that is more important to you than your relationship? (Chapter 5 will dive into why this is essential for her interest).

3. **The Conflict Audit:** When things get tense, do you "withdraw" (shut down) or "explode" (lose control)? Or do you lead the conversation back to a place of resolution?

Summary: The Journey to Mastery

Book 5 is the "Graduate Level" of the Natural's journey. It takes the "Magic" of the initial meeting and turns it into the "Power" of a lasting legacy. You are no longer just learning how to "get" the girl; you are learning how to **be the man** that a high-value woman never wants to leave.

By the end of this book, you will understand the deep psychology of commitment, the maintenance of desire, and the art of leading a shared life with purpose and passion.

CHAPTER 1

ESTABLISH HEALTHY BOUNDARIES EARLY

In the previous books, we focused heavily on the "Engine" of attraction—the spark, the banter, and the physical escalation. But if attraction is the engine, **Boundaries are the Chassis.** Without a solid frame to hold the power, the vehicle eventually shakes itself apart.

The most common mistake men make when they finally meet a woman they truly like is the **"Boundaries Eclipse."** Because the dopamine spike is so high, they begin to trade their personal standards, time, and values for the "Reward" of her presence. They become overly agreeable, they stop seeing their friends, and they tolerate behavior they would never accept from anyone else.

This is a biological catastrophe for attraction. In this chapter, we will explore why the female nervous system is hardwired to test your boundaries and how establishing "Non-Negotiables" early is the ultimate act of high-value leadership.

1. The Neurobiology of the "Boundary Test"

To a woman, a man without boundaries is a man who cannot protect her. Evolutionarily, a man who is "pushed over" by a woman he likes is likely to be "pushed over" by a competitor or a threat in the environment.

The Amygdala and the "Strength Check"

When a woman "tests" you—whether through a playful challenge, a minor emotional provocation, or a request that encroaches on your values—her **Amygdala** is scanning for your reaction.

- **The Weak Response:** If you become defensive, angry, or immediately submissive, her brain registers "Low Stability." This triggers a drop in her **Oxytocin** and a spike in her own **Cortisol**. She feels less safe because you are easily rattled.

- **The Strong Response:** If you remain calm, grounded, and firm in your boundary, her brain registers "High Stability." This triggers a **Limbic Release**. She feels she can relax because she has found a "limit" to her own influence.

The "Mirror Neuron" Effect

If you don't respect your own time and values, her **Mirror Neurons** will adopt that same lack of respect for you. You are essentially training her nervous system on how to value you. A man who says "No" with kindness and conviction is teaching her that his "Yes" actually carries weight.

2. Identifying Your "Non-Negotiables"

You cannot establish boundaries if you don't know where your "Property Line" begins. High-value men operate from a place of **Internal Validation**. They have a set of core principles that exist independently of who they are dating.

The Three Pillars of Boundaries:

1. **Time & Purpose:** Your mission, work, and personal growth.
2. **Social Circles:** Your relationships with family, friends, and mentors.
3. **Self-Respect:** How you allow yourself to be spoken to and treated.

The Boundary Category	The "Nice Guy" Failure	The High-Value Standard
Time	Cancels gym / work / friends whenever she calls.	Maintains his schedule; integrates her into his life, doesn't revolve around hers.
Communication	Tolerates "ghosting," late-night drama, or disrespect.	Calmly addresses behavior: "I enjoy talking to you, but I don't do drama via text."
Values	Changes his opinions to match hers to avoid "conflict."	Respectfully disagrees: "I see it differently, and that's okay. I like that we're different."

3. The Art of the "Calibrated No"

The "No" is the most powerful word in the Natural's vocabulary. However, in Book 5, we use the **"Calibrated No."** This isn't about being a jerk or being stubborn; it's about being **Grounded**.

The Anatomy of a High-Value Boundary:

1. **Neutral Tonality:** No anger, no defensiveness. You are stating a fact, like the weather.

2. **The "Positive Redirect":** You state the boundary but offer an alternative that maintains the connection.

3. **Zero Justification:** High-value men don't write "paragraphs" explaining why they have a boundary. Explaining is a form of seeking permission.

   o **Example:** She asks you to skip a long-standing commitment with your friends to hang out with her last minute.

   o **Low-Value:** "Oh, I guess I can tell the guys I'm sick... I'd rather see you anyway." (Loss of respect).

   o **High-Value:** "I'd love to see you, but Thursday is my night with the guys. Let's do Saturday instead. I'll pick you up at eight."

Why this works:

She now knows two things: You are a man of your word (Reliability), and you are not "starved" for her attention (Abundance). This actually increases her **Dopamine** because you are a "Moving Target" that she has to work to stay close to.

4. Establishing the "Respect Frame" Early

In the first 90 days of a relationship, the "Culture" of the couple is established. This is the **Social Imprinting Phase**. If you allow "Micro-Disrespects" to pass without comment now, they will become "Macro-Conflicts" later.

The "Gentle Call-Out"

If she is late without an apology, or speaks to you with a "sharp" tone, you must use a **State-Break**.

- **The Technique:** Stop the conversation. Look her in the eyes with a calm, neutral expression.

- **The Line:** *"I really like your fire, but I'm not the kind of guy who gets spoken to like that. Let's try that again."*

- **The Result:** You aren't "fighting." You are "Standard-Setting." You are showing her where the "Fence" is. Most high-value women will actually find this incredibly attractive because it demonstrates **Emotional Self-Regulation**.

5. Boundaries with Yourself: The "Internal Guardrail"

The hardest boundaries to keep are the ones you set for yourself. To keep her interested long-term, you must have the discipline to not "over-pursue."

The "Pacing" Boundary

Even if you are head-over-heels in love, your **Anterior Cingulate Cortex (ACC)** must maintain control over your impulses.

- **Don't double-text.**

- **Don't provide "Free Therapy" for hours on end.**

- **Don't become her "Assistant."**

By maintaining your "Internal Guardrail," you prevent the relationship from becoming "Enmeshed." Enmeshment is the death of desire. By keeping your "Self" intact, you allow space for the **Rubber Band Effect** (Book 4, Conclusion) to continue working. She needs to "miss" you to feel attraction. You cannot be "missed" if you have no boundaries on your availability.

6. When Boundaries are Challenged: The "Test of Resolve"

She *will* push back. It is a biological necessity. She needs to know if your "Fence" is made of steel or paper.

Handling the "Push-Back":

- **If she gets upset:** Do not "Fix" her emotion. Allow her to feel it. If you rush to apologize for having a boundary, the boundary is gone.

- **The Phrase:** *"I understand you're frustrated, and I hear you. But this is how I'm handling this. I'm going to go [to the gym/to work/to sleep], and we can talk more later when things are calmer."*

This is the **"Vagal Brake"** in action. You are demonstrating that your internal state is not "shaken" by her external emotionality. This is the ultimate "Green Light" for long-term safety.

7. Action Steps: The "Boundary Integration" Drill

1. **Define Your Top 3 Non-Negotiables:** Write down three things you will never compromise on (e.g., your Tuesday night hobby, how you are spoken to, your sleep schedule).

2. **The "No" Practice:** The next time she (or anyone) makes a request that slightly inconveniences a core value, say "No" without an explanation. Observe the "Social Pressure" you feel and breathe through it.

3. **The "Respect Audit":** Look at your current interactions. Are there "Micro-Disrespects" you've been ignoring? Practice a "Gentle Call-Out" this week.

Summary: The Strength of the Frame

- Boundaries build Respect; Respect builds Attraction: You cannot have the latter without the former.

- **Tests are Opportunities:** Every time she tests a boundary, it's an opportunity for you to demonstrate "Masculine Stability."

- **The "Calibrated No" is a Gift:** It tells her that you are a man of character and purpose.

- **Ownership of State:** Never apologize for having standards. A man who knows his worth doesn't need to shout it; he simply lives it.

By establishing healthy boundaries early, you are not pushing her away. You are building a "Sacred Space" where a high-value relationship can actually grow. You are showing her that you are a man who can lead himself—which is the only type of man a high-value woman will follow for the long term.

CHAPTER 2

SUPPORT HER AMBITIONS AND LIFE GOALS

In the preceding chapters, we established the **Masculine Frame**—those essential boundaries that ensure you are respected and that your mission remains the primary axis of your life. However, a high-value relationship is not a fortress where you sit in isolation; it is a dynamic alliance. To keep a sophisticated, high-achieving woman interested for the long term, you must move beyond the roles of "lover" or "provider" and become her **Chief Strategic Ally.**

There is a pervasive and damaging misconception in some circles of "dating advice" that suggests "holding the frame" requires a cold indifference to a woman's individual world. In reality, the most magnetic and sustainable masculine presence is one that provides a **Secure Base.** In the world of developmental psychology and adult attachment theory, a secure base is a person who provides the emotional stability and

248

psychological safety necessary for another individual to take bold risks, explore new territories, and grow into their fullest potential.

When you support her ambitions, you aren't simply "being a nice guy." You are engaging in a high-level form of **Social Engineering.** You are activating her brain's reward circuitry and linking her personal self-actualization—the highest tier of Maslow's hierarchy—directly to your presence.

1. The Neurobiology of the Secure Base

Human beings are biologically wired for a perpetual trade-off between **Security** and **Exploration.** This is managed by the delicate balance between the **Amygdala** (the fear center) and the **Prefrontal Cortex** (the center for planning and ambition).

The "Safe-to-Soar" Mechanism

When an individual feels unsupported, criticized, or socially isolated, their brain's Amygdala remains in a state of hyper-vigilance. This chronic "background noise" of stress floods the system with **Cortisol**, which physically stifles the creative centers of the brain. You cannot think about "changing the world" or "scaling a business" if your nervous system is preoccupied with "survival" or "social abandonment."

By providing a secure base, you act as a "Biological Buffer." When she knows that you are her unwavering ally, her cortisol levels drop, allowing her **Ventral Striatum** and **Nucleus Accumbens**—the areas responsible for goal-directed behavior and the pursuit of rewards—to fire at their peak capacity.

The Michelangelo Phenomenon: Sculpting the Ideal Self

In social psychology, the "Michelangelo Phenomenon" describes how partners "sculpt" each other over time. Michelangelo famously said that he didn't "create" his statues; he simply chipped away the excess stone to reveal the figure that was already inside.

As a high-value man, you perform this same service for her. When you see her not just as she is, but as her **Ideal Self**, and you consistently reinforce that vision, her brain begins to release **Dopamine** and **Oxytocin** in association with your presence. She doesn't just love you; she loves *the person she becomes when she is with you.*

How you respond to her "Good News" is actually more predictive of long-term relationship health and her continued attraction than how you respond to her "Bad News." This is based on the groundbreaking research of **Dr. Shelly Gable**.

Many men believe that being a "Rock" means being stoic and unemotional when a woman succeeds. They think that by showing too much excitement, they are "chasing" or losing their frame. This is a catastrophic misunderstanding of social value. A man who is truly high-value is so secure in his own success that he can afford to be the loudest cheerleader for hers.

The Four Quadrants of Responding:

To keep her interest, you must move exclusively into the **Active-Constructive** quadrant:

- **The Scenario:** She tells you she finally landed the high-profile client she's been chasing for six months.

- **Passive-Destructive:** "Cool. Hey, did you see the game last night?" (You are stealing her "Dopamine Moment" and replacing it with your own agenda).

- **Active-Destructive:** "That's a lot of work. Are you sure you can handle that on top of everything else? You're going to be stressed out." (You are activating her Amygdala and associating your presence with fear and doubt).

- **Passive-Constructive:** "That's great, babe. You worked hard. What do you want for dinner?" (This is "Dopamine Neutral." It's polite, but it lacks the "Social Reinforcement" required for a deep bond).

- **Active-Constructive (The Natural):** "That is incredible! I knew that client would eventually see what I see in you. We are absolutely celebrating tonight. Tell me every detail—how did you close the deal? What was the moment you knew you had them?"

Why ACR Builds Long-Term Interest:

When you respond this way, you are providing **Social Magnification.** You are taking her internal joy and reflecting it back to her, making it bigger. This signals that you are an **Expansive Partner.** A woman will stay interested in a man who makes her world feel larger, not smaller.

3. The "Strategic War-Room" Method

Supporting her ambitions does not mean becoming a passive "Yes-Man." A high-value woman is often frustrated by people who only tell her what she wants to hear. She is attracted to the man who can provide a **Grounded Masculine Perspective**—logic, stoicism, and long-term vision.

The "Ask vs. Tell" Protocol

One of the greatest sources of conflict in relationships is a man trying to "fix" a problem when a woman just wants to be "heard," or vice versa. To avoid this, use the **Ask vs. Tell Protocol**:

When she comes to you with a professional or personal challenge, stop and ask:

> *"Do you want me to just listen so you can vent and process this, or do you want us to 'War-Room' this and find a strategic solution?"*

This simple question is a massive display of **Emotional Intelligence (EQ).** If she wants to vent, you provide the "Vagal Brake" (calm listening). If she wants a solution, you switch into "Strategic Ally" mode.

The Belief Mirror: Combating Imposter Syndrome

High-achieving women often suffer from "Imposter Syndrome"—the fear that their success is a fluke. In these moments, her **Anterior Cingulate Cortex (ACC)** is over-active with error-detection and self-doubt.

You must act as the "Belief Mirror." Remind her of her objective "Wins" and her unique competencies. You aren't just giving a hollow compliment; you are providing **Evidence-Based Support.** ---

4. Avoiding the "Enabler" and "Caretaker" Traps

There is a fine, high-stakes line between being a "Supportive Ally" and being a "Caretaker." If you cross this line, the **Polarity** of the relationship—and her attraction to you—will collapse.

- **The Ally (High Value):** You encourage her to do the work, take the risk, and face the challenge. You are the **Coach** on the sidelines.

- **The Caretaker (Low Value):** You do the work for her. You protect her from the consequences of her choices. You become her "Personal Assistant."

The Neurobiology of the "Damsel Frame"

If you "over-care" for a woman, you are training her brain to be helpless. This kills the "Sexual Frame" because you move from being her **Lover/Peer** to being her **Parent.** Once a woman views you as a "Parental Figure," the erotic tension—which requires a degree of "Risk" and "Independence"—evaporates.

To maintain attraction, she must still see you as an independent entity with your own mission (Chapter 5). You should be her most powerful asset, but you must never be her "Crutch."

5. Cultivating the "Autonomy Spark"

One of the greatest killers of long-term interest is "Couples-Merge"—the process where two individuals become a single, boring, predictable unit. This happens when partners stop pursuing individual goals and start doing everything together.

The "Gap" and the "Return"

Attraction requires **Distance.** You cannot feel "drawn" to something that is already permanently attached to you. To keep the spark alive, you must encourage her **Individual Identity.**

- **Encourage Solo Pursuits:** If she wants to take a weekend retreat, go to a solo seminar, or join a high-level mastermind group that doesn't include you, **encourage it.**

- **The Neurochemistry of Absence:** When she is away pursuing her own growth, your brain—and hers—undergoes a "Dopamine Reset." When she returns, she brings new information, new energy, and new "Mystery" (Chapter 4) back into the relationship.

By being the man who is "Secure enough to let her go," you become the man she "Chooses to return to."

6. The "Power Couple" Dynamic: Shared Missions

While you must maintain individual identities, the most successful long-term bonds often involve a "Shared Mission" or a "Joint Vision." This moves the relationship from a "Consumer Dynamic" (what can you do for me?) to a "Creative Dynamic" (what can we build together?).

The Annual "State of the Union"

High-value men don't just "let life happen." They lead. Once a year, sit down with your partner and discuss the **Joint Vision.**

- **What are your individual goals?**
- **How can the relationship serve those goals?**
- **What is our "Shared Mission" for the next 12 months?**

This aligns your **Prefrontal Cortex** activity. You are no longer just "dating"; you are "Partners in Excellence." This creates a bond of **Cognitive Interdependence**—a psychological state where your lives are so effectively integrated toward success that leaving the relationship would be a massive "Strategic Loss" for both of you.

7. Somatic Validation: The Non-Verbal Support

Support isn't just about what you say; it's about how your body reacts when she is in the "Arena" of her life.

The "Steady Hand" Technique

When she is in a high-stress period, your physical presence must become more "Grounded."

- Slow your speech.
- Lower your tonality.
- Maintain prolonged, calm eye contact.
- Use the "Anchor Touch" (Chapter 3, Book 4) on the small of her back or her shoulder.

This physical "Grounding" signals to her nervous system that regardless of the chaos in her professional life, the "Base" is secure. This is the **Protective Masculine** energy that women find deeply addictive over long periods of time.

8. Handling Her "Failures" with Grace

The true test of your support isn't when she's winning; it's when she's losing. How you handle her professional or personal setbacks will define the "Safety Rating" of the relationship.

The "Non-Judgmental Anchor"

If she fails a goal or makes a mistake, avoid the temptation to say "I told you so" or to offer unsolicited criticism. In that moment, her **Insular Cortex** (which processes social pain and embarrassment) is on fire.

- **The Move:** Provide "Limbic Comfort" first. Let her process the emotion.
- **The Shift:** Only once she is calm do you move into "Strategic Ally" mode to help her analyze the "Data" of the failure and plan the "Next Strike."

A man who can sit with a woman in her failure without judging her or being "scared" of her emotions is a man she will trust with her life.

9. Action Steps: The "Ally" Integration Plan

To move this from theory to reality, implement these three drills over the next 30 days:

1. **The "Success Audit":** Ask her this week: *"What is the one goal you're most excited about right now, and what is the biggest 'hidden' obstacle you're facing?"* Listen for the subtext, and then offer one specific, high-value resource or piece of advice (if she asks for it).

2. **The ACR 100% Rule:** Commit to **Active-Constructive Responding** for every single piece of good news she shares—no matter how small. Even if she just found a parking spot, practice the "Magnification" of her joy.

3. **The "Independence Day":** Proactively suggest that she take a day or a night to do something entirely for herself, without you. Show her that your security is so high that you don't need to be part of her every waking moment.

Summary: The Indispensable Ally

- **Support is a "Secure Base":** You provide the psychological safety that allows her to be her best self.
- **The Michelangelo Phenomenon:** You don't "change" her; you help reveal the "Ideal Version" of her.
- **ACR is the "Dopamine Anchor":** How you handle her wins determines how much she values your presence.

- **Avoid the Caretaker Trap:** Remain the **Coach**, not the **Crutch.** Maintain your own mission to keep the polarity alive.

By becoming her Chief Strategic Ally, you are doing more than just "keeping her interested." You are building a relationship where your value is tied to her highest growth. You become the one man who truly "Sees" her, "Challenges" her, and "Supports" her—making you an indispensable force in her life.

CHAPTER 3

MANAGE CONFLICTS USING EMOTIONAL INTELLIGENCE

Conflict is the "Stress Test" of a relationship's structural integrity. Many men believe that a "perfect" relationship is one without arguments, but from a neurobiological and psychological standpoint, this is a myth. A lack of conflict usually indicates **Emotional Suppression** or a lack of investment. High-value connections are built between two individuals with strong identities and varying perspectives; therefore, friction is inevitable.

The goal is not to avoid conflict, but to master the art of **High-Value Resolution**. When managed with Emotional Intelligence (EQ), an argument can actually become a "Dopamine Anchor" that increases trust and intimacy. When managed poorly, it triggers a "Cortisol Spiral" that erodes attraction and destroys the **Respect Frame** we established in Chapter 1. In this chapter, we will deconstruct the mechanics of the "Fight-or-Flight" response in relationships and learn how to lead through the storm with grounded, masculine poise.

1. The Neurobiology of "Flooding": The Amygdala Hijack

To manage conflict, you must first understand what is happening inside the human brain when an argument escalates. This is a state known as **"Flooding,"** a term coined by Dr. John Gottman.

The Amygdala Hijack

When a conversation turns into an argument, the **Amygdala**—the brain's alarm system—takes control. It perceives the emotional threat as a physical threat. This triggers the **Sympathetic Nervous System**, flooding the body with **Adrenaline** and **Cortisol**.

- **The Result:** The **Prefrontal Cortex** (the logical, empathetic part of the brain) essentially "shuts down." You lose the ability to think creatively, listen accurately, or feel empathy.

The "Vagal Brake" Failure

In a state of flooding, your heart rate typically rises above 100 beats per minute. At this point, you are no longer "talking" to your partner; you are two nervous systems in a state of primal defense. A high-value man recognizes this physiological shift in himself and his partner and knows that **no productive resolution can happen while the brain is flooded.**

2. The "State Shift" Technique: Leading the Nervous System

As the leader of the relationship's emotional tone, your first priority in a conflict is not to "win" the argument, but to **De-escalate the Physiology**.

The 20-Minute "Self-Soothing" Rule

If you feel your heart racing or your voice rising, you must call a "Tactical Timeout."

- **The High-Value Move:** *"I can feel that we're both getting heated, and I don't want to say anything that disrespects you or our relationship. I'm going to take 20 minutes to clear my head, and then I'm coming back so we can solve this together."*

- **The Science:** It takes approximately 20 to 60 minutes for the body to metabolize the cortisol and adrenaline released during an Amygdala Hijack. By stepping away, you allow the **Parasympathetic Nervous System** to re-engage the "Vagal Brake."

Maintaining the "Grounded Pillar"

During the conflict, your body language is your most powerful tool. If she is escalated, you must remain the "Grounded Pillar."

- **Keep your voice low and slow. * Maintain open body language (no crossed arms).**
- **Stay in the room (unless you are flooded).**

Through **Neural Mirroring**, your calm state will eventually "pull" her out of her reactive state. This is the ultimate display of **Protective Masculinity**—being the man who is not shaken by her emotional storm.

3. Communicating with "I" Statements: Avoiding the Accusation Loop

When we are in conflict, we naturally move toward "You" statements: *"You always do this,"* or *"You're being crazy."* This is a direct attack on her **Identity Center**, which forces her brain deeper into a defensive posture.

The "Vulnerability Formula"

To maintain the **Connection Frame**, use the "I" Statement formula. This shifts the focus from her "Faults" to your "Experience."

1. **The Observation:** "When [Specific Action] happens..."
2. **The Feeling:** "...I feel [Emotion]."
3. **The Need:** "What I need is [Positive Action]."

- **Low-Value Accusation:** "You're always late and you don't respect my time!"
- **High-Value Communication:** "When we show up 30 minutes late to dinner, I feel like our plans aren't a priority. It's important to me that we're on time so we can enjoy the night without rushing. Can we agree to leave earlier next time?"

The "Softened Start-up"

Research shows that the first three minutes of a conflict determine how the rest of the conversation will go. A "Hard Start-up" (criticism or contempt) leads to failure 94% of the time. A "Softened Start-up" (expressing a need without blame) keeps the **Prefrontal Cortex** engaged.

4. The "Four Horsemen" of Relationship Decay

To keep her interested long-term, you must eliminate the four behaviors that Dr. John Gottman identified as the "Four Horsemen" of the apocalypse for relationships. These behaviors don't just hurt feelings; they cause a **"Neuro-Chemical Withdrawal"** of attraction.

The Horseman	The Low-Value Behavior	The High-Value Antidote
Criticism	Attacking her character: "You're so selfish."	**Complaint:** "I'm frustrated that the dishes weren't done."
Contempt	Sarcasm, eye-rolling, acting superior.	**Culture of Appreciation:** Focus on what she does right.
Defensiveness	Making excuses, "Yes, but..."	**Take Responsibility:** Find the 10% of the problem you own.
Stonewalling	Shutting down, ignoring, "The Silent Treatment."	**Physiological Self-Soothing:** Take a break, then return.

Contempt: The "Attraction Killer"

Contempt is the most dangerous Horseman because it involves looking down on your partner. It activates the **Insular Cortex** in the same way that physical disgust does. You cannot feel "Attraction" and "Disgust" simultaneously. To keep her interested, you must treat her with a baseline of **Inherent Respect**, even when you disagree.

5. Seeking the "Underlying Dream": Deep Listening

Most arguments are not about what they seem to be about. The argument about "the dishes" is actually about "feeling unsupported." The argument about "being late" is actually about "feeling undervalued."

The "Vent and Validate" Drill

Before you offer a solution (The War-Room Method from Chapter 2), you must provide **Validation**.

- **Validation is NOT Agreement.** You can validate her feeling without agreeing that her logic is correct.
- **The Phrase:** *"It sounds like you're feeling [Emotion] because [Reason]. Did I get that right?"*
- **The Science:** When a person feels heard and understood, their brain releases **Oxytocin**. This "Bio-Chemical Bridge" lowers the defensive walls and allows for actual problem-solving.

6. Repair Attempts: The Secret of "Resilient" Couples

The difference between successful couples and those who fail isn't that successful couples don't fight; it's that they are better at **Repair Attempts**. A repair attempt is any statement or action—silly or serious—that de-escalates the tension.

Examples of High-Value Repair:

- **Humor:** A playful face or a callback to an inside joke (if timed correctly).
- **Physical Touch:** Reaching out to hold her hand during the heat of the moment.
- **The "I Over-reacted" Admission:** "Hey, I realize I was a bit sharp just then. I'm sorry. Let's start over."

A man who can "Repair" shows that he values the **Connection** more than his **Ego**. This is a massive high-status signal. It shows you are "Grounded" enough to admit a mistake without your identity crumbling.

7. Resolving without Damaging the "Sexual Frame"

One of the biggest risks of conflict is that it can move the relationship into a "Stagnant/Platonic" zone. If you argue like "siblings" or "roommates," the erotic tension disappears.

The "Post-Conflict Re-connection"

Once a conflict is resolved, do not remain "Cold." Use the resolution as a springboard for intimacy.

- **The Logic:** Conflict creates a spike in **Arousal** (high heart rate, high focus). If you resolve the issue and then move into physical touch or deep eye contact, that high arousal can be "re-channeled" into sexual attraction. This is the biological basis for "make-up sex"—the brain translates the "Relief" of resolution into "Passionate Desire."

8. Action Steps: The EQ Conflict Drill

To master your emotional intelligence during friction, implement these three practices:

1. **The "Pulse Check":** In your next disagreement, stop and mentally check your heart rate. If you feel "the buzz" of adrenaline, immediately implement the **20-minute Timeout**.

2. **The "10% Rule":** In any argument, find the 10% of the situation that you are responsible for, and admit it out loud. *"I realize I didn't communicate the time clearly, and that's on me."* Watch how quickly her defensiveness drops.

3. **The "Soft Start-up" Practice:** Next time you have a complaint, spend 60 seconds planning your "Soft Start-up." Focus on your *need* rather than her *flaw*.

Summary: The Master of the Storm

- **Conflict is a Physiological Event:** Manage the "Flooding" before you try to manage the "Argument."

- **The Amygdala Hijack is the Enemy:** Use the "Vagal Brake" (calming breath and slow speech) to lead her nervous system back to safety.

- **Avoid the Four Horsemen:** Especially Contempt. Maintain a baseline of respect to preserve the "Sexual Frame."

- **Validation is the Bridge:** Make her feel heard before you make her feel "Correct."

- **Repair Quickly:** The speed of your repair is a measure of your social value and emotional strength.

By managing conflict with Emotional Intelligence, you prove to a woman that you are a man of **Ultimate Reliability**. She learns that even when things get difficult, you are the "Anchor" who will not drift. This deep sense of safety is the fertile soil in which long-term interest and passionate attraction grow.

CHAPTER 4

KEEP MYSTERY AND SPONTANEITY ALIVE

In the previous chapters, we focused on the "Structural" elements of a relationship—boundaries, support, and conflict resolution. These provide the **Security** (Oxytocin) that a woman needs to stay. However, security alone is the primary cause of "Relationship Desiccation." If you are 100% predictable, you are 0% exciting.

To keep a woman *interested*—meaning she is still thinking about you when you aren't there and still feels a spark of adrenaline when you walk through the door—you must battle the most formidable enemy of long-term desire: **Neural Habituation.** This chapter is about maintaining the "Dopamine Edge" of the relationship by purposefully integrating mystery, spontaneity, and "Strategic Distance."

1. The Neurobiology of Habituation: The "Boredom" Circuit

The human brain is an efficiency machine. Once it has "mapped" a stimulus (a song, a food, or a partner), it stops allocating significant neural resources to it. This is why the first time you kissed her, her brain was a fireworks display of activity, but the 100th time, it barely registers as a "social greeting."

The Reward Prediction Error

Dopamine is not the chemical of "Pleasure"; it is the chemical of **"Anticipation" and "Novelty."** It fires most intensely when there is a "Reward Prediction Error"—when something better or different happens than what was expected.

- **The Routine:** If you go to the same restaurant every Friday at 7:00 PM, her brain's **Nucleus Accumbens** stops firing. The event is "pre-processed."

- **The Spontaneous:** If you tell her on a Tuesday afternoon to be ready in 20 minutes with a jacket because you're going to a rooftop observatory you've never visited, the "Uncertainty" triggers a massive Dopamine surge.

The Cooling of the Ventral Striatum

Studies show that in long-term couples, the **Ventral Striatum** (associated with intense "New Love") often shows decreased activity. To re-ignite this, you must introduce "Novel Stimuli" that force her brain to "re-map" you as a source of excitement rather than just a source of comfort.

2. The Power of "Strategic Distance"

One of the greatest paradoxes of intimacy is that **Desire requires Space.** In her famous work *Mating in Captivity*, Esther Perel notes that "Fire needs air." If you are constantly "available," "predictable," and "merged" with her life, there is no "Gap" for her imagination to inhabit.

The "Individual" Mystery

Mystery isn't about lying or being "shady"; it's about having a life that she doesn't fully "own."

- **The Mistake:** Reporting every detail of your day, every thought you have, and every person you speak to.

- **The Natural:** Having "Solo Missions." You have hobbies, friends, and intellectual pursuits that you do without her. When she asks, "How was your day?" you give her the "Highlights," but you keep the "Deep Process" for yourself. This makes her realize there is still "Territory" in your mind that she hasn't explored.

The "Absence" Spike

Absence facilitates **Emotional Synthesis.** When you are away, her brain "re-plays" memories of you. This strengthens the neural pathways of attraction. If you never leave, she never has the opportunity to "miss" you.

3. Combatting the "Domestic Drift"

Domesticity is the process where a "Lover" slowly transforms into a "Roommate." This happens through the accumulation of "Micro-Routines."

The "State-Break" Spontaneity

To keep her interested, you must purposefully "Break the State" of the domestic routine.

- **The Random Call:** Calling her in the middle of the day just to say, "I was just thinking about that dress you wore last night. You looked incredible. See you at six," and then hanging up.
- **The "Blindfolded" Date:** Don't ask her where she wants to go. Tell her what to wear and drive her there yourself. Taking the "Executive Load" off her brain while providing a surprise is a high-value double-win.

4. Intellectual Spontaneity: The "Ever-Evolving" Man

The most sustainable form of mystery is **Personal Growth.** If you are the same man with the same opinions, same stories, and same skills that you were three years ago, she has "finished the book."

Becoming a "Moving Target"

- **New Inputs:** Read books she hasn't read. Learn a language. Take up a new physical skill (like Brazilian Jiu-Jitsu or sailing).
- **The "Opinion Shift":** As you learn, your perspectives should evolve. When you share a new, sophisticated thought on a topic

you've discussed before, she realizes that you are a "Dynamic System."

- **The Science:** The **Posterior Cingulate Cortex** is involved in how we perceive the "Self" of others. By changing your "Self-Data" through growth, you keep her brain in a state of "Social Discovery."

5. Physical Mystery: Re-introducing the "Tension"

In a long-term bond, touch often becomes "Functional" (a hug hello, a pat on the back). To keep the spark, you must return to the **Haptic Escalation** of Book 4.

The "Unfinished" Touch

Incorporate touch that doesn't "lead" anywhere. A lingering touch on the neck while she's cooking, or a deep, 5-second look (Chapter 4, Book 4) in the middle of a mundane conversation about groceries.

- **The Goal:** To remind her nervous system that you are still her **Lover**, not just her "Life Partner."

- **Spontaneous Intimacy:** Don't wait for "Date Night" or the bedroom. High-value spontaneity is about bringing the "Erotic Frame" into the "Everyday Frame."

6. The "Push-Pull" of Long-Term Commitment

Even in a committed relationship, the **Push-Pull** technique (Chapter 2, Book 4) remains vital.

- **The Pull:** Deep vulnerability, support, and "Us" time.

- **The Push:** Prioritizing your mission, going out with the guys, or being "Too Busy" for a trivial request.

This isn't about being mean; it's about **Maintaining Polarity.** If you are always "leaning in," she will naturally "lean out" to maintain balance. By occasionally "leaning out" to focus on your own world, you create the "Vacuum" that pulls her back toward you.

1. **The "20% Surprise" Rule:** Look at your upcoming week. Identify one routine moment (e.g., Friday night dinner) and change it by at least 20% (different location, different activity, or a surprise guest).

2. **The "Mission Update":** This week, do something for your own personal growth that you haven't told her about yet. Share the "Result" with her only after you've made progress.

3. **The "Context Shift":** Take her somewhere she has never seen you "In Command." Whether it's a professional event, a sports competition, or a social gathering where you are the "host," seeing you in a different high-status context re-sets her perception of you.

Summary: The Art of the Perpetual Discovery

•   **Habituation is the Enemy:** Routine kills the Dopamine response; Novelty revives it.

- **Mystery requires Distance:** Keep a "Private Room" in your mind and your life that she doesn't fully inhabit.

- **Growth is the Ultimate Spark:** By evolving as a man, you ensure that the "Book" of you is never finished.

- **Spontaneity is Leadership:** Taking the lead on surprises removes her "Executive Load" and triggers the "Reward Prediction Error."

By keeping mystery and spontaneity alive, you transform your relationship from a "Settled Fact" into a "Continuing Adventure." You become the man who provides the **Security** she needs to rest, but the **Excitement** she needs to feel alive.

CHAPTER 5

LEAD WITH PURPOSE AND RELIABILITY

We have explored the "Soft" skills of long-term maintenance—the support, the conflict resolution, and the spark of mystery. However, none of these can exist without the "Hard" infrastructure of **Masculine Leadership.** In this chapter, we address the two traits that act as the structural steel of a relationship: **Purpose** and **Reliability.**

If you lack a personal mission (Purpose), you will eventually become "relationship-centric," which smothers attraction. If you lack the ability to follow through on your word (Reliability), you will trigger her "Limbic Alarm," which destroys safety. To keep her interested long-term, you must be a man who is moving toward a horizon and a man who can be trusted to hold the line.

1. The Neurobiology of the "North Star"

A man with a purpose provides a "Predictable Vector." This is essential for the female brain's sense of long-term security.

The Dopamine of the Hunt

When you are actively pursuing a mission—whether it's a career milestone, a physical feat, or a community project—your brain is in a **High-Dopamine State.** This state is contagious. Through **Neural Mirroring**, she feels the energy of your pursuit.

- **The Attraction Factor:** A woman is naturally drawn to the "Wake" of a man who is moving forward. When you stop moving, the "Wake" disappears, and the relationship becomes a stagnant pool.

The Role of the Ventral Tegmental Area (VTA)

The VTA is the root of the brain's reward system. When a man has a purpose, his VTA is consistently firing as he hits "micro-goals." A man who is "Winning" in his own life is neurochemically more attractive than a man who has made his partner his only source of "Wins."

2. The Mission-Relationship Hierarchy

One of the most counter-intuitive truths of long-term attraction is that **the relationship must never be your #1 priority.**

The "Orbit" Paradox

- **Low-Value Orbit:** The man makes the woman the center of his universe. He changes his schedule, his goals, and his personality to keep her happy. Paradoxically, she loses respect for him because he has no "Gravitational Pull" of his own.

- **High-Value Orbit:** The man's **Purpose** is the sun. He is moving toward his goal. The woman chooses to "Orbit" him, joining him on his journey. She is an essential part of his life, but she is not the *source* of his life.

The "Executive Load" Shift

When you have a purpose and a plan, you reduce the **Executive Load** on her Prefrontal Cortex. She doesn't have to "steer the ship" because she knows you have a compass. This allows her to relax into her feminine energy, which is the primary driver of long-term sexual polarity.

3. Reliability: The Foundation of Limbic Safety

If Purpose is the "Direction" of the ship, Reliability is the "Integrity of the Hull." In the brain, reliability is processed in the **Prefrontal Cortex** (evaluating consistency) and the **Insular Cortex** (processing trust and social betrayal).

The "Say-Do" Ratio

A high-value man maintains a 1:1 "Say-Do" Ratio.

- If you say you will call at 8:00, you call at 8:00.

- If you say you will handle the vacation booking, it gets handled.

- If you say you are going to get in shape, she sees you in the gym.

The Cost of "Micro-Breaches"

Every time you break a small promise, you trigger her **Amygdala.** It's a "Micro-Betrayal." Her nervous system registers that you are "Unpredictable." To a woman, unpredictability in a partner is a threat to her survival and the survival of the bond. Over time, these micro-breaches erode the foundation until she no longer feels she can "lean" on you.

4. Leading Through "Decisive Action"

Leadership is not about "dominance"; it is about **Decision-Making. ####** The "Choice" Fatigue In the modern world, women are often in "High-Executive" roles at work, making thousands of decisions a day. When she is with you, the most attractive thing you can provide is **Relief from Choice.**

- **Low-Value:** "What do you want to do tonight? I don't know, what do you want to do?" (This adds to her executive load).

- **High-Value:** "I've made a reservation at that Italian place you liked, and afterward, we're going for a walk by the pier. I'll pick you up at seven."

Strategic Leadership

Leadership also means being the one to initiate the "Heavy" conversations. If there is an elephant in the room, the leader addresses it first. This shows you are not afraid of the "Truth," which increases her **Oxytocin** levels because she feels she doesn't have to "manage" you.

5. Integrity: The "Internal Compass"

Integrity is "Reliability when no one is looking." It is having a code of ethics that you do not break for anyone—including her.

The "Standard-Setter"

When you have a high level of personal integrity, you become a **Standard-Setter.** * You don't lie to your boss.

- You don't gossip about your friends.
- You are honest even when it's inconvenient.

This signals to her that your "System" is stable. She knows that if you are honest with the world, you will be honest with her. This provides a deep, "Somatic Peace" that allows her to fully commit her heart to the relationship.

6. The "Anchor" in Times of Chaos

Life will eventually throw a crisis at you—health issues, financial loss, or family tragedy. This is the moment where **Leadership and Reliability** become the only things that matter.

The "Stoic Filter"

In a crisis, the leader processes the "Data" before he reacts to the "Emotion."

1. **Analyze:** What is the actual problem?
2. **Plan:** What are the next three steps?
3. **Execute:** Lead the way.

While she may be emotionally expressive during a crisis (which is healthy), she needs you to be the **Grounded Center.** By remaining reliable and purposeful in the face of chaos, you cement your status as her "Hero" for life.

7. Action Steps: The "North Star" Integration

1. **Define Your Mission:** If you don't have a mission outside of your relationship, spend this weekend alone. What would you do if you were 10% braver? What is the one thing you want to "build"?

2. **The "Say-Do" Audit:** For the next seven days, do not make a single promise (even "I'll do the dishes") that you do not fulfill 100%. Watch how she responds to your increased consistency.

3. **The "Lead-the-Night" Challenge:** Plan one entire evening from start to finish. Don't ask for her input. Take care of every detail. Observe the look of "Relief" on her face when she realizes she doesn't have to "think" for the night.

Summary: The Captain of the Soul

- **Purpose is the Gravity:** It keeps the relationship in orbit and prevents you from becoming "needy."

- **Reliability is the Safety:** Consistency in small things builds the foundation for trust in big things.

- **Say-Do Ratio:** Your word is your currency. Spend it wisely.

- **Lead by Relieving:** High-value leadership reduces her "Executive Load" and allows for "Limbic Ease."

By leading with purpose and reliability, you provide the "Frame" in which she can flourish. You become the man who doesn't just "talk" about a great life, but the man who is actively building one. This is the ultimate "Drip-Feed" of attraction that keeps a woman interested for a lifetime.

CONCLUSION

KEEP THE SPARK BURNING

We have reached the final summit of **Book 5**. You have traveled from the tactical maneuvers of early attraction—the "sparks" and "banter" of the initial meeting—into the sophisticated, multi-layered architecture of a lasting bond. You have learned that a high-value relationship is not a trophy to be won and placed on a shelf; it is a living, breathing biological system that requires constant, calibrated input.

In the modern world, we are often sold a "Disney" version of love: a story that ends at the wedding or the commitment. But for the Natural, the commitment is where the real "work" of excellence begins. To keep a woman *interested*—not just present, but genuinely, viscerally drawn to you—for the long term, you must master the ultimate paradox of the high-value man: the ability to provide **Total Safety** while maintaining **Total Autonomy**. This conclusion serves as the "Grand Synthesis." We will bridge the gap between the neurobiology of the brain and the daily habits of the heart, ensuring that the flame you ignited in Book 1 never flickers into the cold ash of "roommate syndrome."

1. The Neurobiology of the "Long-Term Spark"

To understand how to keep the spark burning, we must look at what happens to the human brain over years of partnership. As we discussed in the Introduction, the early stages of love are dominated by the "Lust and Attraction" chemicals: **Dopamine**, **Norepinephrine**, and **Phenylethylamine (PEA)**. These are "Stress-Arousal" chemicals. They make you feel high, but they are metabolically expensive.

The "Attachment" Transition

Over time, if the relationship is healthy, the brain transitions into the "Attachment Phase," governed by **Oxytocin** and **Vasopressin**. These chemicals create a sense of calm, trust, and "Pair-Bonding."

- **The Danger:** Many men allow the Oxytocin to completely replace the Dopamine. When this happens, the "Erotic Spark" dies because there is no more "Urgency" or "Uncertainty."

- **The Solution:** You must learn to "Pulsate" between the two states. You must be the man who provides the warm "Oxytocin Blanket" of reliability and support, but who occasionally throws open the windows to let in the cold, exhilarating "Dopamine Wind" of mystery and challenge.

The "Satiation" Effect

The brain's **Ventral Striatum** is designed to habituate to rewards. If you give a woman 100% of your attention 100% of the time, the "Reward Value" of your attention drops to zero. To keep the spark burning, you must maintain a degree of "Relative Scarcity." You must have a life (Chapter 5) that is so full and purposeful that your "Presence" remains a high-value event, not a background noise.

2. Protecting the "Erotic Third"

One of the most profound insights into long-term desire comes from the work of **Esther Perel**. She argues that for desire to exist, there must be a "Bridge" to cross. If two people become "One"—sharing every password, every thought, and every minute of their day—the bridge disappears.

The Architecture of the "Third Space"

In Book 5, we've focused on "You" (the leader) and "Her" (the ally). But there is a third entity: **The Relationship itself. * Individual Sovereignty:** You must maintain a "Private Room" in your mind. This is the place where your deepest mission and your individual growth live. When she realizes there is still a part of you she hasn't "conquered" or "mapped," she remains curious. Curiosity is the precursor to desire.

- **The "Gap" of Longing:** Long-term interest requires the "Rubber Band Effect" (Book 4, Conclusion). You must occasionally "Pull Away" to focus on your mission. This creates the "Vacuum" that she naturally wants to fill with her own effort and attraction.

3. The "State of Grace" and the Culture of Appreciation

While mystery and distance provide the "Spark," the "Fuel" is provided by **Appreciation.** In Chapter 3, we discussed the "Four Horsemen" that destroy relationships. The antidote to all of them is a **Culture of Appreciation.**

The "Gottman Ratio" as a Leadership Tool

Dr. John Gottman's research found that stable, happy couples have a ratio of **5:1 positive-to-negative interactions.** * **The Natural's Application:** As the leader of the emotional tone, you should aim for a **10:1 ratio.** Why? Because as the man, your "Neutral" state is often perceived by women as "Slightly Negative" or "Withdrawn."

- **Active-Constructive Appreciation:** Don't just say "thanks." Use the **ACR technique** from Chapter 2. When she does something that aligns with your values or brings you joy, "Magnify" it.
    - *"I really noticed how you handled that situation with your family today. Your poise was incredible. I'm proud to have you on my team."*

The "Dopamine Anchor" of Recognition

When you catch her "doing something right" and you acknowledge it from a place of high-value leadership, her brain releases a spike of **Dopamine** and **Serotonin.** You are essentially "Training" her nervous system to associate "Pleasing You" and "Being Her Best Self" with a massive chemical reward. This is how you "Keep Her Interested"—by making the relationship the most rewarding place on Earth for her to be.

4. Sustaining Polarity: The Masculine and Feminine Dance

Polarity is the "Electrical Tension" between two opposites. In long-term bonds, this tension tends to neutralize. The man becomes "softer" and more "domesticated"; the woman becomes "harder" and more "managerial."

The "Frame" as a Polarity Stabilizer

Your **Masculine Frame** (Chapter 1) is what maintains the polarity.

- When you take the "Executive Load" off her (Chapter 5) and make a decision, you allow her to move from her "Masculine/Doing" brain into her "Feminine/Being" brain.

- This shift is biologically relaxing for her. It lowers her **Cortisol** and allows her **Oxytocin** to flow.

- **The Result:** When a woman feels "Led," she feels "Safe." When she feels "Safe," she feels "Sexy." This is the fundamental cycle of long-term attraction.

The "Stoic Filter"

To keep the spark, you must remain the "Grounded Center." If you become as emotionally volatile as she is, the polarity snaps. By maintaining your **Emotional Intelligence** (Chapter 3) and your **Reliability** (Chapter 5), you remain the "Mountain" that she can swirl around like the wind. The mountain doesn't move; the wind is attracted to the mountain's stability.

5. The "Novelty Protocol": Battling Neural Habituation

In Chapter 4, we discussed the "Enemy of the Routine." To keep her interested, you must be the "Architect of Novelty."

The "State-Break" Strategy

Habitual routines move the relationship into the **Basal Ganglia** (automatic processing). To keep it in the **Prefrontal Cortex** (active engagement), you must "Break the State."

- **The "Blind Date" Re-mastery:** Once a month, take her on a date where she has no idea where she is going or what she is doing. This triggers "Reward Prediction Error"—the highest form of Dopamine release.

- **The "Context Shift":** See each other in different environments. Seeing you lead a team at work, or seeing you excel in a hobby (Jiu-Jitsu, public speaking, hiking), forces her brain to "Re-map" you. It reminds her that you are a multifaceted man with high social value in the "outside world," not just her "guy at home."

The "Growth Requirement"

You must be a "Moving Target." If you are the same man this year that you were last year, you have become a "Solved Puzzle."

- **Physical Growth:** Keep your body as a "High-Value Asset."

- **Intellectual Growth:** Read, learn, and challenge your own opinions.

- **Purposeful Growth:** Scale your mission.

A woman stays interested in a man who is "Ascending." As long as you are climbing your own "Mountain of Purpose," she will stay interested in the view.

6. Managing the "Long-Term Conflict" Loop

Every long-term relationship has "Perpetual Problems"—issues that will likely never be fully "solved" because they are based on personality differences.

The "High-Value Acceptance"

The Natural doesn't try to "fix" his partner's personality. He uses his **Emotional Intelligence** (Chapter 3) to manage the friction.

- **The 69% Rule:** Gottman's research shows that 69% of relationship conflicts are unresolvable.

- **The Leadership Move:** You decide which 31% you will solve and which 69% you will handle with humor, boundaries, and "Vagal Regulation."

- When you stop trying to "Change" her and instead "Lead" the dynamic, the resentment that kills the spark disappears. You create a "Culture of Peace," and peace is the prerequisite for passion.

7. Somatic Intimacy: Beyond the Bedroom

To keep her interested, you must maintain a "High-Touch" environment that is not always "Goal-Oriented" toward sex.

The "Micro-Touch" Architecture

In Book 4, we learned the **Escalation Ladder**. In Book 5, we use the "Affection Loop." * **The Anchor Touch:** A hand on the small of her back as you walk through a door.

- **The "Neck Linger":** A kiss on the neck while she's working at her desk.
- **The 6-Second Hug:** Long enough to trigger a massive Oxytocin dump.

The "Primal Gaze"

Never stop looking at her the way you did in Chapter 4 of Book 4. Even after five years, your "Grounded Gaze" should communicate: *"I see you, I want you, and I am completely unimpressed by your attempts to distract me from my mission."* This combination of **Desire and Sovereignty** is the most addictive "Drug" a man can provide a woman.

8. The "Legacy" of the Natural: A Life of Excellence

As we conclude this 5-Book journey, it is important to realize that "Keeping her interested" is a byproduct of **Living an Excellent Life.** A man who is:

1. **Socially Unlocked** (Book 1)
2. **Biologically Aware** (Book 2)
3. **Conversationally Fluent** (Book 3)
4. **Flirtatiously Grounded** (Book 4)
5. **Purposefully Reliable** (Book 5)

...is a man that 99% of women will never want to lose. You are no longer "performing" a role; you have **Integrated the Identity.** #### The "Self-Sustaining" Spark The spark doesn't stay alive because you "do" things to her; it stays alive because you **are** a man of value. Your interest in yourself, your mission, and your world is what fuels her interest in you.

To ensure the lessons of Book 5 become your "New Normal," implement this "Weekly Maintenance Protocol":

1. **The "Ally" Audit (Monday):** Ask her: *"What's your biggest 'Win' this week, and what's the biggest 'Weight' on your shoulders? How can I help with the weight?"*

2. **The "Mystery" Injection (Wednesday):** Do one thing for your own mission/growth that you don't tell her about. Let her see the "Result" later.

3. **The "Leadership Night" (Friday):** You plan everything. No questions, no "what do you want to do." You lead; she follows.

4. **The "Gratitude Dump" (Sunday):** Tell her three specific things she did this week that made you respect or desire her more. Use **Active-Constructive** language.

10. Summary: The Master of the Long-Term

- **Balance the Chemicals:** Combine the **Oxytocin** of safety with the **Dopamine** of novelty.

- **Maintain the "Third Space":** Never become so enmeshed that there is no distance to bridge.

- **Lead the Polarity:** Stay in your "Masculine Frame" to allow her to stay in her "Feminine Flow."

- **Evolve or Die:** Your personal growth is the ultimate "Drip-Feed" of attraction.

- **Be the Secure Base:** When she feels she can "Rest" in your strength, she will have the energy to "Desire" your presence.

You have now completed the tactical and philosophical journey from "Socially Anxious" to "Master Natural." You have the tools to attract, connect with, and keep the woman of your dreams. But remember: **The "Natural" is a path, not a destination.** Continue to lead. Continue to learn. Continue to love with purpose.

REFLECTION QUESTIONS

CHECK YOUR PROGRESS

You have reached the final intellectual milestone of **Book 5**. By now, you understand that long-term attraction is not a lucky accident—it is the result of a deliberate, neurobiologically informed leadership style. However, the transition from "learning" to "embodying" requires a process called **Metacognition**: the ability to think about your own thinking and monitor your own behavior.

This chapter is your **Long-Term Readiness Audit**. These questions are designed to challenge your ego, reveal your hidden insecurities, and calibrate your "Relationship Compass." To gain the maximum benefit, answer these questions through the lens of your current relationship or your most recent long-term partnership. Be brutally honest; the **Prefrontal Cortex** cannot optimize a system based on false data.

Establishing a frame is easy during a first date; maintaining it over three years is where most men fail.

1. The "Resentment" Compass

- **The Question:** "Do I currently harbor any 'Quiet Resentments' toward my partner, and if so, can I trace them back to a boundary I failed to set early on?"

- **The Science:** Resentment is the result of a **Boundary Violation**. When you allow someone to infringe on your values without a "Calibrated No," your **Insular Cortex** registers a loss of self-respect.

- **Reflection:** Think of a recurring argument. Is the argument actually about her behavior, or is it about your lack of a clear standard? How would the dynamic shift if you set a firm, calm boundary tomorrow?

2. The Approval-Seeking Metric

- **The Question:** "When my partner is in a 'Bad Mood,' do I immediately feel the need to 'Fix' it or apologize, even if I haven't done anything wrong?"

- **The Science:** This is a sign of **Emotional Enmeshment**. If your nervous system is entirely dependent on her emotional state, you have lost your "Grounded Pillar" status.

- **Reflection:** Can you sit in the same room with her while she is frustrated, remain supportive and calm, and not let her "Cloud" enter your "Atmosphere"?

Section 2: The Strategic Ally Audit (Chapter 2)

Being an ally means elevating her without becoming her caretaker.

3. The ACR (Active-Constructive) Reality Check

- **The Question:** "Can I recall the last three times my partner shared 'Good News'? How exactly did I respond?"

- **The Science:** Recall **Dr. Shelly Gable's** quadrants. If your responses were "Passive-Constructive" (a simple "that's nice"), you are missing opportunities to build **Oxytocin** and **Dopamine** anchors.

- o **Reflection:** Does her success feel like a "Win" for the team, or do you feel a subtle pang of competitive anxiety? A high-value man's status is never threatened by his partner's ascent.

4. The "Secure Base" Simulation

- o **The Question:** "Does my partner feel she can take a 'High-Risk' career or personal move because of the stability I provide, or does she feel she has to 'Play it Safe' because our relationship is too fragile?"
- o **The Science:** This is the **Dependency Paradox**. The more "Securely Attached" she feels to you, the more independent she will act in the world.
- o **Reflection:** When was the last time you acted as a "Belief Mirror" for her? Do you know her current #1 life goal, and what are you doing specifically to fuel it?

Section 3: The Emotional Intelligence Audit (Chapter 3)

Conflict is the forge of loyalty. If you fear conflict, you cannot lead.

5. The "Flooding" Awareness

- o **The Question:** "During an argument, at what specific point do I feel my 'Vagal Brake' fail? What are my physical 'Tell-Tale' signs of an Amygdala Hijack?"
- o **The Science:** Knowing your heart rate or muscle tension cues allows you to call a **Tactical Timeout** before the **Prefrontal Cortex** shuts down.
- o **Reflection:** In your last "big fight," did you say things you later regretted? If so, you were "Flooded." What is your plan to communicate the need for a 20-minute break next time the heat rises?

6. The "Repair Attempt" Inventory

- o **The Question:** "Am I usually the first to initiate a 'Repair Attempt' after a clash, or do I wait for her to apologize first?"
- o **The Science:** The speed of repair is a measure of **Relationship Resilience**. Waiting for her to "submit" is a low-value ego play. Leading the repair is a high-value leadership move.

- o **Reflection:** Can you "Repair" using humor or a "Soft Start-up" without feeling like you are "losing" the argument? Remember: The goal is **Resolution**, not **Victory**.

Section 4: The Mystery & Spontaneity Audit (Chapter 4)

Predictability is the "Slow Poison" of desire.

7. The "Solved Puzzle" Assessment

- o **The Question:** "If my partner were asked to describe my daily routine and my top 3 opinions, could she do it with 100% accuracy?"
- o **The Science:** If the answer is "Yes," you have become **Neuro-Habituated**. You have no "Dopamine Edge."
- o **Reflection:** When was the last time you did something that genuinely surprised her? Not a gift, but a **State-Break**—a change in your behavior, a new hobby, or a spontaneous adventure.

8. The "Erotic Third" Evaluation

- o **The Question:** "Do I have a 'Private Room' in my life—a mission, a group of friends, or a project—that she has zero influence over?"
- o **The Science:** Long-term desire requires **Distance**. If you have no "Separate Self," there is no "Bridge" for her to cross to find you.
- o **Reflection:** Are you "Over-sharing"? Do you report every minor detail of your day? Try withholding 10% of the mundane "Data" and replacing it with a focused, mysterious pursuit of a new goal.

Section 5: The Purpose & Reliability Audit (Chapter 5)

This is the bedrock of your value. Without this, the other chapters are merely "performance."

9. The "North Star" Trajectory

- o **The Question:** "If my partner left me tomorrow, would my 'Mission' in life change, or would it continue on the same path?"

- o **The Science:** A man who is **Mission-Centric** is inherently more attractive than a man who is **Relationship-Centric**. Your **VTA (Ventral Tegmental Area)** should be fueled by your purpose.
  - o **Reflection:** Do you find yourself "waiting" for her to decide the direction of your life? Or are you a ship that is already moving, inviting her to join the journey?

10. The "Say-Do" Audit

- o **The Question:** "In the last 30 days, how many 'Micro-Promises' have I broken?" (e.g., "I'll fix that," "I'll be home at six," "I'll start that diet.")
- o **The Science:** Micro-breaches of reliability trigger the **Amygdala**. They signal that you are "Unstable."
- o **Reflection:** Does she "lean" on you with full weight, or does she "double-check" your work? If she double-checks, you have a reliability leak. How will you plug it this week?

Section 6: The Long-Term Spark Synthesis (Conclusion)

11. The "70/30" Balance

- o **The Question:** "In my current dynamic, am I leaning too far into 'Oxytocin/Comfort' (The Roommate) or too far into 'Dopamine/Tension' (The Tease)?"
- o **The Science:** Most long-term men fail by becoming 100% Oxytocin.
- o **Reflection:** What is one "Tension-Building" activity you can re-introduce this week? (e.g., The "Primal Gaze," a deeper level of flirting, or a challenging "Push-Pull" interaction).

12. The Legacy Perspective

- o **The Question:** "Am I acting like the man I was when we first met, or have I evolved into a more sophisticated version of that man?"
- o **The Science:** The **Posterior Cingulate Cortex** tracks the "Evolution of the Self." Stagnation is a signal of declining value.
- o **Reflection:** What is the "Sequel" to the story of you? If she has finished the first book of your relationship, what does the next volume look like?

Imagine it is one year from today. You have applied every principle in **Book 5**. Walk through this mental rehearsal:

1. **The Morning:** You wake up and immediately focus on your **Mission** for 2 hours before engaging with her. She feels your "Purposeful Energy" before you even speak.

2. **The Conflict:** She is stressed and "snaps" at you. You don't snap back. You use the **Vagal Brake**, validate her stress, and hold your **Respect Frame**. Within 10 minutes, she is leaning into you for comfort.

3. **The Spontaneity:** You've planned a weekend getaway that you haven't mentioned. You simply tell her to pack a bag for "Adventure." Her **Nucleus Accumbens** is firing with anticipation.

4. **The Result:** She looks at you not with the "comfortable" gaze of a roommate, but with the "hungry" gaze of a woman who is still discovering the man she loves.

The Reflection: Which part of this simulation feels the most "Unnatural" to you? That is your **Mastery Gap**. Focus your attention there.

Summary of Book 5

If you can answer these questions with integrity, you are no longer a "student" of attraction; you are a **Practitioner of Long-Term Excellence**. Book 5 is about moving from the "Excitement of the Hunt" to the "Power of the Legacy." You are the man who can build a kingdom and keep it.

FINAL CONCLUSION

YOUR NEW PATH FORWARD

You stand now at the end of a journey that has spanned the entirety of the human social experience. From the foundational neurobiology of the "Spark" to the sophisticated architecture of a lifelong bond, you have deconstructed the silent language of the nervous system and reconstructed yourself into a man of high value, high empathy, and high purpose. But as we close this final chapter, it is essential to realize that this is not an "end." In the world of the Natural, there are no finish lines—only new horizons.

This final conclusion, "Your New Path Forward," is designed to transition you from the world of **Deliberate Practice** to the world of **Unconscious Competence**. We are moving from the "What" and the "How" into the "Who." This is the integration phase, where the techniques of the previous five books cease to be "tools" you pick up and instead become the very fabric of your character.

1. The Four Stages of Social Mastery

To navigate your path forward, you must understand where you sit on the spectrum of mastery. Learning a new way of being follows a predictable neurological path.

Stage I: Unconscious Incompetence

This is where many men begin. You didn't know what you didn't know. You moved through the world unaware of the **Vagal Brake**, the **Mirror Neuron System**, or the **Dopamine Reward Loop**. Social failures felt like "bad luck" or "personal flaws" rather than systemic errors in calibration.

Stage II: Conscious Incompetence

This occurred during your first reading of Book 1 and Book 2. You suddenly saw the "Matrix." You realized where you were leaking value, why your body language was triggering "threat" signals in others, and why your conversations were hitting dead ends. This stage is often uncomfortable; it is characterized by the "Aha!" moments followed by the frustration of not yet being able to execute perfectly.

Stage III: Conscious Competence

This is likely where you are now. You can navigate a social interaction successfully, but it requires **Prefrontal Cortex** effort. You have to remind yourself to breathe, to maintain eye contact, to use "Push-Pull" (Book 4), and to lead with purpose (Book 5). You are effective, but you are still "thinking" about being effective.

Stage IV: Unconscious Competence (The Natural)

This is the destination of the path forward. At this stage, your **Basal Ganglia** has fully integrated these behaviors. You no longer "try" to be high-value; you simply *are*. Your nervous system has been re-wired. You respond to conflict with grounded poise because it is your nature. You spark attraction because your presence is inherently "Dopaminergic." This is the stage where the "Technique" disappears and only the "Man" remains.

2. The Integration of the Five Books: The Master Synthesis

To move forward, you must carry the core pillars of this curriculum not as separate lessons, but as a unified "Operating System." Let us look at how these pillars interact in the "Real World."

The Grounded Foundation (Books 1 & 2)

Your path forward is built on **Somatic Presence**. A man who is not "in his body" cannot lead. You must continue the practices of vagal regulation and biological awareness. When you walk into a room, your first priority is your own internal state. If you are grounded, the room will ground itself around you. This is the "Gravity" of the high-value man.

The Fluid Connection (Book 3)

Conversation is the "Circulatory System" of your social life. Moving forward, you must view every interaction as an opportunity for "Social Discovery." Use the **Open-Ended Loop** and the **Emotional Echo** not to "get" something from people, but to truly map the landscape of their minds. A Natural is, above all, a master of curiosity.

The Polarized Spark (Book 4)

Attraction is the "Electricity" of the human experience. You must never lose your "Edge." Even in a long-term bond, the ability to play with tension, to use the "Rubber Band Effect," and to communicate desire through the "Primal Gaze" is what separates the "Lover" from the "Roommate." You are the man who is comfortable with the "Fire."

The Purposeful Legacy (Book 5)

Finally, your path is defined by your **North Star**. Without a mission, a man is just a "Social Actor." Your relationship, your social circle, and your career are all "Orbits" around the sun of your purpose. To keep her—and the world—interested, you must never stop ascending your own mountain.

3. The "Drip-Feed" of Excellence: Daily Habits for the Path Forward

Mastery is not maintained through "Grand Gestures"; it is maintained through "Micro-Inputs." To ensure you do not regress into old patterns, adopt the following daily rituals:

- **The Morning "State-Set":** Before you check your phone or engage with the world, engage with your nervous system. 5 minutes of box breathing or cold exposure to "Set the Vagal Brake." Start your day in a state of **Parasympathetic Dominance**.

- **The "Social Warm-up":** Interact with three "low-stakes" people every day (the barista, the doorman, a stranger in the elevator). Use one technique from Book 3 (e.g., the "Cold Read"). This keeps your conversational muscles "Warm."

- **The "Purpose Audit":** Every evening, ask yourself: *"Did I move the needle on my mission today, or did I merely react to the world?"* A Natural is proactive, not reactive.

- **The "Polarity Check":** If you are in a relationship, ensure you have provided at least one "State-Break" of spontaneity or a "Deeper Gaze" of attraction. Do not let the "Domestic Drift" settle in.

4. Navigating the "Shadow Side" of Mastery

As you become more effective, you will encounter new challenges. High-value men attract not just high-value women, but also "Energy Vampires," envious competitors, and the "Paradox of Choice."

The Envy of the Un-Mastered

When you begin to move with the ease of a Natural, those who are still stuck in "Conscious Incompetence" may feel threatened. You may face "Social Tests" from men trying to knock you off your "Grounded Pillar."

- **The Move:** Do not become defensive. Defensive behavior is a signal of low value. Use the **Stoic Filter**. Smile, agree with the grain of truth in their "jab," and move on. Your silence and lack of "reactivity" is the ultimate display of power.

The Paradox of Choice

As your "Attraction Value" increases, you will have more options. The danger here is the "Grass is Greener" syndrome—a constant Dopamine-seeking that prevents deep, long-term bonding.

- **The Move:** Use the **Screening Principles** from Book 1. Look for "Character" and "Neuro-Somatic Alignment" over mere physical novelty. A high-value man knows that "Depth" is ultimately more rewarding than "Breadth."

5. The Role of Failure on the Path Forward

You will fail. You will have nights where your "Vagal Brake" fails and you become reactive. You will have dates where the "Conversation Flow" hits a wall. You will have moments in your relationship where you lose the "Spark."

The "Reframing" of the Natural

The difference between a "Nice Guy" and a "Natural" is how they handle failure.

- **The Nice Guy** sees failure as proof that he is "not enough." He spirals into **Cortisol-driven** self-criticism, which further lowers his value.

- **The Natural** sees failure as "Data." He analyzes the interaction like a scientist. *"Ah, I see—I lost the frame there because I was seeking approval. My heart rate spiked, and I stopped listening. Good to know. I'll recalibrate next time."*

Failure is simply the "Friction" required for growth. Embrace it. Each "No" is a lesson; each "Clash" is a forge.

6. The "Sovereign Man": Freedom from the Outcome

The ultimate realization of this journey is that **your value is independent of the social world.**

Throughout these five books, we have taught you how to attract others, but the "Secret" at the center of the curriculum is this: **You attract others most effectively when you don't "need" them.**

The Neurobiology of Non-Attachment

When you operate from a place of "Need," your brain is in a **Scarcity State**. This produces "Leaky" body language, "High-Pitch" tonality, and "Approval-Seeking" conversation. People can "smell" the neediness; it triggers their "Repulsion Response."

When you operate from **Sovereignty**, your brain is in an **Abundance State**. You are "Outcome Independent." You want the connection, but you don't "need" it to feel whole. This state produces the most attractive "Signal" a human can emit. It is the signal of a man who is "Complete" within himself.

7. Final Words: The Responsibility of the Natural

You now possess a set of "Social Superpowers." You have the ability to influence emotions, to spark desire, and to lead the nervous systems of those around you. With this power comes a deep responsibility.

A true Natural is not a "manipulator." A manipulator uses these tools to take value from others. A High-Value Natural uses these tools to **provide value**.

- When you ground yourself, you give others the "Gift of Safety."
- When you flirt with edge, you give a woman the "Gift of Feeling Alive."
- When you support her ambitions, you give her the "Gift of Excellence."

The path forward is one of **Service through Strength**. By becoming the best version of yourself, you create a "Ripple Effect" that elevates everyone in your orbit. You are the "Anchor" in a chaotic world. You are the "Spark" in a dull world. You are the "Leader" that the modern landscape so desperately needs.

8. The "Mastery Checklist" for the Path Forward

As you move into the world, keep this mental checklist as your "Pre-Flight" ritual for every social interaction:

1. **State Check:** Is my breath deep? Is my body relaxed? Am I grounded?
2. **Outcome Independence:** Am I okay if this person likes me? Am I okay if they don't?

3. **Presence:** Am I listening to the "Subtext" or just the "Text"?

4. **Polarity:** Am I leaning in (seeking) or am I holding my center (attracting)?

5. **Purpose:** Does this interaction serve my "North Star"?

The Final Vision

Imagine yourself five years from today. You are walking through a crowded room. You don't have to "think" about your posture; it is naturally tall and open. You don't have to "think" about what to say; your curiosity drives the conversation effortlessly. People are drawn to you like moths to a flame, not because of what you are "doing," but because of the **Frequency** you are emitting.

Beside you is a woman who is not only beautiful but who is deeply "Integrated" with you. She respects your boundaries, fuels your mission, and looks at you with a gaze that has only deepened over time. You are the master of your internal state and the architect of your social world.

THE SUCCESS BLUEPRINT

A PRINT AND KEEP CHECKLIST

You have navigated the deep waters of the "Path of the Natural." You have moved from the mechanical understanding of social dynamics to the biological mastery of the human nervous system. However, the greatest enemy of mastery is not a lack of knowledge, but the erosion of execution. In the heat of the moment—when a conflict arises, when a high-value woman enters the room, or when your mission feels heavy— the brain tends to revert to its oldest, most practiced neural pathways.

This **Success Blueprint** is designed to prevent that regression. It is a comprehensive, distilled checklist of every critical trigger we have covered across the five books. This is your "Flight Manual." Use it to audit your behavior daily, weekly, and monthly. By systematically checking these points, you move the concepts from your **Prefrontal Cortex** (conscious effort) into your **Basal Ganglia** (automatic habit).

Phase 1: The Daily "Somatic" Reset (The Foundation)

Before you interact with the world, you must master the vessel. A man who is internally chaotic cannot lead an external dynamic.

- **The Vagal Brake Check:** Have you engaged in at least five minutes of deliberate breathwork today? (e.g., Box breathing or 4-7-8 breathing). This ensures your **Parasympathetic Nervous System** is dominant, allowing for "Social Engagement" rather than "Fight-or-Flight."

- **Postural Sovereignty:** Check your physical stance. Are your shoulders back and down, heart open, and chin neutral? Remember that **Body Language** is a two-way street; by adopting a high-power pose, you are lowering your **Cortisol** and raising your **Testosterone** endogenously.

- **Eye Contact Calibration:** In your first three "low-stakes" interactions of the day, did you maintain eye contact long enough to register the person's eye color? This trains the **Mirror Neuron System** to recognize you as a "non-threatening but high-status" presence.

- **Tonality Audit:** Speak your first sentence of the day out loud. Is it ending with a downward inflection (authority) or an upward inflection (seeking approval)? Aim for the "Grounded Baritone."

Phase 2: The Social Entry Checklist (Book 1 & 3)

When you enter a social environment, your "Initial Signal" determines how much effort you will have to expend later.

- **The "Entrance Pause":** Did you stop at the threshold for three seconds to scan the room before moving? This signals to the room's **Amygdala** that you are a predator/leader (secure) rather than prey (rushed).

- **Proximity Control:** Are you maintaining the "Golden Ratio" of personal space—close enough to signal intimacy but far enough to avoid triggering a "Threat Response"?

- **The Emotional Echo:** In your first conversation, did you repeat the last three words of the other person's sentence? This activates their **Dorsolateral Prefrontal Cortex**, making them feel "seen" and "heard" without you having to provide complex logic.

- **Open-Ended Loop Initiation:** Have you asked at least one "How" or "What" question that requires an emotional narrative rather than a factual "Yes/No" answer?

- **Cold Reading over Interrogation:** Instead of asking "Where are you from?", did you use an observation? (e.g., "You have a very relaxed energy; I'm guessing you're from the coast.") Even if you are wrong, the **Misattribution of Arousal** creates an instant "Spark" of connection.

Phase 3: The Attraction & Romantic Frame Checklist (Book 4)

Attraction is the result of **Polarity**. If the tension is gone, the interest dies.

- **The Push-Pull Metric:** Have you delivered a "Push" (a playful challenge or teasing disagreement) followed immediately by a "Pull" (a genuine compliment or a lingering look)? This keeps the **Dopamine** levels in her brain fluctuating, preventing habituation.

- **The Primal Gaze:** When looking at her, are you maintaining the "Triangular Gaze" (Eye-Eye-Mouth) or the "Deep Hold" (looking past the eyes)? This communicates sexual intent without the need for verbal "creepiness."

- **Haptic Escalation (The Ladder):** Have you established "Phase 1" touch (non-intimate areas like the shoulder or forearm)? If yes, have you tested for a **Positive Compliance Response** before moving to "Phase 2"?

- **Outcome Independence Check:** If she were to walk away right now, would your internal "State" remain unchanged? If you feel "anxious" or "needy," you must immediately re-center your breath and return to your **Mission**.

- **The "Executive Load" Shift:** Did you make at least one definitive decision today regarding a shared activity? (e.g., "We are going here at 8:00," rather than "What do you want to do?").

Phase 4: Long-Term Relationship Maintenance (Book 5)

Keeping her interested is about the balance between **Safety (Oxytocin)** and **Mystery (Dopamine)**.

- **The 5:1 (or 10:1) Appreciation Ratio:** Have you given her at least five genuine, "Active-Constructive" compliments today for every one "Complaint" or "Correction"?

- **The Boundary Audit:** Has there been an instance where you said "No" to a request that encroached on your **Mission** or **Values**? Remember, a man without boundaries is a man without a frame.

- **The "Secure Base" Action:** Have you proactively supported her in an ambition or goal that has nothing to do with you? (e.g., "I know you have that big meeting; I've handled dinner so you can focus.")

- **The "State-Break" Spontaneity:** When was the last time you did something that was a "Reward Prediction Error"? (A surprise trip, a random deep conversation, or a new context for a date).

- **The "Say-Do" Integrity Check:** Did you fulfill every promise you made today, down to the smallest detail? Reliability is the "Limbic Anchor" of her trust.

Arguments are the "Stress Test" of your leadership.

- **The Heart Rate Monitor:** During a disagreement, did your heart rate exceed 100 BPM? If so, did you call a **Tactical Timeout** (20 minutes) to allow the **Adrenaline** to metabolize before continuing?

- **Validation before Solution:** Did you say the phrase: "I understand why you feel [Emotion] because [Reason]. Did I get that right?" This lowers her **Cortisol** and allows her **Prefrontal Cortex** to re-engage.

- **Ownership of the 10%:** Even if you feel 90% in the right, have you identified and apologized for the 10% that was your fault (e.g., your tone, your timing, your lack of clarity)?

- **Avoiding the "Four Horsemen":** Did you catch yourself using **Contempt** (eye-rolling/sarcasm) or **Stonewalling** (ignoring)? If so, did you immediately "Repair" the interaction?

Phase 6: The "Sovereign Man" Mission Audit (Overall Synthesis)

The Natural is defined by what he does *outside* of the relationship.

- **Mission Dominance:** Is your current "Mission" (career, fitness, or personal growth) still your primary priority, or has your relationship become your "Sun"?

- **The "Moving Target" Factor:** What new skill, piece of knowledge, or physical improvement have you gained this month? If you aren't growing, you are becoming a "Solved Puzzle."

- **The Social Circle Radius:** Have you maintained your relationships with your "Tribes" (friends, mentors, and peers)? A man who is socially isolated is a man who is high-risk for **Enmeshment**.

- **Internal Validation vs. External Seeking:** Did you do something today purely because *you* valued it, regardless of whether she (or anyone else) would notice or praise you for it?

The Mastery Affirmation (Read Weekly)

"I am a man of grounded presence. My value is inherent and independent of the outcome of any single interaction. I lead with purpose, I speak with intent, and I maintain my frame through the storms of emotion and the lulls of routine. I am the 'Secure Base' for those I love and a 'Moving Target' for the world. My mission comes first, my boundaries are absolute, and my growth is perpetual. I am the Natural."

Final Blueprint Summary

1. **Ground the Body:** Breath, Posture, and Vagal Tone.
2. **Lead the Interaction:** Pausing, Scanning, and Open-Ended Loops.
3. **Spark the Tension:** Push-Pull, The Gaze, and Decisive Action.
4. **Sustain the Bond:** Active-Constructive Responding, Reliability, and Spontaneity.
5. **Defend the Mission:** Boundaries, Self-Respect, and Constant Evolution.

Print this checklist. Keep it in your workspace or your journal. Audit yourself every Sunday evening. The path of the Natural is not a destination you reach; it is a standard of excellence you choose to live by every single day.

THE MASTER RESOURCE LIST

Introduction

Books:

- Robin Dunbar, (1996), Grooming, Gossip, and the Evolution of Language
- Stephen W. Porges, (2011), The Polyvagal Theory: Neurophysiological Foundations of Emotions, Attachment, Communication, and Self-regulation
- Albert Bandura, (1997), Self-Efficacy: The Exercise of Control
- Carol S. Dweck, (2006), Mindset: The New Psychology of Success
- Amy Cuddy, (2015), Presence: Bringing Your Boldest Self to Your Biggest Challenges
- Alexander Todorov, (2017), Face Value: The Irresistible Influence of First Impressions
- Robert A. Glover, (2003), No More Mr. Nice Guy

Online Resources:

- https://www.science.org/doi/10.1126/science.1089134
- https://www.cigna.com/about-us/newsroom/news-and-views/studies-and-reports/loneliness-epidemic-america
- https://newsroom.ucla.edu/releases/is-technology-making-people-less-social
- https://journals.sagepub.com/doi/abs/10.1177/0146167297234003
- https://psychology.cornell.edu/news/the-spotlight-effect
- https://www.scientificamerican.com/article/the-mirror-neuron-revolution/

Book 1

Introduction

Books:

- Albert Bandura, (1997), Self-Efficacy: The Exercise of Control
- Carol S. Dweck, (2006), Mindset: The New Psychology of Success
- Amy Cuddy, (2015), Presence: Bringing Your Boldest Self to Your Biggest Challenges
- Nathaniel Branden, (1994), The Six Pillars of Self-Esteem
- David D. Burns, (1980), Feeling Good: The New Mood Therapy
- Stephen W. Porges, (2011), The Polyvagal Theory: Neurophysiological Foundations of Emotions, Attachment, Communication, and Self-regulation
- Norman Doidge, (2007), The Brain That Changes Itself

Online Resources:

- https://www.health.harvard.edu/staying-healthy/understanding-the-stress-response
- https://www.psychologytoday.com/us/basics/self-efficacy
- https://hbr.org/2012/10/how-body-language-shapes-who-you-are
- https://www.self-compassion.org/the-research
- https://www.nature.com/articles/427311a
- https://academic.oup.com/cercor/article/14/6/603/433300

Chapter 1

Books:

- Michael Merzenich, (2013), *Soft-Wired: How the New Science of Brain Plasticity Can Change Your Life*
- Daniel Goleman, (2006), *Social Intelligence: The New Science of Human Relationships*
- Rick Hanson, (2013), *Hardwiring Happiness: The New Brain Science of Contentment, Calm, and Confidence*

- Daniel J. Siegel, (2010), *Mindsight: The New Science of Personal Transformation*
- John B. Arden, (2010), *Rewire Your Brain: Think Your Way to a Better Life*
- Joseph LeDoux, (2015), *Anxious: Using the Brain to Understand and Treat Fear and Anxiety*
- Norman Doidge, (2007), *The Brain That Changes Itself*
- Michelle G. Craske, (2014), *Cognitive-Behavioral Therapy*
- Robert Sapolsky, (2017), *Behave: The Biology of Humans at Our Best and Worst*

Online Resources:

- https://www.health.harvard.edu/blog/anxiety-or-excitement-the-power-of-relabeling-201312236946
- https://www.sciencedirect.com/topics/neuroscience/hebbian-theory
- https://www.ncbi.nlm.nih.gov/pmc/articles/PMC6132381/
- https://www.apa.org/monitor/2010/10/neuroplasticity
- https://www.psychologytoday.com/us/blog/the-brain-and-emotional-intelligence/201112/amygdala-hijacks
- https://www.brainfacts.org/thinking-sensing-and-behaving/learning-and-memory/2020/the-power-of-the-mental-rehearsal-061120

Chapter 2

Books:

- David Givens, (2005), *Love Signals: A Practical Field Guide to the Body Language of Courtship*
- Amy Cuddy, (2015), *Presence: Bringing Your Boldest Self to Your Biggest Challenges*
- Alex Pentland, (2008), *Honest Signals: How They Shape Our World*
- Edward T. Hall, (1966), *The Hidden Dimension* (Foundational text on Proxemics)
- Paul Ekman, (2003), *Emotions Revealed: Recognizing Faces and Feelings to Improve Communication and Emotional Life*

- Joe Navarro, (2008), *What Every BODY is Saying: An Ex-FBI Agent's Guide to Speed-Reading People*
- Desmond Morris, (1977), *Manwatching: A Field Guide to Human Behaviour*

Online Resources:

- https://www.hbs.edu/faculty/Pages/item.aspx?num=43061
- https://www.psychologytoday.com/us/blog/spy-catcher/201206/comfortable-in-your-own-skin
- https://www.sciencedirect.com/science/article/abs/pii/S0092656605000078X
- https://www.nature.com/articles/s41598-019-44001-3
- https://www.paulekman.com/resources/micro-expressions/
- https://social-dynamics-lab.mit.edu/

Chapter 3

Books:

- Aaron T. Beck, (1979), Cognitive Therapy and the Emotional Disorders
- Eric Berne, (1964), Games People Play: The Psychology of Human Relationships
- Jeffrey E. Young, (1994), Reinventing Your Life: The Breakthrough Program to End Negative Behavior... and Feel Great Again
- Kristin Neff, (2011), Self-Compassion: The Proven Power of Being Kind to Yourself
- Steven C. Hayes, (2005), Get Out of Your Mind and Into Your Life: The New Acceptance and Commitment Therapy
- Judson Brewer, (2021), Unwinding Anxiety: New Science Shows How to Break the Cycles of Worry and Fear to Heal Your Mind
- Russ Harris, (2007), The Happiness Trap: How to Stop Struggling and Start Living

Online Resources:

- https://www.psychologytoday.com/us/basics/cognitive-distortions

- https://www.sciencedirect.com/topics/neuroscience/default-mode-network
- https://www.self-compassion.org/the-research
- https://www.health.harvard.edu/staying-healthy/understanding-the-stress-response
- https://www.frontiersin.org/articles/10.3389/fpsyg.2018.02018/full
  https://www.ncbi.nlm.nih.gov/pmc/articles/PMC3181887/
- https://hbr.org/2013/12/emotional-agility

Chapter 4

Books:

- **Joseph Wolpe**, (1958), Psychotherapy by Reciprocal Inhibition
- **Michelle G. Craske**, (2014), Cognitive-Behavioral Therapy
- **Albert Ellis**, (1962), Reason and Emotion in Psychotherapy
- **Daniel J. Siegel**, (1999), The Developing Mind
- **David H. Barlow**, (2021), Anxiety and Its Disorders: The Nature and Treatment of Anxiety and Panic.
- **Stephen W. Porges**, (2017), The Pocket Guide to the Polyvagal Theory: The Transformative Power of Feeling Safe.
- **Edmund J. Bourne**, (2020), The Anxiety and Phobia Workbook.

Chapter 5

Books:

- **Nathaniel Branden**, (1994), The Six Pillars of Self-Esteem
- **Robert Sapolsky**, (2017), Behave: The Biology of Humans at Our Best and Worst
- **Robert Glover**, (2003), No More Mr. Nice Guy
- **David Buss**, (2019), Evolutionary Psychology: The New Science of the Mind
- **Mark Manson**, (2011), Models: Attract Women Through Honesty
- **Brené Brown**, (2012), Daring Greatly
- **Jordan Peterson**, (2018), 12 Rules for Life: An Antidote to Chaos

Online Resources:

- https://greatergood.berkeley.edu/article/item/is_social_status_the_secret_to_happiness
- https://www.ncbi.nlm.nih.gov/pmc/articles/PMC2603061/
- https://humanbiology.stanford.edu/
- https://www.psychologytoday.com/us/blog/head-games/201310/the-power-admitting-mistakes
- https://www.scienceofpeople.com/vocal-authority/
- https://journals.sagepub.com/home/evp
- https://www.self-compassion.org/

Conclusion

Books:

- **Viktor Frankl**, (1946), Man's Search for Meaning
- **Nassim Nicholas Taleb**, (2012), Antifragile: Things That Gain from Disorder
- **Marcus Aurelius**, (180 AD), Meditations
- **Mihaly Csikszentmihalyi**, (1990), Flow: The Psychology of Optimal Experience
- **Maxwell Maltz**, (1960), Psycho-Cybernetics
- **Ryan Holiday**, (2016), Ego is the Enemy

Online Resources:

- https://dailystoic.com/what-is-stoicism-a-definition-3-key-strategies-to-help-you-live-a-better-life/
- https://www.ted.com/talks/amy_cuddy_your_body_language_may_shape_who_you_are
- https://www.psychologytoday.com/us/blog/the-power-self-identity/201706/the-power-self-identity
- https://humanbiology.stanford.edu/resources/videos
- https://greatergood.berkeley.edu/topic/resilience/definition
- https://www.pnas.org/doi/10.1073/pnas.1112064109

Reflection Questions

Books:

- **Stephen C. Hayes**, (2019), A Liberated Mind: How to Pivot Toward What Matters

- **Daniel Kahneman**, (2011), Thinking, Fast and Slow

- **James Clear**, (2018), Atomic Habits

- **Norman Doidge**, (2007), The Brain That Changes Itself

- **Tasha Eurich**, (2017), Insight: The Surprising Truth About How Others See Us

- **Maxwell Maltz**, (1960), Psycho-Cybernetics

Online Resources:

- https://positivepsychology.com/metacognition/

- https://greatergood.berkeley.edu/quizzes/take_quiz/self_compassion

- https://www.hubermanlab.com/episode/the-science-of-mindset-and-behavior-change

- https://www.therapistaid.com/therapy-worksheets/cbt/none

- https://www.scientificamerican.com/article/the-neurobiology-of-the-self/

- https://act.psychology.org/

Book 2

Introduction

Books:

- **Malcolm Gladwell**, (2005), Blink: The Power of Thinking Without Thinking

- **Keith Ferrazzi**, (2005), Never Eat Alone

- **Vanessa Van Edwards**, (2017), Captivate: The Science of Succeeding with People

- **Leil Lowndes**, (1999), How to Talk to Anyone

- **Robert Cialdini**, (2016), Pre-Suasion: A Revolutionary Way to Influence and Persuade

- **Nicholas Boothman**, (2002), How to Make People Like You in 90 Seconds or Less
- **Matthew Lieberman**, (2013), Social: Why Our Brains Are Wired to Connect

Online Resources:

- https://www.gottman.com/blog/want-to-improve-your-relationship-start-paying-attention-to-bids/
- https://www.psychologytoday.com/us/blog/the-modern-man/201210/the-3-second-rule
- https://www.gsb.stanford.edu/insights/art-small-talk
- https://www.ncbi.nlm.nih.gov/pmc/articles/PMC3520144/
- https://www.scienceofpeople.com/first-impressions/
- https://behavioralscientist.org/

Chapter 1

Books:

- **Joe Navarro**, (2008), What Every Body Is Saying
- **Daniel Goleman**, (2006), Social Intelligence: The New Science of Human Relationships
- **Allan & Barbara Pease**, (2004), The Definitive Book of Body Language
- **Paul Ekman**, (2003), Emotions Revealed
- **Edward T. Hall**, (1966), The Hidden Dimension
- **Robert Greene**, (2001), The Art of Seduction

Online Resources:

- https://www.scienceofpeople.com/body-language/
- https://www.paulekman.com/micro-expressions-training-tools/
- https://www.nature.com/articles/nn1017
- https://www.psychologytoday.com/us/blog/sexual-personalities/201806/the-science-eye-contact-and-attraction
- https://www.scienceofpeople.com/proxemics/
- https://www.socialpsychology.org/

Chapter 2

Books:

- **Bill McGowan**, (2014), *Pitch Perfect: Say It Right the First Time, Every Time*
- **Terry Felber**, (2006), *Am I Making Myself Clear?*
- **Chris Voss**, (2016), *Never Split the Difference*
- **Don Gabor**, (2011), *How to Start a Conversation and Make Friends*
- **Gerry Spence**, (1995), *How to Argue and Win Every Time*
- **Judith Humphrey**, (2014), *Impromptu: Leading in the Moment*

Online Resources:

- https://www.theschooloflife.com/article/the-secret-of-better-small-talk/
- https://www.scienceofpeople.com/how-to-start-a-conversation/
- https://hbr.org/2018/05/the-surprising-power-of-questions
- https://www.psychologytoday.com/us/blog/the-modern-man/201210/the-false-time-constraint
- https://socialpronow.com/blog/vocal-tonality/
- https://plato.stanford.edu/entries/common-knowledge/

Chapter 3

Books:

- **Kate Murphy**, (2020), *You're Not Listening: What You're Missing and Why It Matters*
- **Chris Voss**, (2016), *Never Split the Difference: Negotiating As If Your Life Depended On It*
- **Michael P. Nichols**, (2009), *The Lost Art of Listening*
- **Daniel Goleman**, (2006), *Social Intelligence: The New Science of Human Relationships*
- **Celeste Headlee**, (2017), *We Need to Talk: How to Have Conversations That Matter*
- **William Ury**, (2015), *Getting to Yes with Yourself*

Online Resources:

- https://www.gottman.com/blog/the-power-of-active-listening/
- https://www.scientificamerican.com/article/the-neuroscience-of-being-on-the-same-wavelength/
- https://hbr.org/2016/07/what-great-listeners-actually-do
- https://www.psychologytoday.com/us/blog/the-art-closeness/201901/how-use-cold-reading-build-rapport
- https://www.mindtools.com/az439cn/active-listening
- https://www.frontiersin.org/articles/10.3389/fpsyg.2013.00311/full

Chapter 4

Books:

- **Jia Jiang**, (2016), *Rejection Proof: How I Beat Fear and Became Invincible Through 100 Days of Rejection*
- **Guy Winch**, (2013), *Emotional First Aid: Healing Rejection, Guilt, Failure, and Other Everyday Hurts*
- **Nassim Nicholas Taleb**, (2012), *Antifragile: Things That Gain from Disorder*
- **Mark Manson**, (2016), *The Subtle Art of Not Giving a Fck**
- **Albert Ellis**, (1962), *Reason and Emotion in Psychotherapy*
- **Susan Cain**, (2012), *Quiet: The Power of Introverts in a World That Can't Stop Talking*

Online Resources:

- https://www.ncbi.nlm.nih.gov/pmc/articles/PMC3108544/
- https://greatergood.berkeley.edu/article/item/how_to_deal_with_rejection
- https://www.ted.com/talks/jia_jiang_what_i_learned_from_100_days_of_rejection
- https://www.psychologytoday.com/us/blog/the-modern-man/201201/how-handle-rejection
- https://www.scienceofpeople.com/resilience/
- https://www.apa.org/monitor/2012/04/rejection

Chapter 5

Books:

- **Vanessa Van Edwards**, (2017), *Captivate: The Science of Succeeding with People*

- **Robert Greene**, (2001), *The Art of Seduction*

- **Daniel Goleman**, (1995), *Emotional Intelligence: Why It Can Matter More Than IQ*

- **Leil Lowndes**, (1999), *How to Talk to Anyone: 92 Little Tricks for Big Success in Relationships*

- **Keith Ferrazzi**, (2005), *Never Eat Alone*

- **Oren Klaff**, (2011), *Pitch Anything*

Online Resources:

- https://www.scienceofpeople.com/deep-questions/

- https://www.theschooloflife.com/article/on-small-talk/

- https://hbr.org/2017/01/the-neuroscience-of-trust

- https://www.psychologytoday.com/us/blog/the-power-us/202104/the-power-shared-identity

- https://www.ncbi.nlm.nih.gov/pmc/articles/PMC3401037/

- https://greatergood.berkeley.edu/article/item/the_36_questions_that_lead_to_love

Conclusion

Books:

- **Malcolm Gladwell**, (2005), *Blink: The Power of Thinking Without Thinking* **Olivia Fox Cabane**, (2012), *The Charisma Myth: How Anyone Can Master the Art and Science of Personal Magnetism*

- **Amy Cuddy**, (2015), *Presence: Bringing Your Boldest Self to Your Biggest Challenges*

- **Jordan Peterson**, (2018), *12 Rules for Life: An Antidote to Chaos*

- **Nassim Nicholas Taleb**, (2012), *Antifragile: Things That Gain from Disorder* **Robert Greene**, (2018), *The Laws of Human Nature*

Online Resources:

- https://www.ted.com/talks/amy_cuddy_your_body_language_may_shape_who_you_are
- https://www.psychologytoday.com/us/blog/the-power-self-identity/201706/the-power-self-identity
- https://hbr.org/2013/07/connect-then-lead
- https://www.scienceofpeople.com/vocal-authority/
- https://www.ncbi.nlm.nih.gov/pmc/articles/PMC4241340/
- https://greatergood.berkeley.edu/article/item/how_to_be_more_present_in_your_daily_life

Reflection Questions

Books:

- **Tasha Eurich**, (2017), *Insight: Why We're Not as Self-Aware as We Think, and How Seeing Ourselves Clearly Helps Us Succeed*
- **Ray Dalio**, (2017), *Principles: Life and Work*
- **Daniel Kahneman**, (2011), *Thinking, Fast and Slow*
- **James Clear**, (2018), *Atomic Habits*
- **Charles Duhigg**, (2012), *The Power of Habit*
- **Carol Dweck**, (2006), *Mindset: The New Psychology of Success*

Online Resources:

- https://www.self-compassion.org/
- https://www.hubermanlab.com/episode/the-science-of-mindset-and-behavior-change
- https://www.authentichappiness.sas.upenn.edu/
- https://www.psychologytoday.com/us/blog/the-power-metacognition
- https://www.scienceofpeople.com/self-awareness/
- https://greatergood.berkeley.edu/article/item/how_to_be_more_self_aware_in_relationships

Book 3

Introduction

Books:

- **Mihaly Csikszentmihalyi**, (1990), *Flow: The Psychology of Optimal Experience* **Daniel Kahneman**, (2011), *Thinking, Fast and Slow*
- **Keith Johnstone**, (1979), *Impro: Improvisation and the Theatre*
- **Steven Kotler**, (2014), *The Rise of Superman*
- **Robert Greene**, (2012), *Mastery*
- **Judith Glaser**, (2014), *Conversational Intelligence*

Online Resources

- https://www.psychologytoday.com/us/blog/the-power-flow
- https://www.hubermanlab.com/episode/the-science-of-creativity-and-flow
- https://www.scienceofpeople.com/conversational-flow/
- https://hbr.org/2015/06/the-neurochemistry-of-positive-conversations
- https://www.ted.com/talks/mihaly_csikszentmihalyi_flow_the_secret_to_happiness
- https://www.frontiersin.org/articles/10.3389/fpsyg.2021.641545/full

Chapter 1

Books:

- **Edward de Bono**, (1970), *Lateral Thinking: Creativity Step by Step*
- **Tony Buzan**, (1993), *The Mind Map Book*
- **Keith Johnstone**, (1979), *Impro: Improvisation and the Theatre*
- **Daniel Kahneman**, (2011), *Thinking, Fast and Slow*
- **Leonard Mlodinow**, (2018), *Elastic: Flexible Thinking in a Time of Change*
- **Steven Pinker**, (1994), *The Language Instinct*

Online Resources

- https://www.psychologytoday.com/us/blog/the-power-lateral-thinking
- https://www.mindtools.com/pages/article/newCT_00.htm
- https://www.scienceofpeople.com/how-to-be-witty/
- https://www.ted.com/talks/tim_brown_tales_of_creativity_and_play
- https://hbr.org/2014/12/the-art-of-the-pivot-in-conversation
- https://www.neuroscience.org.uk/the-associative-cortex-and-social-intelligence/

Chapter 2

Books:

- **Warren Berger**, (2014), *A More Beautiful Question: The Power of Inquiry to Spark Breakthrough Ideas*
- **Edgar Schein**, (2013), *Humble Inquiry: The Gentle Art of Asking Instead of Telling*
- **Chris Voss**, (2016), *Never Split the Difference: Negotiating As If Your Life Depended On It* (Specifically the framework of "Calibrated Questions")
- **James Pennebaker**, (2011), *The Secret Life of Pronouns: What Our Words Say About Us*
- **Marilee Adams**, (2004), *Change Your Questions, Change Your Life*
- **Judith Glaser**, (2014), *Conversational Intelligence: How Great Leaders Build Trust and Get Extraordinary Results*

Online Resources:

- https://www.scienceofpeople.com/deep-questions/
- https://hbr.org/2018/05/the-surprising-power-of-questions
- https://www.psychologytoday.com/us/blog/the-art-closeness/201511/36-questions-learn-love-anyway
- https://hbr.org/2015/06/the-neurochemistry-of-positive-conversations
- https://www.neuroscience.org.uk/the-social-brain-and-the-reward-of-self-disclosure/

- https://www.forbes.com/sites/forbescoachescouncil/2017/12/12/the-power-of-open-ended-questions/

Chapter 4

Books:

- **Chris Voss**, (2016), *Never Split the Difference: Negotiating As If Your Life Depended On It*
- **Carl Rogers**, (1961), *On Becoming a Person*
- **Giacomo Rizzolatti**, (2008), *Mirrors in the Brain: How Our Minds Share Actions and Emotions*
- **Judith Glaser**, (2014), *Conversational Intelligence*
- **Daniel Goleman**, (2006), *Social Intelligence*
- **James Pennebaker**, (2011), *The Secret Life of Pronouns*

Online Resources:

- https://www.blackswanltd.com/the-edge/the-power-of-mirroring
- https://www.psychologytoday.com/us/blog/the-psychology-body-language/201309/the-surprising-power-mirroring
- https://www.scienceofpeople.com/mirroring/
- https://hbr.org/2015/04/the-power-of-mirroring-in-negotiations
- https://www.ted.com/talks/uri_hasson_this_is_your_brain_on_communication
- https://www.neuroscience.org.uk/the-superior-temporal-sulcus-and-social-perception/

Chapter 5

Books:

- **Rob Walker**, (2019), *The Art of Noticing*
- **Amy Herman**, (2016), *Visual Intelligence*
- **Derren Brown**, (2007), *Tricks of the Mind*
- **Erving Goffman**, (1959), *The Presentation of Self in Everyday Life*
- **Alexandra Horowitz**, (2013), *On Looking: A Walker's Guide to the Art of Observation.*

Online Resources:

- https://www.psychologytoday.com/us/blog/the-power-noticing
- https://www.scienceofpeople.com/how-to-be-more-observant/
- https://hbr.org/2014/12/the-power-of-noticing
- https://www.ted.com/talks/amy_herman_a_lesson_on_looking
- https://www.neuroscience.org.uk/the-parietal-lobe-and-spatial-awareness/

Conclusion

Books:

- **Mihaly Csikszentmihalyi**, (1990), *Flow: The Psychology of Optimal Experience*
- **Stephen Nachmanovitch**, (1990), *Free Play: Improvisation in Life and Art*
- **Malcolm Gladwell**, (2005), *Blink: The Power of Thinking Without Thinking*
- **Keith Johnstone**, (1979), *Impro: Improvisation and the Theatre*
- **George Lakoff**, (1980), *Metaphors We Live By*
- **Steven Kotler**, (2021), *The Art of Impossible*
- **Daniel Coyle**, (2009), *The Talent Code*

Online Resources:

- https://www.psychologytoday.com/us/blog/the-power-flow/201406/the-neuroscience-flow
- https://www.scienceofpeople.com/how-to-talk-to-anyone/
- https://hbr.org/2018/05/the-surprising-power-of-questions
- https://www.ted.com/talks/mihaly_csikszentmihalyi_flow_the_secret_to_happiness
- https://www.neuroscience.org.uk/the-prefrontal-cortex-and-social-inhibition/
- https://www.forbes.com/sites/bryanrobinson/2021/04/13/how-to-enter-a-flow-state-in-your-conversations/

Reflection Questions

Books:

- **Ray Dalio**, (2017), *Principles: Life and Work*
- **Carol Dweck**, (2006), *Mindset: The New Psychology of Success*
- **Daniel Kahneman**, (2011), *Thinking, Fast and Slow*
- **Anders Ericsson**, (2016), *Peak: Secrets from the New Science of Expertise*
- **James Clear**, (2018), *Atomic Habits*

Online Resources:

- https://www.psychologytoday.com/us/blog/the-power-self-reflection
- https://www.scienceofpeople.com/social-skills-test/
- https://hbr.org/2017/03/why-self-reflection-is-the-key-to-effective-leadership
- https://www.mindtools.com/pages/article/reflective-practice.htm
- https://www.neuroscience.org.uk/the-role-of-the-dlpfc-in-self-monitoring/

Book 4

Introduction

Books:

- **David Deida**, (1997), *The Way of the Superior Man*
- **Robert Glover**, (2003), *No More Mr. Nice Guy*
- **Helen Fisher**, (2004), *Why We Love: The Nature and Chemistry of Romantic Love* **Amir Levine & Rachel Heller**, (2010), *Attached*
- **Rollo Tomassi**, (2013), *The Rational Male*
- **Geoffrey Miller**, (2000), *The Mating Mind*

Online Resources:

- https://www.psychologytoday.com/us/blog/the-attraction-doctor/201205/the-evolution-flirting
- https://www.scienceofpeople.com/how-to-flirt/

- https://hbr.org/2015/05/the-neurochemistry-of-trust-and-attraction
- https://www.ted.com/talks/helen_fisher_the_brain_in_love
- https://www.neuroscience.org.uk/the-anterior-cingulate-cortex-and-social-mismatch/
- https://www.forbes.com/sites/bryanrobinson/2020/02/13/the-neuroscience-of-romance/

Chapter 1

Books:

- **Joe Navarro**, (2008), *What Every BODY is Saying* (Ex-FBI agent's guide to speed-reading people).
- **David Givens**, (2005), *Love Signals: A Practical Field Guide to the Body Language of Courtship.*
- **Allan & Barbara Pease**, (2004), *The Definitive Book of Body Language.*
- **Paul Ekman**, (2003), *Emotions Revealed*
- **Edward T. Hall**, (1966), *The Hidden Dimension*
- **Desmond Morris**, (1971), *Intimate Behaviour*

Online Resources:

- https://www.paulekman.com/resources/micro-expressions/
- https://www.psychologytoday.com/us/blog/spycatcher/201112/the-body-language-attraction
- https://www.scienceofpeople.com/female-body-language/
- https://hbr.org/2015/01/the-neuroscience-of-trust
- https://www.neuroscience.org.uk/the-autonomic-nervous-system-and-social-behavior/
- https://www.scientificamerican.com/article/the-secret-language-of-feet/

Chapter 2

Books:

- **Scott Weems**, (2014), *Ha! The Science of When We Laugh and Why*

- **John Morreall**, (2009), *Comic Relief: A Comprehensive Philosophy of Humor.*
- **Peter McGraw & Joel Warner**, (2014), *The Humor Code: A Global Search for What Makes Things Funny.*
- **David Deida**, (1997), *The Way of the Superior Man*
- **Robert Greene**, (2001), *The Art of Seduction*
- **Charlie Houpert**, (2016), *Charisma on Command*

Online Resources:

- https://www.psychologytoday.com/us/blog/the-attraction-doctor/201206/playful-teasing-and-attraction
- https://www.scienceofpeople.com/how-to-be-funny/
- https://hbr.org/2014/03/the-value-of-humor-in-the-workplace
- https://www.ted.com/talks/andrew_tarvin_the_skill_of_humor
- https://www.neuroscience.org.uk/the-neuroscience-of-social-play/
- https://www.scientificamerican.com/article/the-science-of-wit/

Chapter 3

Books:

- **Matthew Hertenstein**, (2013), *The Tell: The Little Clues That Reveal Big Truths about Who We Are*
- **Tiffany Field**, (2001), *Touch*
- **Ashley Montagu**, (1971), *Touching: The Human Significance of the Skin*
- **Joe Navarro**, (2008), *What Every BODY is Saying*
- **David Deida**, (1997), *The Way of the Superior Man*
- **Dacher Keltner**, (2009), *Born to Be Good*

Online Resources:

- https://www.psychologytoday.com/us/blog/the-power-touch
- https://www.scienceofpeople.com/touching/
- https://hbr.org/2015/01/the-neuroscience-of-trust
- https://www.ted.com/talks/tiffany_field_the_power_of_touch

- https://www.neuroscience.org.uk/c-tactile-afferents-and-social-touch/
- https://www.nature.com/articles/nrn2633

Chapter 4

Books:

- **Michael Argyle**, (1988), *Bodily Communication*
- **Joe Navarro**, (2008), *What Every BODY is Saying*
- **Paul Ekman**, (2003), *Emotions Revealed*
- **Malcolm Gladwell**, (2005), *Blink*
- **Nicholas Epley**, (2014), *Mindwise*
- **Simon Baron-Cohen**, (2003), *The Essential Difference*

Online Resources:

- https://www.psychologytoday.com/us/blog/the-power-gaze
- https://www.scienceofpeople.com/eye-contact/
- https://hbr.org/2012/03/the-science-of-eye-contact
- https://www.ted.com/talks/jim_canterucci_the_power_of_eye_contact
- https://www.neuroscience.org.uk/the-superior-temporal-sulcus-and-social-perception/
- https://www.scientificamerican.com/article/the-eyes-have-it-how-eye-contact-facilitates-social-flow/

Chapter 5

Books:

- **David Deida**, (1997), *The Way of the Superior Man*
- **Irwin Altman & Dalmas Taylor**, (1973), *Social Penetration: The Development of Interpersonal Relationships.*
- **Robert Greene**, (2001), *The Art of Seduction*
- **Brené Brown**, (2012), *Daring Greatly*
- **Esther Perel**, (2006), *Mating in Captivity*
- **Stan Tatkin**, (2011), *Wired for Love*

Online Resources:

- https://www.psychologytoday.com/us/blog/the-attraction-doctor/201202/shifting-the-friend-zone-romance
- https://www.scienceofpeople.com/build-intimacy/
- https://hbr.org/2014/12/the-neurochemistry-of-intimacy
- https://www.ted.com/talks/brene_brown_the_power_of_vulner ability
- https://www.neuroscience.org.uk/the-vmpfc-and-emotional-valuation/
- https://www.scientificamerican.com/article/the-science-of-social-penetration/

Conclusion

Books:

- **David Deida**, (1997), *The Way of the Superior Man*
- **Eckhart Tolle**, (1997), *The Power of Now*
- **Mark Manson**, (2011), *Models: Attract Women Through Honesty*
- **Stephen Porges**, (2011), *The Polyvagal Theory*
- **Robert Glover**, (2003), *No More Mr. Nice Guy*
- **Viktor Frankl**, (1946), *Man's Search for Meaning*

Online Resources:

- https://www.psychologytoday.com/us/blog/the-attraction-doctor/201205/outcome-independence-the-secret-social-success
- https://www.scienceofpeople.com/how-to-be-relaxed/
- https://hbr.org/2015/01/the-neuroscience-of-trust-and-respect
- https://www.ted.com/talks/amy_cuddy_your_body_language_m ay_shape_who_you_are
- https://www.neuroscience.org.uk/polyvagal-theory-and-human-connection/
- https://www.scientificamerican.com/article/the-science-of-outcome-independence/

Reflection Questions

Books:

- **Daniel Kahneman**, (2011), *Thinking, Fast and Slow*
- **James Clear**, (2018), *Atomic Habits*
- **Josh Waitzkin**, (2007), *The Art of Learning*
- **Maxwell Maltz**, (1960), *Psycho-Cybernetics*
- **Anders Ericsson**, (2016), *Peak: Secrets from the New Science of Expertise*
- **Marcus Aurelius**, (180 AD), *Meditations*

Online Resources:

- https://www.psychologytoday.com/us/blog/the-power-self-reflection
- https://www.scienceofpeople.com/social-skills-audit/
- https://hbr.org/2016/03/the-power-of-deliberate-practice
- https://www.ted.com/talks/tasha_eurich_increase_your_self_awareness_with_one_simple_fix
- https://www.neuroscience.org.uk/the-medial-prefrontal-cortex-and-the-self/
- https://www.scientificamerican.com/article/how-mental-rehearsal-changes-the-brain/

Book 5

Introduction

Books:

- **John Gottman**, (1999), *The Seven Principles for Making Marriage Work*
- **David Deida**, (1997), *The Way of the Superior Man*
- **Stan Tatkin**, (2011), *Wired for Love*
- **Helen Fisher**, (2004), *Why We Love: The Nature and Chemistry of Romantic Love*
- **Amir Levine & Rachel Heller**, (2010), *Attached*
- **Esther Perel**, (2006), *Mating in Captivity*

Online Resources:

- https://www.gottman.com/blog/the-emotional-bank-account/
- https://www.psychologytoday.com/us/blog/the-attraction-doctor/201205/maintaining-attraction-in-long-term-relationships
- https://www.scienceofpeople.com/oxytocin/
- https://www.ted.com/talks/esther_perel_the_secret_to_desire_in_a_long_term_relationship
- https://www.neuroscience.org.uk/oxytocin-vasopressin-and-social-bonding/
- https://www.scientificamerican.com/article/the-neuroscience-of-lasting-love/

Chapter 1

Books:

- **Henry Cloud & John Townsend**, (1992), *Boundaries: When to Say Yes, How to Say No to Take Control of Your Life.*
- **Mark Manson**, (2011), *Models*
- **Robert Glover**, (2003), *No More Mr. Nice Guy*
- **Nedra Glover Tawwab**, (2021), *Set Boundaries, Find Peace: A Guide to Reclaiming Yourself.*
- **Jordan Peterson**, (2018), *12 Rules for Life*
- **David Deida**, (1997), *The Way of the Superior Man*

Online Resources:

- https://www.psychologytoday.com/us/blog/the-attraction-doctor/201302/establishing-boundaries-in-relationships
- https://www.gottman.com/blog/the-importance-of-boundaries-in-relationships/
- https://www.scienceofpeople.com/how-to-set-boundaries/
- https://hbr.org/2016/01/the-price-of-agreeableness
- https://www.neuroscience.org.uk/the-prefrontal-cortex-and-social-boundaries/
- https://www.scientificamerican.com/article/the-science-of-saying-no/

Chapter 2

Books:

- **Shelly Gable**, (2004), *What Do You Do When Things Go Right?*
- **Amir Levine**, (2010), *Attached*
- **John Gottman**, (2011), *The Science of Trust.*
- **Sheryl Sandberg**, (2013), *Lean In*
- **Carol Dweck**, (2006), *Mindset*
- **David Deida**, (1997), *The Way of the Superior Man*

Online Resources

- https://www.gottman.com/blog/the-michelangelo-phenomenon/
- https://www.psychologytoday.com/us/blog/the-attraction-doctor/201208/active-constructive-responding
- https://www.scienceofpeople.com/how-to-support-your-partner/
- https://hbr.org/2017/01/how-dual-career-couples-make-it-work
- https://www.neuroscience.org.uk/the-neurobiology-of-social-support/
- https://www.scientificamerican.com/article/the-power-of-the-secure-base/

Chapter 3

Books:

- **John Gottman**, (2015), *The Seven Principles for Making Marriage Work*
- **Daniel Goleman**, (1995), *Emotional Intelligence*
- **Stan Tatkin**, (2016), *Wired for Dating*
- **Marshall Rosenberg**, (2003), *Nonviolent Communication*
- **Douglas Stone & Sheila Heen**, (2010), *Difficult Conversations.*
- **Harville Hendrix**, (1988), *Getting the Love You Want*

Online Resources:

- https://www.gottman.com/blog/the-four-horsemen-recognizing-criticism-contempt-defensiveness-and-stonewalling/
- https://www.psychologytoday.com/us/blog/the-attraction-doctor/201211/handling-conflict-in-relationships
- https://www.scienceofpeople.com/emotional-intelligence/
- https://hbr.org/2017/01/how-to-manage-your-emotional-triggers
- https://www.neuroscience.org.uk/the-amygdala-and-emotional-regulation/
- https://www.scientificamerican.com/article/the-science-of-conflict-resolution/

Chapter 4

Books:

- **Esther Perel**, (2006), *Mating in Captivity: Unlocking Erotic Intelligence.*
- **Robert Greene**, (2001), *The Art of Seduction*
- **David Deida**, (1997), *The Way of the Superior Man*
- **Gregory Berns**, (2005), *Satisfaction: The Science of Finding True Fulfillment*
- **Alain de Botton**, (2016), *The Course of Love*
- **Siri Hustvedt**, (2010), *The Shaking Woman*

Online Resources:

- https://www.psychologytoday.com/us/blog/the-attraction-doctor/201305/keeping-the-spark-alive-in-relationships
- https://www.gottman.com/blog/the-importance-of-novelty-in-relationships/
- https://www.scienceofpeople.com/how-to-be-more-spontaneous/
- https://www.ted.com/talks/esther_perel_the_secret_to_desire_i n_a_long_term_relationship

- https://www.neuroscience.org.uk/the-nucleus-accumbens-and-novelty/
- https://www.scientificamerican.com/article/why-novelty-is-the-key-to-happiness/

Chapter 5

Books:

- **David Deida**, (1997), *The Way of the Superior Man*
- **Jocko Willink**, (2015), *Extreme Ownership*
- **Viktor Frankl**, (1946), *Man's Search for Meaning*
- **Ryan Holiday**, (2016), *Ego is the Enemy*
- **James Clear**, (2018), *Atomic Habits*
- **Nathaniel Branden**, (1994), *The Six Pillars of Self-Esteem*

Online Resources:

- https://www.psychologytoday.com/us/blog/the-attraction-doctor/201201/reliability-the-secret-successful-relationships
- https://www.gottman.com/blog/the-importance-of-trust-in-relationships/
- https://www.scienceofpeople.com/leadership-qualities/
- https://hbr.org/2019/02/the-neuroscience-of-trust
- https://www.neuroscience.org.uk/the-prefrontal-cortex-and-decision-making/
- https://www.scientificamerican.com/article/the-science-of-integrity/

Conclusion

Books:

- **John Gottman**, (2015), *The Seven Principles for Making Marriage Work*
- **Esther Perel**, (2006), *Mating in Captivity*
- **David Deida**, (1997), *The Way of the Superior Man*
- **Stan Tatkin**, (2012), *Wired for Love*
- **Helen Fisher**, (2004), *Why We Love*
- **Mark Manson**, (2011), *Models*

Online Resources:

- https://www.gottman.com/blog/the-magic-six-hours-a-week/
- https://www.psychologytoday.com/us/blog/the-attraction-doctor/201402/keeping-the-passion-alive-in-long-term-relationships
- https://www.scienceofpeople.com/how-to-keep-a-relationship-exciting/
- https://www.ted.com/talks/esther_perel_the_secret_to_desire_i n_a_long_term_relationship
- https://www.neuroscience.org.uk/the-long-term-effects-of-oxytocin-on-bonding/
- https://www.scientificamerican.com/article/the-science-of-lasting-love/

Reflection Question

Books:

- **Daniel Kahneman**, (2011), *Thinking, Fast and Slow*
- **John Gottman**, (2011), *The Science of Trust*
- **James Clear**, (2018), *Atomic Habits*
- **Ray Dalio**, (2017), *Principles*

Online Resources:

- https://www.gottman.com/blog/category/column/the-sound-relationship-house/
- https://www.psychologytoday.com/us/blog/the-power-self-reflection/2021
- https://www.scienceofpeople.com/relationship-goals/
- https://hbr.org/2016/03/the-power-of-deliberate-practice-in-leadership

Final Conclusion

Books:

- **George Leonard**, (1991), *Mastery: The Keys to Success and Long-Term Fulfillment.*
- **Robert Greene**, (2012), *Mastery.*

- **Mihaly Csikszentmihalyi**, (1990), *Flow: The Psychology of Optimal Experience.*
- **Stephen Porges**, (2011), *The Polyvagal Theory: Neurophysiological Foundations of Emotions, Attachment, and Self-regulation.*
- **Barry Schwartz**, (2004), *The Paradox of Choice: Why More Is Less.*
- **James Clear**, (2018), *Atomic Habits: An Easy & Proven Way to Build Good Habits & Break Bad Ones.*
- **Viktor Frankl**, (1946), *Man's Search for Meaning.*
- **Daniel Goleman**, (1995), *Emotional Intelligence: Why It Can Matter More Than IQ.*

Online Resources:
- https://www.hubermanlab.com/episode/controlling-your-dopamine-for-motivation-focus-satisfaction
- https://www.gottman.com/blog/the-magic-ratio-the-positive-perspective/
- https://www.psychologytoday.com/us/basics/habit-formation
- https://www.scienceofpeople.com/body-language-science/
- https://hbr.org/2016/01/why-you-should-be-less-attached-to-outcomes
- https://neurosciencenews.com/mirror-neurons-social-behavior-23425/
- https://www.nature.com/articles/s41583-018-0002-6
- https://www.scientificamerican.com/article/the-science-of-resilience/

The Success Blueprint

Books:
- **James Clear**, (2018), *Atomic Habits: An Easy & Proven Way to Build Good Habits & Break Bad Ones.*
- **Jocko Willink**, (2015), *Extreme Ownership: How U.S. Navy SEALs Lead and Win.*
- **John Gottman**, (1999), *The Marriage Clinic: A Scientifically Based Marital Therapy.*

- **Daniel Kahneman**, (2011), *Thinking, Fast and Slow.*
- **Steven Pressfield**, (2002), *The War of Art: Break Through the Blocks and Win Your Inner Creative Battles.*
- **Ryan Holiday**, (2016), *Ego Is the Enemy.*

Online Resources:

- https://www.gottman.com/blog/the-magic-ratio-the-positive-perspective/
- https://www.hubermanlab.com/topics/neuroplasticity-and-habit-formation
- https://www.psychologytoday.com/us/blog/the-power-self-reflection/202111/how-audit-your-personal-growth
- https://hbr.org/2019/02/the-neuroscience-of-trust
- https://www.scienceofpeople.com/leadership-traits/
- https://www.neuroscience.org.uk/the-basal-ganglia-and-habit-integration/

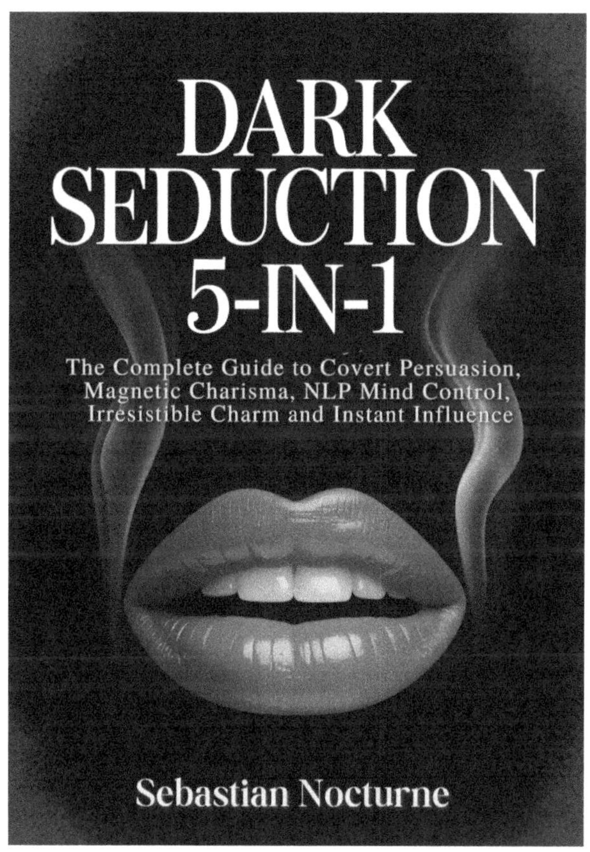
DARK
SEDUCTION
5-IN-1
The Complete Guide to Covert Persuasion,
Magnetic Charisma, NLP Mind Control,
Irresistible Charm and Instant Influence
Sebastian Nocturne

www.ingramcontent.com/pod-product-compliance
Lightning Source LLC
Chambersburg PA
CBHW060637080726

47818CB00004B/174